Making and Molding
Identity in Schools

SUNY Series, Power, Social Identity, and Education
Edited by Lois Weis

# Making and Molding Identity in Schools

*Student Narratives on Race, Gender, and Academic Engagement*

Ann Locke Davidson

STATE UNIVERSITY OF NEW YORK PRESS

Published by
State University of New York Press, Albany

© 1996  State University of New York

For information, address State University of New York Press,
State University Plaza, Albany, N.Y., 12246

Production by Cathleen Collins
Marketing by Nancy Farrell

**Library of Congress Cataloging-in-Publication Data**

Davidson, Ann Locke.
    Making and molding identity in schools : student narratives on
race, gender, and academic engagement / Ann Locke Davidson.
        p.    cm. — (SUNY series, power, social identity, and
education)
    Includes bibliographical references and index.
    ISBN 0-7914-3081-2 (hardcover : alk. paper). — ISBN 0-7914-3082-0
(pbk. : alk. paper)
    1. High school students—California—Social conditions—
Longitudinal studies. 2. Ethnicity—California—Longitudinal
studies. 3. Identity (Psychology)—California—Longitudinal
studies. I. Title. II. Series.
LC205.5.C2D38  1996
370.19′342′09794—dc20
                                                                    95-47050
                                                                    CIP

10   9   8   7   6   5   4   3   2   1

# Contents

## Contents

# Tables

# Acknowledgments

As I reflect on the making and molding of this book, it becomes evident that texts, like projections of self, are highly relational constructions. While the individual name on this book's cover signifies a solitary accomplishment, in fact it embodies the help and advice of many.

My first and greatest debt is to the young men and women who allowed me to share their lives. "Carla," "Johnnie," "Marbella," "Ryan," "Sonia," "Patricia," and the other adolescents with whom I spent time were patient, warm, and forthcoming, to a degree that I would not have anticipated. As they introduced me to friends, looked after me while at school, and answered my many questions, they subverted the myth of the alienated, self-centered adolescent.

School personnel, generous with their time and frank in assessing their own and others' actions, also were critical to the completion of this work. Their insights were essential, not only for helping me understand their school environments, but also for making clear the critical links between teachers' and students' working conditions. Though there were times when my views and assumptions about the social world differed from those with whom I spoke, the concerns that I raise in this text are not meant to denigrate, but rather to generate, conversations about whether and how schools might work differently for both adults and youths.

During the years that I conducted this study, I benefited from the example and intellect of many. Elliot Eisner's strong commitment to qualitative forms of inquiry and his ideas concerning the ecology of schooling had an integral influence on my conceptualization of this project and in my approach to writing this text. George and Louise Spindler introduced me to the anthropology of education, reframing my perspectives on my own and other's actions and enabling me to see schools as cultural institutions. David Tyack revealed how schools have evolved as sorting institutions and helped convince me that this was a study worth doing. Jane Collier introduced me to poststructural social theory and was instrumental in helping me complete the proposal for this research. Finally, Milbrey McLaughlin and Joan Talbert reminded me of the many ways in which context may matter for engagement, not only for students but for teachers as well.

I owe a special debt to Patricia Phelan. As director of the Students' Multiple Worlds Study, Pat taught me how to ask and listen, exemplifying the craft of interviewing through teaching and example. Her sensitive insights into human behavior, gentle yet pointed questions, and creative approaches to the analysis of the social world have continued to be essential. She has spent hundreds of hours discussing the lives of the youths I describe. From the instigation of the study to the completion of this manuscript, Pat's support and encouragement have been integral.

I am also grateful for the generous financial support I received as a graduate student, both from the Center for Research on the Context of Secondary School Teaching (CRC) at Stanford University and from the Spencer Foundation, in the form of a yearlong dissertation fellowship. Milbrey McLaughlin and Joan Talbert, directors at CRC, welcomed and encouraged my project, voiced their enthusiasm throughout the process, helped me develop my ideas, and provided material support for fieldwork expenses. A heartfelt thanks to them.

Finally, I thank significant others for their ever present support, including my parents, Ted and Adele, my brother Bill and my husband Howard. Howard in particular served as a sounding board for ideas, critiqued drafts, and helped in fieldwork by carrying out interviews in Spanish and translating them when my ear and memory failed me. There were less tangible contributions as well, not the least of which were patience and encouragement as I struggled to find my way in transforming data to book.

For their assistance, patience, and unflagging support, I dedicate this book to Howard Davidson and Patricia Phelan.

# Introduction

## *Way to an Inquiry*

Being Black and going to school in St. Louis
doesn't really exist. ....We even got sent to juvenile
cause it was like, that was back in the days when
everything was just crazy and we didn't care. And
before we realized who we were, where we were
going, we were just, you know, out there, floating
around.

But now, [since I moved here] it's changed. ....
I don't tolerate that anymore. I just say forget it,
you know. That was a long time ago, that was the
*old* me. .... This year I surprised myself, I made
honor roll! (RA27STC:696–697; RA27STB:
139–151, 482–485, 1345–1346)*

—Johnnie Betts,
high school sophomore

This book focuses on the relationship between ethnic/racial identity and ✓
academic engagement, examining in particular the role that schools and

---

* Here and elsewhere, quotations are identified by file code. These interviews are part
of a public-use file that will eventually be made available to interested researchers through
Stanford's Center for Research on the Context of Secondary School Teaching. Conventions
used when quoting interview segments are as follows:

• Brackets ([]) mark text that has been inserted for the purpose of clarification.
• Four ellipses ( .... ) indicate that a segment of protocol has been omitted.
• Three ellipses ( ... ) indicate a pause in the dialogue.

classrooms play in shaping this relationship. My inquiry grew out of conversations with youths like Johnnie, who speaks above of his transition from
an inner-city middle school in St. Louis to an urban high school in California. As an eighth grader, Johnnie explained, the "old me" learned
through interactions with teachers and observations of his community that
being Black meant unemployment and certain failure. As such, attending
school and working to succeed academically were, as Johnnie termed it, a
"sucker's" choice. As a student of curriculum and anthropology, I recognized this part of the tale. Like the politically savvy students portrayed by
Fordham and Ogbu (1986) and other social theorists (Willis, 1977;
MacLeod, 1987), Johnnie and his peers adopted oppositional practices to
resist schooling, partly because they believed that effort devoted to schoolwork would not pay off.

It was the second half of the story that sounded new. As Johnnie
compared his experiences at a central California high school to those at his
middle school, he implied that the meaning of social categories can vary
substantially across school settings, with significant implications for academic engagement. In a school where teachers communicate high expectations and African American students see school involvement as legitimate,
being Black can mean something different Johnnie explained. Speaking
African American English vernacular and having African American friends
can go alongside doing well in school and expressing pride about making
the honor roll. In Johnnie's case, movement across school settings had
uncoupled the problematic link between academic success and selling out.

Following Johnnie's lead, this book delves into the lives of students to
ask how they conceptualize and assert their ethnic and racial identities
across varied curricular settings. When speaking of identity, I am referring to
presentation of self in a matrix of social relationships—a pattern of social
assertion that significant others recognize and come to expect. I focus particularly on links between ethnic/racial self-conceptions, academic engagement, and factors within school settings. As expressed in the title of this
book, my purpose is to illuminate factors and practices that work to mold
students as they go about making identities.

In conducting this inquiry, my intent is to approach a familiar topic
from a novel angle. Over the past twenty years, most research on diverse
students has looked at academic engagement through the lens of group
membership, asking how cultural differences or the group's minority status
(immigrant or involuntary) shape behaviors and perceptions. Thus, the
emphasis has been on external forces—primarily familial socialization to

cultural practices or the perception of historical circumstances by group members. With regard to the relationship between identity and academic engagement, for example, anthropologists have argued that the nature of the history, subordination, and exploitation of a group affects the meanings that its members attach to ethnic and racial differences, and thus the willingness of group members to assert an academic identity (Ogbu, 1987, 1994; Suarez-Orozco & Suarez-Orozco, 1993). Ethnographies of African American and Mexican American students (Fordham & Ogbu, 1986; Matute-Bianchi, 1986) have helped lead to the hypothesis that "involuntary" minorities—peoples who were originally brought to the United States through slavery, conquest, or colonization—develop an oppositional identity in which succeeding in school is viewed as selling out to one's oppressors. (This perspective, in turn, is said to derive from historical experiences with inequities in American labor and political markets.) In contrast, immigrant minorities, having chosen voluntarily to come to the United States, perceive America as a land of opportunity, believe the effort devoted to schoolwork will pay off, and consider academic success as additive learning. In this latter case, adoption of an academic identity is not viewed as antithetical to maintenance of ethnic/racial identity; in fact, in some cases the two may be viewed as complementary (Gibson, 1987; Suarez-Orozco & Suarez-Orozco, 1993).

Such work is useful not only for advancing the dialogue concerning differences in minority group achievement, but also for conceptualizing the role that broader historical and economic circumstances play in day-to-day classroom activity. Taken to an extreme, however, it implies that the meanings, behaviors, and perceptions associated with a specific background are relatively fixed, exerting a constant influence on students' academic work until they leave. I reframe the question by considering the role of school and classroom processes in nurturing, resisting, or shaping the meanings students bring with them to school. For example, can an immigrant orientation be transformed in a school environment that offers little to its immigrant students? Can the oppositional practices associated with involuntary minority status be manifested differently in less constraining settings? In so doing, my intent is not only to further theory development, but also to identify and reveal the relations of power and knowledge that structure social categories, thereby contributing to the selves youths reveal across different contexts.

I will argue for a fluid conception of social categories, showing through in-depth case studies that ethnic and racial identities are dependent on the range of cultural and intercultural phenomena that individuals mediate within varied social matrices. Consistent with contemporary theories of ethnicity and race (Anzaldúa, 1987; Clifford, 1988; Hall, 1987; hooks, 1992; Okamura, 1981; Roosens, 1989; Rosaldo, 1989), adolescents' voices reveal that identity is constantly recreated, coming forward or retreating to the background in response to the politics and relations that characterize changing social situations. School-based settings, as primary cultural arenas in which issues of diversity are enacted, thus structure and guide the meaning of social categories and the construction of ethnic and racial identities. The voices and experiences of high school students demonstrate the connections between identity and academic engagement, therefore demonstrating the critical need to consider school-based practices and processes in analyses of student action.

## POWER AND IDENTITY FROM A
## POSTSTRUCTURAL PERSPECTIVE

Recent work in anthropology, sociology, and education has been influenced by poststructural notions of power, particularly ideas concerned with the means by which power is put into operation and its impact on the actions and conceptions of others. Positing that the selves we create are embedded in disciplinary relationships laced with power and meaning (Kondo, 1990; Foucault, 1983; Giroux, 1992), poststructuralism offers an alternative approach to conceptualizing the politics and aesthetics of identity in American high schools.

Poststructuralism's emphases on disciplinary technology (isolating, ordering, systematizing practices) and serious speech acts (truth claims asserted by an expert in an area) are two concepts relevant to my analysis. Disciplinary technology and serious speech acts both contribute to a definition of what is "normal" in advance and, therefore, can be viewed as practices that teach, or "discipline" participants to the meaning of institutional (and social) categories, for example, prisoner, soldier, teacher, student. In schools, for example, the taken-for-granted, "objective" division of students into academic tracks can be viewed as a disciplinary technology, in that tracking highlights differences and disciplines students and teachers to particular conceptions about the meaning of high- and low-achieving students (particularly when one considers that European American and Asian American students tend to dominate these courses). Similarly, a disciplinary system that gives unlimited authority to send students from the classroom to in-school suspension marks students as total subordinates and teaches that good students discern and conform to adult rules, arbitrary or not.

Likewise, because students may view certain adults (e.g., guidance counselors, teachers, etc.) as privileged authorities with specific knowledge about higher education, life chances, and so on, their assertions may be viewed as serious speech acts—knowledge to be studied, repeated, and passed on to friends. A network of serious speech acts may come to constitute a discursive system; that is, a system that works to control both what is said and how others are conceptualized. For example, an administration's creation and publication of a policy that bans students from wearing colors associated with the activities of one specific ethnic or racial group labels members of that group as particularly dangerous. Similarly, counselors and teachers may pronounce certain behaviors frequently associated with middle-class European American youth (e.g., student council, school-based activities) as necessary for college acceptance, thereby rendering youths, who do well academically, yet spend free time working, less confident about their futures.

A second theme relevant to this analysis is the poststructural conception of power as an "action upon an action" (Foucault, 1983:221). Power does not determine others but rather structures the possible field of action, "guiding the course of conduct and putting in order the possible outcome" (Foucault, 1983:220). Embodied and enacted in personal relationships, power relations are present as individuals make active efforts to force others into comprehensible categories. At the same time, individuals are not inert objects; rather, individuals can and do resist the meanings they encounter even as others seek to push them toward comprehensible categories. In short, power is not a system of domination that leaves no room for resistance, but rather practices and discourse that define normality in advance.

From this perspective, identity can be conceptualized as a process that develops in a matrix of structuring social and institutional relationships and practices. Presentations of self, ranging from resistance to assimilation, are linked not only to minority status and perceptions of labor market opportunities but also to disciplinary technologies, serious speech acts, and other factors at the institutional level. Because schools participate in negotiating the meanings students attach to identity, the ways in which teachers and schools handle power and convey ethnically and racially relevant meanings become relevant to the conceptualization of students' behaviors. Further, while school-based practices and factors may reflect broader societal factors and definitions, it becomes possible to conceptualize the orchestration of resistance among a network of teachers, or at the broader school level.

## BACKGROUND TO THE STUDY

This book evolved out of a three-year longitudinal investigation of adolescents' sociocultural worlds. The Students' Multiple Worlds Study, carried out at Stanford University's Center for Research on the Context of Secondary School Teaching (CRC),[1] focused on fifty-five students who were selected to represent some of the diversity found in four of California's large urban high schools.[2] The research team included Patricia Phelan, senior research associate and project director, and Hanh Cao Yu and myself, both graduate students at the time. As a team, we were concerned generally with students' perspectives about factors that impact academic and social engagement within the school community. This initial approach led to the development of a model and typology that illustrate the diverse ways in which meanings drawn from youths' family, peer, and school worlds combine to influence students' actions (Phelan, Davidson & Yu, 1993). This book departs slightly from this more holistic emphasis in that it emphasizes the school as a context for meaning. At the same time, the case studies of individual students reflect this perspective, as each incorporates information about the meanings students bring to school as a result of immersion in family and peer group settings. Thus, the reader is able to consider the role of school-level practices and factors in light of meanings and practices derived from the students' experiences outside of school.

Initially invited to describe school factors that affect engagement with learning, the teens frequently and spontaneously referred to a variety of features relevant to their feelings about school. References to race and ethnicity and their implications for engagement were common. For example, "Andrea," a Vietnamese immigrant whose grades began to drop rapidly when she entered high school, spoke of the conflict she perceived between maintaining her ethnicity and the behaviors she viewed as necessary for academic achievement: "Sometimes at home when my grades go down I promise myself 'Okay, I'm not going to hang around them [Vietnamese peers] no more, I just want to hang with all Americans so I'm Americanized so I learn more English and be good. .... [but] when I see Vietnamese hanging around with Americans at school they're always speaking English. ... I mean, if I hate them and I become one of them it's not good (ES48STD: 389–394; 533–539)." Further, students commonly linked aspects of their academic behavior to messages about social differences that were embedded in their school environments. For example, Joyce, a high-achieving African American/Guyanian student, spoke of silencing herself in an advanced track classroom, connecting her behavior to messages internalized about the relationship between race, mathematics achievement, and intelligence: ".... well none of my Black friends want to be in advanced math. .... or maybe they're not smart enough. But sometimes I feel that I shouldn't belong in there because like there's a lot of smart people in that class and I just don't feel like I'm smart enough to be in that class. .... I can never ask a question because everyone is so smart in that class (VA16STD: 1402–1420)."

The study on which this book is based was initiated to delve further into issues such as those raised by Andrea and Joyce. The investigation relied on ethnographic methods: intensive interviews, carried out over a two-year period; observations in and out of the classroom; and analyses of school (e.g., statistical data on tracking, suspension rates) and individual record data (e.g., attendance patterns, grades). In addition to drawing on information collected from the larger sample of fifty-five participants, I selected twelve sophomore students from whom we collected additional case study data. The research team spent time with these youths and their friends as participant-observers: hanging out before and after school, attending classes, going to lunch, and visiting their homes. In addition, we interviewed these students about the norms, behaviors, expectations, and values they perceived as being specific to their ethnic or racial backgrounds.

Yu, herself a Vietnamese immigrant, worked with the two Vietnamese immigrant females in the study. Phelan worked with Ryan Moore, a European American male. I paired myself with the remaining nine students, splitting my time among them. Together, we spent approximately sixty-five days attending high school. As displayed in Table I.1, the study included students from the four major social groups represented at these high schools (African American, European American, Latino, and Vietnamese); of these students, three could be classified as "involuntary" and nine as "voluntary" immigrants. Table I.1 also provides an overview of the students' academic backgrounds a) upon entering high school and b) during their freshman and sophomore years of high school, demonstrating the diversity in their academic experiences.

Table I.1. Students Included in the Ethnicity Study

| | | | Average GPA | |
| | | Immigrant | Middle | High |
| Student | Race/Ethnicity | Status | School | School |
| --- | --- | --- | --- | --- |
| Edward Abatta | Italian American | Voluntary | 3.71 | 2.75 |
| Johnnie Betts | African American | Involuntary | 0.80 | 2.89 |
| Donna Carlota | Mexican/European American | Involuntary | 2.81 | 2.29 |
| Carla Chávez | Mexican/Cuban American | Voluntary | 3.97 | 3.75 |
| Joyce Cunningham | African/Guyanian American | Voluntary | 3.82 | 3.67 |
| Sonia Gonzales | Mexican American | Voluntary | 2.60 | 0.54 |
| Trinh Le | Vietnamese Immigrant | Voluntary | 4.00 | 4.00 |
| Ryan Moore | European American | Voluntary | 3.92 | 3.84 |
| Joey Nelson | African American | Involuntary | 2.67 | 1.67 |
| Marbella Sanchez | Mexican Immigrant | Voluntary | 3.00 | 3.34 |
| Patricia Schmidt | Mexican/Chinese/European American | Voluntary | 3.58 | 3.37 |
| Andrea Wong | Vietnamese/Chinese Immigrant | Voluntary | 3.70 | 2.52 |

Committed to the concept of "triangulation," we did not rely solely on students' perspectives but also collected data relevant to understanding the disciplinary technology and serious speech acts operating at each of the high schools. Thus, we collected district statistical data on academic tracking, suspension rates, fulfillment of college requirements, and high school graduation rates. In addition, I and other CRC staff interviewed faculty, staff, and administrators (thirty to forty adults at each high school). Interview data collected by other CRC research personnel provided general contextual information: school history, teachers' perceptions of desegregation, and teachers' perceptions of student needs. In my interviews, I concentrated on factors and themes which emerged during student interviews, asking questions relevant to understanding the disciplinary technologies employed and the level of differentiation observed at each high school. Thus, the interviews were designed to provide basic information about factors such as the school's mission with regard to diversity, tracking procedures, the communication and availability of information regarding college and careers, and student discipline. In addition, I sought to elicit adults' working social theories about social conflict, approaches to student discipline, sources of academic/social differentiation, and the behavior of diverse youth. Finally, I interviewed teachers from classrooms which students identified as places where they were most and least likely (or able) to engage academically. Here I was interested in gaining insight into teacher characteristics or practices which students identified as empowering or enabling.

I am often asked how I became interested in these research questions and the extent to which students were willing to help me answer them (e.g., "Why do you care about students who are so different from you?" "Did the students talk to you?"). Such questions are typically connected to my position as an European American, middle-class woman, as well as to my age (twenty-seven at the time of the study). I became concerned about the relationship between the politics of difference and cognition as a result of varied learning experiences in two countries. During 1984, as a student in a small French city, I found myself increasingly aware of my national identity as Reagan voiced anti-Russian rhetoric and "Dynasty" figured prominently on local television stations. As the most conventionally American-looking among us heard derogatory comments that seemed to connect to the political situation, and as my accented attempts at French drew looks of impatience, I tried to shift the political meanings underlying social interactions by telling people that I was Swedish or German (a strategy that proved only somewhat useful given my accent). Often, I chose to remain silent.

Three years later, the politics of being an American in China were quite different. In 1987, China was arguably at the peak of its latest historical swing toward ideas associated with technologically developed countries such as the United States. Here, nationality and race became a political asset—light hair and blue eyes marked me as a harbinger of information about a world many were eager to discuss, and I was treated as a curiosity worthy of attention (which perhaps accounts for patience with my grammatical errors and heavy accent). While one might predict an easier transition and more successful language learning experience in a European country, in fact the political meanings attached to my nationality rendered the acquisition of language and border-crossing skills more difficult in this setting. In France, I grew hesitant to speak and avoided conversations with strangers; in China, I spoke publicly and without hesitation.

Yet, while providing points of reference, such experiences clearly differ greatly from those of the youths I describe in this volume. (For example, I could leave and return to a home country where my culture has been defined as "mainstream.") The question "Did the students talk to you?" might better be framed as "What did you miss?", as the ethnic, class and gender differences between myself and the students with whom I spent time added another layer of complexity to social interactions. For example, I couldn't go with males into the bathroom or locker room, nor could I participate in pick-up basketball games during lunch. Such gender issues are reflected in the predominant place of females in this book, as I saw and consequently knew more about the females than the males in my study. Likewise, though my comprehension of Spanish is fair, students would have spoken Spanish more than they did had I known the language fluently and, as such, revealed more aspects of their ethnicity. Complicating this factor was the diversity in linguistic practices that I encountered, with youths moving from standard Mexican Spanish, to dialect, to various urbanisms (ranging from Chicano street slang or "Caló" to "Spanglish") as the occasion demanded. Thus, sometimes during lunchtime gatherings I lost the thread of conversation, leaving holes in my field notes. Though individuals often filled me in after the fact, it is clear that the situation would have been better had I had perfect understanding of the language. Finally, on a general level, being an adult European American woman among teens structured their behavior in a variety of ways. I know, for example, that youths with sporadic attendance patterns were more likely to attend class when I was with them. Students may also have censored or exaggerated some of their descriptions and conversations. Though it was possible to corroborate many students' descriptions with teacher interviews, record data, and statements made by other students, it is doubtful that events always occurred as youths perceived them.

Nevertheless, the forthcoming data will show that the teens were generous and engaged in our discussions. Over and over again, students told me and other members of our team that most adults do not take the time to hear or ask about the difficulties they face. They were eager to talk and full of questions. Though social differences were relevant to our interactions, they did not impede a desire for communication.

A second question that arises in my conversations with others about this research concerns the choice of case study youth; that is, how did I choose the students that I describe in the following chapters? To respond, I explain that I sought first to illustrate three general patterns of identity construction—unconventional, conformist, and transcultural—that emerged during this research. When selecting students to illustrate these three general categories, I wanted also to choose individuals who clearly illuminated disciplinary technologies, discourses, and other practices that work both to reproduce and resist social categories. After selecting three initial students (one for each category), I then sought diversity, both in terms of demographic characteristics (racial, ethnic, or nationality) and in terms of academic experiences. So, for example, when choosing adolescents to illustrate conformist identities, I initially selected an European American-born male enrolled in the advanced academic track. I then selected a counterpart student, a Mexican American-born female enrolled in general courses. In all, as summarized in the overview of this text which follows, I describe three pairs of youth who vary in terms of academic placement and in terms of either race, ethnicity, or nation of origin.

## OVERVIEW OF THE TEXT

Discourse concerning diversity and its implications for schooling have long been of concern to educators (Davidson & Phelan, 1993). Certain forms of "difference" have usually been the focus, with these differences typically framed as static variables with predictable and specific influences on students' academic engagement. This book seeks to shed light on an area that has received relatively little attention, considering how school practices affect youths' sense of their racial and ethnic backgrounds, and thus the relationship between identity and academic engagement. Much of the story will be told through the use of case studies, designed to draw the reader into the world of adolescents.

I begin, however, at a distance. Chapters 1 and 2 deepen and advance the discussion that I began in this introductory chapter. In chapter 1, I start with a critical historical overview of the ways in which scholars have conceptualized the relationship between diverse youth and schooling. By juxtaposing a discussion of structural factors, relevant to the construction of identity, with research that suggests that schools can negotiate effectively for the attention of oppositional students, I lay the foundation for going beyond portraits in which individuals appear as static and rather helpless entities. In chapter 2, I turn to youth, allowing them to argue for incorporating consideration of school-based factors into analyses of resistance and accommodation. Using data collected from the fifty-five participants in the Students' Multiple Worlds Study, I describe and discuss five school-level factors that adolescents describe as contributing to student alienation, particularly among members of marginalized racial and ethnic groups. These include: patterns that emanate from academic tracking, negative expectations, differential treatment of social groups, bureaucratized relationships and practices, and barriers to information.

*emphasis on resistance*

In Part II, "Disciplinary Technologies Resisted: Unconventional Identities," I look more closely at individuals, with the intent of revealing more specifically how identity is molded in relation to distinctive curricular environments. I describe two students who seek to challenge the social categories and stereotypes that emanate from disciplinary technologies in their environments. The first case (chapter 3) describes Marbella Sanchez, a recent Mexican immigrant enrolled in courses for learners of English as a Second Language. Marbella is a student who is committed to the projection of an ethnic identity that is at once pro-academic and oppositional. At the same time, strong sorting mechanisms and rigid disciplinary policies limit her ability to project and assert this identity. Chapter 4 describes Carla Chávez, a high-achieving Latina who is enrolled in advanced track classes. Born in the United States to Cuban and Mexican parents, Carla's story reveals how participation in the advanced track can enable realization of political goals, while at the same time generate feelings of isolation and dependency. Even as Carla participates, she feels compelled to mask her ethnic voice and limit her academic engagement.

From this emphasis on resistance, in Part III, "Dominant Discourses Accepted: Conformist Identities," I move to consider the observance of social categories. My emphasis here is on how disciplinary technologies and practices work to divide and separate youths into the successful and the deviant. Cases reveal how two students come to read and embrace definitions they see as relevant to their backgrounds, thus reproducing social categories. Chapter 5 describes Sonia Gonzales, the American-born daughter of Mexican immigrants. Once a strong student, during the first two years of high school, Sonia becomes increasingly involved in "crazy" behavior which she defines as characteristic of what it means to be Mexican. With this, Sonia's grades plummet, and she appears as the stereotype of the disengaged oppositional youth. Ryan Moore, described in chapter 6, in many ways appears to be the antithesis of Sonia. Defined by those in his environment as the embodiment of the all-American student, Ryan is a high-achieving European American youth who is committed to northern American middle-class values. Yet, in many ways, Ryan's response to his situation is identical to Sonia's. Like Sonia, Ryan conforms to the categorical meanings present in his environment, sometimes at the expense of his personal desires and feelings. Distancing himself from those who are perceived as different, Ryan argues also that all of the students around him should "try to grow and get better and fit in."

Part IV, "Empowering Speech Acts: Encouraging Transcultural Identities," focuses on varying types of speech acts that students perceive as powerful enough to counteract other messages they have encountered about their ethnic or racial backgrounds. Two cases are presented. In chapter 7, I return to the story of Johnnie Betts. Johnnie's case reveals how movement into a new high school environment—in which graduation and engagement are expected of African American and European American students alike—caused a fundamental reorientation in the way in which he conceptualized his racial identity in relation to his schooling. At the same time, because the speech acts that Johnnie encounters are not oriented toward altering academic differentiation at his high school or toward the empowerment of youth of color, their long-term impact on the school as a whole is limited. Thus, Johnnie's case raises questions about the long-term significance of acts that are not oriented toward affecting the school as a system. This situation is compared to that at a second high school, described in chapter 8. Here, I discuss how Patricia Schmidt, a young woman of multiethnic descent, benefits from significant speech acts that comprise the ideology of a program oriented toward the empowerment of low-income students and students of color. I explain how adults work to employ these speech acts to successfully combat messages emanating from the disciplinary technologies of the high school. Additionally, I describe how the program affects academic differentiation at the high school, thereby challenging some of the categorical meanings in the environment.

Part V, the epilogue, links ethnographic data to educational and theoretical questions. I concentrate particularly on the implications of the data for debates concerning the potential for ethnic flexibility, approaches to multicultural education, curricular reorganization of schools, and alternative approaches to discipline.

The work here is employed both to problematize dominant views of the relationship between social background and academic identity and to further conversation. The youths that I portray bring meanings with them to school—meanings that can be traced to community politics as well as to family and peer group norms. But such meanings exist in relation to those encountered at school, contributing to the set of conditions that constrain the manner in which individuals craft their identities.

# PART I

# Frames on Identity
# and Academic Engagement

CHAPTER 1

# The Politics of Identity

## *Historical and Theoretical Contexts*

As a text concerned with the politics of ethnic and racial self-expression in the 1990s, the data and conclusions that emerge in this work must be read as artifacts of both a theoretical legacy and a specific history. During the past decade, Americans have witnessed the greatest rise in immigration since the turn of the century. With immigrants—the majority from Asia, Latin America, and Mexico—arriving at the rate of more than one million per year, today's America has been described as "a truly multicultural society marked by unparalleled diversity" ("America's Immigrant Challenge," p. 3). Nowhere is this more apparent than California, the site for this study. Paralleling this has been an upsurge of discussion about diversity among domestic Americans, with Americans of color pushing for broader representation within the political and public spheres. This is reflected particularly in discourse concerning public education, with debates raging around the content of the curriculum, the nature of culturally sensitive pedagogy, and the provision of education to immigrant children.

Expanding on issues raised in the introduction to this text, this chapter presents a critical overview of developments in theory, concerning ethnic and racial identities and the politics of engaging diverse school youth. My purpose is to situate this text, providing a framework for the chapters that follow. Though several studies are referenced and discussed, I do not attempt to summarize all relevant research but rather to illuminate and discuss three central themes, each of which has implications for the forthcoming analysis. First, reflecting the discourse in broader American society, scholars have increasingly come to recognize previously unpredicted manifestations of race and ethnicity in American society. With this have come new conceptualizations of the factors and processes that affect their salience and practice, both for groups and for the individual. These ideas, emphasizing the political and relational nature of social categories, have important implications for educational theorists and practitioners. Most notably, they point to the potential for flexibility, with regard to the ways in which individuals practice the racial and ethnic aspects of their social identities, with this practice contingent on a variety of factors, both situational and national. This points to the importance of considering an array of contextual factors when seeking to interpret and explain student behavior.

Second, reflecting a continued desire to explain and ameliorate the reproduction of social inequality along ethnic and racial lines, educational anthropologists have increasingly moved beyond explanations that emphasize differences in cultural behaviors. Previous explanations have been complemented by theories that incorporate consideration of societal factors. By demonstrating critical connections between social structure, group ideology, and educational engagement, this approach has led to important advances with regard to understanding differences in the engagement of diverse students. At the same time, the global nature of such theories limits their explanatory power on the local and individual level.

To support the latter part of the argument advanced above, in the third section of this chapter I present empirical evidence which suggests that school- and classroom-level factors may also influence the behavior and ideology of diverse students. These findings indicate the importance of moving beyond the primary emphasis on historical and structural factors emphasized in contemporary anthropological theory to incorporate the more fluid, situational conceptions of social categories emphasized by contemporary theorists.


## SHIFTING CONCEPTIONS OF RACE AND ETHNICITY

Debates concerning manifestations of ethnic and racial identities in America have been framed largely around understanding factors relevant to their salience, emergence, and disappearance. Throughout the beginning of the twentieth century, for example, ethnicity in America has been popularly conceptualized as something temporary. Often viewed as a working- and lower-class style that will erode with social and geographical mobility (Alba, 1990), ethnicity and its manifestations (e.g., group solidarity, a sense of ethnic identity) are typically linked to shared culture, experience, and interests, as well as membership in homogenous informal social structures. As immigrants acculturate, this traditional model assumes that manifestations of ethnicity will gradually be replaced by Anglo American traits and a "mainstream" sense of identity. Though race has traditionally been seen as a biological category, similar assumptions have structured policy debates concerning its cultural manifestations. Again, such differences are expected to disappear with time as people of color assimilate to mainstream society.

A variety of factors, however, call this model into question. For one, older scholars assumed that the social and geographic mobility necessary for the dispersal of cultural and social differences associated with race and ethnicity would occur. Yet, while there is evidence that European American immigrants have approached this mobility, even in the third and later generations, educational, occupational, and income differences continue to separate African Americans and Latinos from their European American counterparts (Alba, 1990).

Moreover, there is data to indicate that social mobility changes but does not necessarily eradicate the salience of race and ethnicity. Among Mexican Americans who have attained middle-class status, for example, language use clearly declines. Yet the cultural emphasis on extended familism, reflected in ties to family and community, appears to strengthen over time in the United States (Keefe & Padilla, 1987). Similarly, middle-class African Americans report feeling a stronger bond with African Americans than with their social class; consistent with this, many continue to live in neighborhoods that are primarily African American (Zweigenhaft & Domhoff, 1991). Finally, even among European American groups who have experienced the economic and social mobility presumed necessary for total assimilation, some aspects of ethnicity remain salient (Alba, 1990). For example, large numbers of White ethnics continue to describe themselves in terms of ethnic labels, attach some importance to these, and can point to some ethnically relevant experience in their lives. Among members of this group, manifestations of ethnic identity, reflected in a heightened awareness of ethnic background, knowledge of mother tongue, and social sensitivity to ethnicity, appear to increase with education.

These and other factors have led to increasing recognition that manifestations of race and ethnicity may not follow a linear pattern, with acculturation leading to assimilation, but rather reemerge in new shapes and forms. Consistent with theorists that see race and ethnicity as partially political phenomena (see also Bell, 1975; Glazer & Moynihan, 1975; Nielsen,

1985), anthropologists and other social theorists have increasingly argued that ethnic and racial identities are socially constructed, with such construction tied to political, economic, and personal circumstances. Over time and across settings, groups and individuals may employ cultural symbols in novel ways to construct boundaries and gain material resources (Anzaldúa, 1987; Clifford, 1988; Hall, 1987; hooks, 1989; Kondo, 1990). Clifford (1988), for example, describes the public emergence of tribal identity among Mashpee Native Americans in a small town near Boston. Majority residents until the 1960s, the Mashpee were gradually outnumbered by European Americans. As local government passed from Mashpee control and large tracts of undeveloped land were claimed by European Americans, Mashpee residents became increasingly concerned. The more obvious markers anthropologists and others traditionally associate with culture and ethnicity were also nonexistent; surviving language had not been seen since 1800, and distinct religious and political structure had also disappeared. Yet, in 1976, this seemingly acculturated group organized to sue the federal government for possession of 16,000 acres of land, basing their claim on the argument that they, as a tribe, had been collectively despoiled of lands in the mid-nineteenth century. Referring to this reemergence of identity among Mashpee citizens, Clifford contends:

> Groups negotiating their identity in contexts of domination and exchange persist, patch themselves together in ways different from a living organism. A community, unlike a body, can lose a central "organ" and not die. All the critical elements of identity are in specific conditions replaceable: language, blood, land, leadership, religion. Recognizable, viable tribes exist in which any one or even most of these elements are missing, replaced or largely transformed. (1988:338)

Consistent with Clifford's argument, others have described how groups may develop new and shifting manifestations of race and ethnicity distinctive in cultural form (Anzaldúa, 1987; hooks, 1992; Ogbu, 1994; Rosaldo, 1989). Such patterns emerge in response both to the group's political and economic situation and the desire to maintain identity. Commenting on Chicano Spanish, for example, Gloria Anzaldúa writes: "Chicano Spanish is a border tongue which developed naturally. . . . For a people who are neither Spanish nor live in a country in which Spanish is the first language; for a people who live in a country in which English is the reigning tongue but who are not Anglo . . . what recourse is left to them but to create their own language? A language which they can connect their identity to, one capable of communicating the realities and values true to themselves—a language with terms that are neither español ni inglés, but both" (p. 55).

For individuals, the complex political, economic, and historical relations that give rise to shifting manifestations of race and ethnicity are also manifested on the personal level, shaping projections of identity (Anzaldúa, 1987; Kondo, 1990). Speaking of her position as a Japanese American carrying out fieldwork in Japan, for example, Kondo describes how she was moved toward a more Japanese female role:

> At its most extreme point, I became "the Other" in my own mind, where the identity I had known in another context simply collapsed. The success of our conspiracy to recreate me as Japanese reached its climax one August afternoon. . . . Promptly at four P.M., the hour when most Japanese housewives do their shopping for the evening meal, I lifted the baby into her stroller and pushed her along ahead of me as I inspected the fish, selected the freshest looking vegetables, and mentally planned the meal for the evening. As I glanced into the shiny metal surface of the butcher's display case, I noticed someone who looked terribly familiar: a typical young housewife, clad in slip-on sandals and the loose cotton shirt called "home wear," a woman walking with a characteristically Japanese bend to the knees and sliding feet. Suddenly I clutched the handle of the stroller to steady myself as a wave of dizziness washed over me, for I realized I had caught a glimpse of nothing less than my own reflection. (Kondo, 1990:16–17)

Kondo was able to martial the psychological and material resources to distance herself from consuming pressures to assimilate: "I resolved to move into a new apartment, to distance myself from my Japanese home and Japanese existence" (p. 17). However, others lack access to the power necessary to maintain this delicate balance. In his controversial autobiography, for example, Richard Rodriguez (1982) speaks frankly of the choice he perceived between educational success and maintenance of his home language, arguing that it was necessary to leave his working-class Latino self behind in order to succeed in a Catholic school. Having lost his facility with Spanish, his link to the past, Rodriguez was further driven to compensate for his loss through working to assimilate to academic life: "I never forgot that schooling had irretrievably changed my family's life. That knowledge, however, did not weaken ambition. Instead, it strengthened resolve. Those times I remembered the loss of my past with regret, I quickly reminded myself of all the things my teachers could give me" (p. 50).

Thus, the voices of individual authors and data from whole group studies combine to suggest that manifestations of racial and ethnic identity do not follow a predictable path, but ebb, flow, and reshape in response to the politics and relations that characterize changing national, regional, and local social situations. With individuals and groups ever able to develop new cultural forms conducive to the expression of identity, it becomes relevant to consider contextual conditions that give shape to varied forms of group and self-expression.

## CULTURE, IDENTITY, AND SCHOOLING: ANTHROPOLOGICAL CONCEPTIONS

One of the more enduring cornerstones of American thought is the conviction that education offers a route to social mobility for peoples of all backgrounds. Education is popularly conceptualized as one factor integral to achieving the economic parity and geographic dispersal presumed basic to integrating diverse citizens into American society. Yet, while it is clear that education improves individual chances for social mobility, it is equally apparent that schools work less well for impoverished African American and Latino school children. Overall, African American and Latino youth, as well as children from lower socioeconomic backgrounds, drop out at rates higher than their peers (Rumberger, 1987; National Center for Education Statistics, 1994: Table 103).[1] There are also significant achievement gaps among students of European American, African American, and Latino descent, with European Americans outperforming their peers on tests of reading, writing, and mathematics proficiency (National Center for Education Statistics, 1994: Tables 106, 112, 116). For the many students of color (and women) who do graduate from high school, educational credentialing also falls short of its promise of equal opportunity. Among high school graduates age twenty-two to thirty-four, for example, 8 percent of European American males live in poverty. This compares to 11 percent of European American females, 16 percent of African American males, and 31 percent of African American females (Fine, 1991).[2]

In the context of patterns that suggest education is often more reproductive than transformative, anthropologists have worked since the 1960s to understand and interpret the relationship between diverse youth and schooling. Their efforts have generated a long-running debate concerning the relative influence of cultural and structural factors on student engagement and achievement. Throughout the late 1960s and 1970s, in response to theories implying that impoverished African American children are culturally deprived of stimulating learning environments (Bereiter & Engelmann, 1966; Deutsch, 1967), a series of ethnographic and sociolinguistic studies were employed to demonstrate that students of color encounter stimulating, but culturally different, learning environments. In 1969, for example, sociolinguist William Labov provided detailed descriptions of the conversations of urban African American youth to support his argument that "in fact, Negro children in the urban ghettoes receive a great deal of verbal stimulation, hear more well-formed sentences than middle-class children, and participate fully in a highly verbal culture; they have the same basic vocabulary, possess the same capacity for conceptual learning, and use the same logic as anyone else who learns to speak and understand English" (p. 179). Studies of African American (Heath, 1982), Native Hawaiian (Gallimore, Boggs & Jordan, 1974), and various Native American communities (Cazden & John, 1968; John, 1972; Philips, 1972, 1982) provided further evidence of the rich learning environments that can characterize culturally different homes and communities.

Building on this ethnographic data, initial anthropological explanations of the academic difficulties experienced by children of color emphasized cultural differences in interaction and learning styles.[3] Arguing that verbal and nonverbal communication patterns are culturally learned patterns that generate different and often conflicting expectations between persons of different cultures, anthropologists theorized that cultural differences produce systematic and recurrent miscommunication in the classroom that over time escalates into academic trouble and failure. Because cultural explanations for academic failure do not occur to teachers, educators turn to labels, attributing inherent negative traits to their students, such as laziness. Thus, while failure is in reality co-produced by teachers and students, the explanation of such failure is institutionalized as deficiency.

Missing from such culture-focused arguments, however, were considerations of 1) the structural factors that may contribute to social reproduction, 2) the relationship between inequality and group belief systems, and 3) examination of the fact that many groups with cultural styles different from that of the mainstream succeed in the U.S. educational system (Ogbu, 1978; 1982). In recognition of these difficulties, anthropologists have increasingly considered groups' historical experiences with economic and political inequalities in seeking explanations of social reproduction. Linking historical experiences to the evolution of group ideology, Ogbu (1987, 1994) has developed the notions of oppositional social identity and oppositional cultural frame of reference. Terming peoples who were originally brought to the United States through slavery, conquest, or colonization "involuntary minorities" (African Americans, Native Americans, some Mexican Americans, and Native Hawaiians are examples), Ogbu argues that a long history with oppression and racism has created a skeptical attitude among involuntary minorities toward opportunities for gainful employment and social mobility. Doing well in school, therefore, seems pointless. Cultural differences become markers of identity to be maintained in opposition to the dominant culture; further, groups may develop secondary cultural differences, claiming and exaggerating certain forms of behavior, symbols, events, and meanings as appropriate because they are not characteristic of members of another population (Ogbu, 1987). Providing an oppositional frame of reference that has arisen in response to stigmatization, these factors enter negatively into the process of schooling, affecting engagement and motivation. In this sense, involuntary minority youth manifest an oppositional identity similar to that of the disaffected White working-class British students depicted in Willis' (1977) classic ethnography of social reproduction.

Ogbu applies a similar analysis to consideration of "immigrant" or "voluntary minorities"; peoples who moved more or less voluntarily to the United States because they believed it would bring them greater economic well-being, better overall opportunities, and greater political freedom. Immigrant minorities are said to perceive America as a land of opportunity and believe therefore that the effort they devote to schoolwork will pay off. Academic success, therefore, is seen as additive learning and cultural differences are seen as barriers to be overcome. Further, when economic and political conditions in the United States are better than in their home countries, immigrants may manifest a "dual frame of reference," in which opportunities in the United States are constantly compared and assessed in light of the situation in the country of origin.

Educational ethnographers considering involuntary and immigrant minority students have documented differences in both perceptions and expressions of identity. Fordham and Ogbu (1986), focusing on the ideology and behaviors of thirty-three African Americans at a low-income urban high school, describe how a majority of the youths interviewed perceived several behaviors associated with academics—working hard to get good grades, spending time in the library studying, being on time, and reading and writing poetry—as "acting White." Academic striving brought social (peer group) pressure, including accusations of disloyalty to the group and its cause, which in turn created anxiety about fear of losing one's friends and community.[4] Maria Matute-Bianchi (1986) documented a similar oppositional ideology among second- and third-generation Mexican-descent students.

Ethnographic research on immigrant students also provides evidence of links among group ideology, national experience, and academic engagement (Gibson, 1987; Suarez-Orozco, 1989; Suarez-Orozco & Suarez-Orozco, 1993).[5] Suarez-Orozco describes the ideology of fifty Central American high school students, who, on average, have a lower dropout rate than their Mexican American and Puerto Rican peers.[6] The youths face a number of institutional barriers: "A school atmosphere of drugs, violence, low expectations, the calculated tracking of minority students to nonacademic subjects, bitter teachers, the seductive offers by more acculturated peers to join the street culture, and the need to work to help the family" (Suarez-Orozco, 1987:290). Nevertheless, students describe schooling as the most important means of status mobility, manifesting a "dual frame of reference" in which they compare present opportunities in the United States to the past realities of their war-torn environments. Linking school success to familial obligation, the immigrants, like the individual quoted below, voice a sense of duty to families whom they perceive as having made tremendous sacrifices to send them to the United States:

> She wants to study to become somebody. She wants a career. Her parents are very poor. She wants a career to help her poor parents, so they do not have to suffer so much. She studies hard and becomes somebody. Her parents are so proud of her. (Suarez-Orozco & Suarez-Orozco, 1993:130)

Gibson (1987), in her study of Punjabi Indian youth in the San Joaquin Valley, found a similar drive to achieve, associated with the group's immigrant status, a factor she believes helps to account for this group's superior performance on standardized achievement tests relative to their European American counterparts.

Ogbu's macrosociological theory is attractive both in its breadth and broad explanatory power, and it illustrates the critical role that identity and ideology may play in the schooling process. Nevertheless, studies raise questions about the validity of concentrating purely on immigrant status when considering and predicting manifestations of identity and its meaning among groups. First, it is not clear that opposition necessarily implies academic failure. Contemporary studies of Iranian (Hoffman, 1988), Canadian Jewish (Shamai, 1987), French Algerian (Raissiguier, 1994), and Mexican American (Foley, 1991) students have demonstrated that both immigrant and involuntary youth may express oppositional cultures, while at the same time achieve academically. For example, Hoffman found that her Iranian informants did not view America as a land of opportunity but rather as an inferior alternative to life in Iran. Furthermore, although these students are extremely successful academically, teachers see them as "problem students" because of their perceived lack of respect for the school and its rules. Hoffman argues that Iranian students selectively reject and resist the values and methods of the school, while at the same time accepting its instrumental value—that academic success leads to later economic reward.

Second, consistent with contemporary theories of race and ethnicity, the manifestation and meaning of resistance appears to be shaped not only by immigrant status but also by social class status and the particulars of the local economic and political context (Foley, 1991; Jiobu, 1988; MacLeod, 1987; Weis, 1990).[7] In a study of Mexican American teens in a southwestern Texas town, for example, Foley (1991) describes a group of academically successful middle-class Mexican Americans. While these students are "involuntary minorities" and manifest secondary cultural discontinuities in the form of invented Chicano cultural forms of expression, they also express traditional Mexican behaviors and engage in actions and behaviors conducive to winning favor with school authorities. Foley links this behavior to outcomes associated with the civil rights movement in small South Texas communities. The upwardly mobile Chicano parents of these youths and their peers are increasingly represented in government, professional, and small business positions. In this context, education does not appear superfluous, a factor that may help to account for why an additional 10 percent of students of Mexican descent in the area are finishing college than are their parents.

Finally, there is ample evidence to indicate that schools and the teachers within them can shape the behavior of oppositional youth. Yet, with regard to school-based contextual factors, teachers and schools appear almost incidental in Ogbu's theoretical framework, providing the settings that ensure outcomes but doing little or nothing to shape them. The final section of this chapter thus describes research relevant to the argument that manifestations of identity and academic engagement are shaped not just by broad sociohistorical factors, but also by practices and relationships at the school level.

## IDENTITY, ENGAGEMENT, AND SCHOOL-LEVEL PROCESSES

Literature concerning the relationship between diverse youth and schooling indicates that academic engagement for children of color is complicated and dependent on their situations. Engagement appears to depend not only on historical, economic, and political realities, but also on day-to-day factors and practices at the school and classroom levels. These findings suggest potential relationships between the meaning and practice of identity and the politics and relations that characterize educational contexts.

It is apparent, for example, that school context may shape positive academic outcomes for students whose background characteristics qualify them as "oppositional" (involuntary minorities). There is increasing evidence, for one, that Catholic schools produce higher achievement rates for Latino and African American youth. In tests of student achievement (as measured by performance on HS&B survey tests), Catholic school African Americans and Latinos outperform their comparable African American and Latino public school peers. After controlling for both student ability and socioeconomic indicators (parental education, occupational status, and certain possessions in the home), Catholic schooling in and of itself exerts a moderate but meaningful influence on measured achievement (Keith & Page, 1985). Statistical analyses suggest that the "Catholic school effect" may be due largely to the strong relationship between enrollment in Catholic schools and enrollment in advanced courses. Even after controlling for course enrollment, however, a small Catholic school effect continues to exert itself directly on achievement.[8] There is also evidence that within the public sector, schools differ in terms of the outcomes they produce for both voluntary and involuntary youth of color (Fordham, 1991; Lucas, Henze & Donato, 1990; Tharp & Gallimore, 1991; Tomlinson, 1991). In a study of twenty British urban comprehensive schools, for example, Tomlinson (1991) found striking cross-school differences in attainment for pupils with the same social and ethnic background characteristics.

When explaining such outcomes, scholars look not only to differences in features indicative of disciplinary technologies (e.g., course enrollment), but also to normative practices conducive to the development of alternative discursive systems (Lucas, Henze & Donato, 1990; Fordham, 1991; Metz, 1986). Describing the striking educational turnaround at a primarily African American junior high school in New York City, for example, Fordham (1991) emphasizes practices which foster student solidarity, while simultaneously encouraging competition conducive to academic effort. Cohorts at

Jordan Mott Junior High School are divided into four "teams," each balanced for ability. Classes within teams accrue points based on individuals' academic performance and attendance; these enable all team members to attend basketball games, go on class trips, and be present at class parties. Arguing that a desire to seek self-realization through service to the group is a culturally learned and prized value among African Americans, Fordham hypothesizes that Mott is successful partially because it works to link group cohesion to academic effort, thereby tying identity to school achievement. In contrast, the traditional school's emphasis on division by ability and on one-on-one competition run counter to the African American emphasis on collectivity and joint action. Fordham hypothesizes that these traditional divisionary practices create a dynamic in which academically successful youth feel forced to choose between academic success and racial identity. Similarly, in a study of three desegregated magnet schools, Metz (1986) analyzes the meanings generated by contrasting achievement ideologies, arguing that the extent to which teachers were able to stimulate academic progress in students of color (primarily African American) varied with the pedagogical mission the school adopted. Within a school for the gifted and talented, for example, Metz identifies a dominating ideology of competition and achievement. Here, students of color not only did not work hard, but also engaged in diverting antics that helped them avoid public academic performance. In two other magnet schools, the first dedicated to individually guided education and the second to open education, there were rewards for competence and progress, relative to one's former accomplishments, and a curriculum structured to encourage intense teacher-student interaction. Here, Metz found an increase in the academic engagement of students of color and a noticeable decrease in teacher-student conflict and interracial tensions.

A second pattern of findings also suggests relationships between classroom practice and manifestations of identity. Numerous studies describe changed behaviors in involuntary minority children after the adoption of "culturally appropriate" pedagogical practices and social arrangements (Au, 1980; Au & Jordan, 1981; Heath, 1982; Moll & Diaz, 1987; Tharp & Gallimore, 1991; Vogt, Jordan & Tharp, 1987). Originally manifesting behaviors that might be characterized as "oppositional," these students are described as engaged in changed social arrangements. As part of a research and development effort targeted toward increasing literacy among Native Hawaiian children, for example, the Kamehameha Early Education Project (KEEP) adapted reading instruction that incorporates participation structures characteristic of the "talk-story," a favored form of communication among

Native Hawaiian adults. Microanalyses of classroom discourse indicate that lessons incorporating these culturally congruent participation structures were associated with higher rates of pro-academic student behavior (Au & Mason, 1981). Similarly, Shirley Brice Heath (1982) worked with teachers to incorporate types of questions typically used in the African American community into classroom lessons. Heath found that European American teachers who socialized their own children to language depended heavily on questions conducive to teaching basic analytical skills typical of elementary school discourse. Examples include learning to label, identifying parts of a picture, naming parts of a whole, and talking about parts out of context. (e.g., What color is that coat? What is that?) In contrast, African American parents asked relatively few analytical questions. Rather, children were expected to learn how to respond to questions similar to those used in adult conversation. For example, children were frequently asked to relate to the whole of incidents and the composite characteristics of persons, objects, and events. (e.g., What's happening here? What's that like?) With incorporation of these latter question forms into social studies lessons, previously disengaged African American children "talked, actively and aggressively became involved in the lesson, and offered useful information about their past experiences" (1982:124). Moreover, teachers were able to convince their African American students to learn traditional classroom discourse skills. Heath argues that, as a result of this strategy: "Students caught onto the idea that this [asking analytical questions] was a somewhat strange custom, but one which, if learned, led to success in school activities and, *perhaps most important, did not threaten their ways of talking about things at home"* (1982:125, emphasis mine).

More recently, and consistent with the goals of this study, anthropologists and sociologists have focused directly on identifying links among student ideology, manifestations of academic identity, and features of instructional and programmatic settings. Mehan, Hubbard, and Villanueva (1994), for example, describe the student ideology that arises in a program that is highly successful in preparing low-income "involuntary minorities" for college. The program, functioning as a daily class elective, also places mid- and lower-achieving youth in college-prep courses and supports their academic development through tutoring and college counseling. Students in the program develop an ideology in which discrimination and prejudice are recognized, cultural identity is affirmed, and achievement is valued as a route to occupational success. Mehan and colleagues link this ideology—more like that of immigrants than involuntary minorities—to cultural practices particular to the program. These include those that work to foster group identification (marking group identity in a public manner and isolating group members for one period of the day) and the provision of opportunity to develop friendships with other academically oriented youth of color. Similarly, Weis (1990) demonstrates how school processes work to further the formation of ideology among White working-class high school males in a town where the mill economy has virtually disappeared. In contrast to previous studies of working-class male students, youth here express value for education and adhere to the behavioral norms of the school. However, at the same time, they do little to prepare themselves for college, earn average grades, focus primarily on passing, and evidence little engagement in the content of the curriculum, thereby revealing a "contradictory code" or respect toward schooling. Weis links this ideology to class status, the specifics of the local economy, and school processes. Like students, teachers articulate the instrumental importance of schooling but emphasize form rather than substance in learning. Students encounter a curriculum where routine, order, and following directions are emphasized—following teacher directions and memorizing prepackaged notes rather than engaging in discussions or activities conducive to constructing and challenging knowledge.

Findings from these studies indicate that it is critical for scholars to look at schools as more than stages for cultural and social reproduction. As institutions characterized by disciplinary technologies and discursive systems, schools may themselves play a role in furthering or restructuring the formation of identity among youth. Thus it is critical for those concerned with social change to begin to consider reproduction from multiple contextual perspectives.

## SUMMARY AND DISCUSSION

With a shifting demographic landscape and indications that manifestations of social categories are more complex and multifaceted than previously conceptualized, there have been dramatic developments in the ways in which race and ethnicity are discussed. Once associated with global sets of behaviors and orientations connected to shared culture, today race and ethnicity are increasingly viewed as political and relational social constructions. At the group level, studies have indicated that manifestations of race and ethnicity do not steadily decline but appear to flow in response to shifting economic, political, and local conditions. For individuals, identity manifests itself in complex ways, its salience and meaning shifting also with contextual meanings.

These theoretical developments provide a context for the critique of current dominant anthropological approaches to the relationship between identity and engagement in schooling. Reflecting developments in the field of sociology and statistics that indicate different patterns of academic achievement between minority groups, educational anthropologists have increasingly emphasized the relationship between the meanings youths attribute to their ethnic/racial identity and their group's historical position within the national economic and political structure. These meanings enter into the process of schooling, shaping responses to the education offered. I have suggested that such theory, focused exclusively on larger societal factors, overlooks the role that both local and school contextual factors may play in shaping students' ideology and subsequent engagement. Literature on culturally responsive pedagogy, as well as the successes of individual schools and programs, indicates that teachers and schools can negotiate with students whose sociohistorically produced peer group norms run counter to schooling. Further, there is evidence to suggest that ideology and identity reflect not only broader societal factors, but also features present in the institutional settings where youth act.

The next chapter moves forward with this point. I present data collected from fifty-five diverse students in four urban high schools. My emphasis is school and classroom factors which teens name as relevant to the construction of opposition, particularly among youth of color.

# CHAPTER 2

# Youths' Frames on Engagement

At this point, we have seen that studies of varied groups indicate that the conceptualization and practice of ethnic, racial, and class identities may enter both negatively and positively into the process of schooling. Drawing on literature which indicates that course enrollment, school ethos, and culturally congruent pedagogy may contribute to the process of identity formation among students of color, I have also argued that schools may affect the academic and social engagement of "oppositional" youths. In this chapter, I change course slightly, allowing adolescents to argue for incorporating considerations of school-based factors into analyses of resistance and accommodation to schooling. Drawing on interview data from fifty-five students, I focus on five factors which youth suggest contribute to manifestations of disengagement and alienation, particularly among students of color. These factors include: ① patterns that emanate from academic tracking, ② negative expectations, ③ differential treatment of varied ethnic and racial groups, ④ bureaucratized relationships and practices, and ⑤ barriers to information.

To situate students' perceptions, I draw on a sociological literature concerned with <u>school and workplace alienation</u>. Alienation has been empirically connected to lower academic achievement and to disruptive school behavior (Calabrese, 1987; Trusty & Dooley-Dickey, 1993); many have suggested that alienation contributes to youths' eventual exit from school (Trusty & Dooley-Dickey, 1993). Further, alienation appears to be a multidimensional and situational construct dependent on social isolation, cultural estrangement, powerlessness, and meaninglessness (Calabrese & Schumer, 1986; Mau, 1992; Seeman, 1975).[1] Youths suggest that academic tracking increases their social isolation and can contribute to their sense of cultural estrangement, while negative expectations, differential treatment,

33

bureaucratized relationships and practices, and barriers to information contribute to their sense of powerlessness and meaninglessness. These factors, in
turn, generate manifestations of opposition, including reduced academic
effort, truancy, and verbal/physical expressions of anger and frustration.
Further, because these factors affect individuals from some social groups
more than others, they can contribute to the molding of oppositional or disengaged identities on the group level.

The findings presented emerged from an analysis of interviews with
fifty-five high school students who participated in the Students' Multiple
Worlds Study. The sample, enrolled at four urban desegregated high schools
in California, was selected to represent some of the ethnic, racial, linguistic,
and academic diversity found in today's Californian students. Of the fifty-
five youths, for example, seventeen are European American and thirty-
eight are youths of color. Of the latter, there are seventeen of Latino, eleven
of Asian, four of African American, two of Filipino, one of Palestinian,
and three of multiethnic/racial descent. Of them, twenty-seven report that
a language other than English is spoken at home, nineteen were born outside of the United States, and six are recent immigrants (in the United
States for less than two and one-half years when interviewed).[2] The study
participants also vary substantially in terms of academic placement and
achievement, with individuals of all ethnic and racial backgrounds represented in each category (see endnote three).[3]

Four core interviews with each student over a two-year period, each
audiotaped, coded, and transcribed, were designed to provide in-depth
information on students' perceptions of factors relevant to their academic
and social engagement within the school community. The data presented in
this chapter emerged primarily from questions in which students were asked
1) to describe pressures and problems emanating from features of their
school environments 2) to discuss their reactions to specific school and
classroom components and practices, e.g., pattern of academic classes
attended, disciplinary practices and policies, transportation program, access
to information, and the curriculum and 3) to describe and consider the
sources of division among peer groups.

Before turning to the findings that emerged from the analysis, three
caveats are in order. First, by concentrating on students' perceptions, I take
a subjective approach to social analysis, focusing on "their" understanding of
the world in order to gain local knowledge. Yet, it is also clear that there are
outside factors that influence students' behavior and understandings,
whether youths perceive these influences or not. For example, though none
of the schools in this study had adopted multicultural curricula, no indi-

viduals in the study identified the content of the curriculum as an important concern. Yet, one cannot conclude from this that curriculum is irrelevant to the construction of opposition and engagement; rather, students may have become so adapted to Eurocentered texts over the course of eleven years in school that curriculum was not immediately salient. A central goal of this research is to integrate the subjective with the objective, to situate students' perceptions in a broader analysis of structural factors operating at the school and classroom levels. Thus, in later chapters, I draw also on interviews with adults, my field observations, and school record data to complement student data, constructing a broader portrait of components that contribute to the molding of ethnic and racial identities.

Second, I describe findings for the entire Student Multiple Worlds Study sample in order to illustrate general patterns. However, in reality, the salience of each factor that I describe (patterns that emanate from academic tracking, negative expectations, differential treatment of varied ethnic and racial groups, bureaucratized relationships and practices, and barriers to information) tended to vary with the individual and his or her particular academic situation. For example, differential treatment along racial/ethnic lines was far more apparent to youths of color than to European American students. Similarly, bureaucratic relationships and practices were more relevant 1) for students who, because of their behavior or frustrated efforts to impact their future, had contact with administrators and 2) for students in highly controlling school environments. Given the diversity of the sample and their school environments, it would have been surprising to see a strikingly high percentage of students agreeing about the importance of all of these factors, and indeed this was the case. Instead, each individual tended to name one or two (of the five) factors as important, a tendency which is reflected in the percentages reported in the text that follows.

Third, and finally, while students perceive the factors that follow as relevant, each taken singly is probably limited in terms of its impact on the construction of identity. The case studies that follow will reveal this point, indicating how the factors discussed work with other elements to generate a web of ethnically and racially relevant meanings that individuals respond to as they craft identity in school environments.

*Patterns Emanating from Academic Tracking*

Since the early 1900s, academic tracking has arguably been the most ubiquitous disciplinary technology practiced in American schools, and the practice most conducive to separating youth by race, ethnicity, and social class. Low income as well as African American and Latino students have and continue to be disproportionately represented in lower track classes, while advanced courses are dominated by youth of European American and Asian descent (Persell, 1977; Oakes, 1985). For participants in the Students' Multiple Worlds Study, this was also the case. For example, in Table 2.1 below, I present data indicative of the degree of academic differentiation by race and ethnicity in advanced classrooms across three of the high schools attended by youths participating in the study. The table allows the reader to compare the percentage of fluent English-speaking students from four major groups at each school to their percentage of enrollment in three types of courses: advanced English, advanced mathematics (analysis and calculus), and advanced science (chemistry and physics).

Table 2.1. Academic Tracking by Race/Ethnicity and School: Advanced Courses

|  |  | Percentage of Enrollment | | |
| --- | --- | --- | --- | --- |
| School | Percentage of FEP Population | Advanced English | Advanced Math | Chemistry/ Physics |
| Explorer |  |  |  |  |
| African | 4.7 | 1.5 | 2.3 | 3.1 |
| Asian | 11.0 | 16.8 | 27.6 | 15.3 |
| European | 60.8 | 69.3 | 56.3 | 56.4 |
| Latino | 22.8 | 7.6 | 11.5 | 9.2 |
| Huntington |  |  |  |  |
| African | 5.8 | 3.9 | 1.8 | 3.5 |
| Asian | 15.8 | 34.3 | 40.1 | 37.6 |
| European | 58.2 | 53.2 | 50.1 | 49.7 |
| Latino | 19.2 | 10.6 | 6.6 | 9.2 |
| Maple |  |  |  |  |
| African | 8.5 | 6.5 | 9.4 | 2.8 |
| Asian | 9.3 | 12.5 | 18.8 | 14.8 |
| European | 49.0 | 57.0 | 55.0 | 53.7 |
| Latino | 33.2 | 24.0 | 16.5 | 28.7 |

As indicated, while the degree of differentiation by race and ethnicity varies across school settings, European Americans and youths of Asian descent are disproportionately represented in advanced courses.

In all, 44 percent (twenty-four individuals) of the Students' Multiple Worlds Study sample referred to patterns that emanate from academic tracking, describing this as a factor relevant to producing various components of alienation. In all, students identify three implications for behaviors and/or perceptions. First, study participants characterized academic divisions as contributing to the establishment of social categories by separating groups and defining them as academically or socially different. The divisions generated by tracking produced a powerful set of meanings about the relative intelligence of individuals from different groups and their behavioral tendencies and interests:

> *Joey, African American:*[4] Cause mostly the advanced kids are the real smart students and most of the people here, they ain't.
> *Interviewer:* And who are the real smart students, who do they tend to be?
> *Joey:* Mostly Vietnamese, boys and girls most of them. And girls. Mostly Vietnamese and girls. There's some guys I guess.
> *Interviewer:* Are there any Black students in the advanced track here?
> *Joey:* I think there might be one. Not in my grade level that I know of. (ES51STD:432–448)

> *Wendy, European American:* Most people in accelerated classes are White or Japanese or Vietnamese or Chinese, you hardly ever see a Mexican. If you do it's like, I don't know, they don't stay very long. I don't know if it's because they're graded really hard, but I don't think so. .... I think it's a little bit how they're raised, and they're raised a lot differently. .... mostly Vietnamese or Orientals are extremely smart. They're extremely smart. And there's a few in my class, Orientals in there. Very smart. (ES47STD:1221–1228; 2305–2326)

> *Midori, Japanese American:* Because, you know, how should I say this? They [students who are not in advanced courses] aren't as clean cut perhaps? You know, they might be ruffians, gang members maybe. There are barriers there, you know, it's like 'Ah, drug money, no thanks!' (OR01STD:1783–1790)

In short, youths not only noticed differential patterns of academic representation, but appeared to draw conclusions about groups based on the patterns they observed.

Second, and in accordance with the above, students described tracking as contributing to their social isolation, both by limiting opportunities for interaction and by contributing to the development of antagonistic relationships. For example, Javier, a Mexican immigrant enrolled in the ESL track, commented, "I hardly have contact with Americans. My classes are purely Hispanic" (ES38STA:113–122). Similarly, Ben, a European American enrolled in advanced courses, explained ". . . the ones that aren't really going to be going to college, and there's nothing wrong with that, but they isolate themselves and they just rip apart everyone else who is. And that kind of makes a division between students in school" (OR07STD:734–740).[5]

Finally, students of color from groups concentrated in less prestigious tracks described tracking as contributing to their sense of cultural estrangement. In essence, tracking created zones of privileged academic activity, dominated by middle-class youth of European American and Asian descent. Youth from ethnic and racial groups clustered in less valorized curricular environments were left with doubts about whether they could ever belong to the more academically oriented realms of the school. This was reflected particularly in the discourse of underrepresented youth who challenged social borders by enrolling in the advanced academic track:

> *Carla, Mexican/Cuban American:* Well, I kind of feel uncomfortable. Not many Mexicans and Hispanics are in those [advanced] classes. And so it kind of makes me feel uncomfortable.
> *Interviewer:* What about that makes you feel uncomfortable?
> *Carla:* Because ... they probably think of me as weird, because they think Hispanics, probably they have this view that most Hispanics are dumb or something. Have that opinion, you know, get bad grades. So, I don't know why I feel uncomfortable, I just ... means you're not really with any other ... many people. .... probably by the end [of the year] they might realize I belong. (RA28STD:540–570)

> *Trinh, Vietnamese immigrant female:* Well, the thing with being Vietnamese, it's kind of like there's a lot of Americans in there [in Trinh's advanced classes], that's when I'm more alone. And then, when you're alone, you're nervous, like over little things, more than other people. (RA30STEN:1236–1242)

In all, 32 percent of youths of color in the sample referred to discomfort that emanated from their enrollment in classrooms dominated by racially and ethnically different students.

Thus far, we have seen that from students' perspectives, the academic meanings and social divisions generated by tracking create expectations about who will and who should attend specific types of courses. Further, youths' sense of social isolation is enhanced as individuals from different groups have little opportunity to interact with peers arriving from different communities. Finally, members of academically marginalized groups experience a sense of cultural estrangement, feeling like strangers or guests to the academic realm of the school. On an individual level, youths of color describe these three factors as combining to affect both academic engagement and the expression of identity. First, youths limited their classroom participation, silencing themselves in classrooms where they were in the minority, adapting to the social expectations of others, and masking the expression of their ethnic or racial backgrounds:

> *Joyce, African/Guyanian American:* I can never ask a question [in advanced math] cause everyone is so smart in that class. .... In biology, I could just ask questions with no pressure. I feel better when there's more diversity because there's different people around you. You're not alone, you know. Only one who's not the same as all the rest. (VA16STD: 1736–1738; VA16STEN: 1662–1685)

> *Chieu, Vietnamese immigrant male:* They [the Vietnamese youth in the class] don't want to speak Vietnamese. The ones who have been here awhile, they don't want to speak because they get embarrassed. They're afraid that if you speak Vietnamese loud next to Americans, they'd laugh at us. They're afraid of being embarrassed, so they don't speak. (ES42STD:444–451)

> *Khanh, Vietnamese immigrant male:* You just try to fit in with them. I don't know, I just try to find something that we have in common. (VA15STD:557–559)

Feeling that their race or ethnicity would render them vulnerable to the judgements of peers, youths adopt a situated self (Spindler & Spindler, 1993) that will not draw attention to any indicator of difference.

In a second pattern, students engaged in various forms of active or passive opposition, circumscribing their academic efforts and participation. By skipping class and choosing to remain in easy courses, youths avoided the discomfort of entering segregated classrooms and also felt free to engage in forms of ethnic or racial self-expression:

> *Chieu, Vietnamese immigrant male:* When I go to school, I'm so afraid to go to math class. There's no one to sit close to. In the other classes I have some friends. In math class, I only sit with Americans. They only talk to each other. The Mexicans only

talk to each other. .... ever since sixth grade, I've never cut. But this year, when I get to class, when I don't see anyone to talk to, to eat with .... since that day, I got into the habit of cutting. (ES42STD:415–422; 298–305)

*Andrea, Vietnamese immigrant:* Americans, they don't cut that much [compared to my Vietnamese friends]. Sometimes at home when my grades go down I promise myself 'OK, I'm not going to hang around them no more, I just want to hang with all Americans so I'm Americanized so I learn more English and be good.' .... [But] there's something, OK, when I see Vietnamese hanging around Americans they're always speaking English and they don't speak Vietnamese. I really think those girls, I mean if I hate them and become one of them it's not good. (ES48STD: 389–394; 532–539)

*Donna, Mexican/European American:* [When my teacher asked if I would like to move to the general track] I just said that I'll take it [remedial English]. It really helps me understand more. .... And you know, being with my friends, since all my friends are in there. Sometimes it was really easy for me. I know everything in the book. (RA52STA:558–564; 612–617)

This pattern is in accordance with research concerning the effects of subtle prejudice on African Americans. Scholars link both the interpersonal stress, which emanates from isolation in work settings dominated by European Americans, and discrepancies in the performance evaluations of African American and European American job holders to African Americans' tendency not to apply for, accept, or keep jobs in fields and organizations with small minority representations (Pettigrew & Martin, 1987). Data from the Students' Multiple Worlds Study supports this contention. Study participants suggest that manifestations of opposition can reflect an assessment of the costs associated with entering environments where students will be vulnerable to stereotypes and pressures from a dominant majority.

*Significant Speech Acts Concerning Diversity:*
*Negative Expectations and Differential Treatment*

Numerous studies have demonstrated the subtle yet powerful ways in which perceptions of social difference play into behavior. Social psychologists have looked extensively at interactions between European Americans and African Americans, showing that European Americans tend to provide less assistance and to engage in more aggressive or avoidance behaviors toward their African American counterparts (Pettigrew & Martin, 1987). With regard to classroom interactions, studies indicate that European American teachers' relationships with youths of color differ from their relationships with culturally similar students. Teachers look for and reinforce achievement behaviors in European American students more than they do in youths of color, attribute achievement-oriented behavior among European American students to effort and motivation, and attribute like behaviors to factors that youths of color cannot control, such as parental encouragement (Baron, Tom & Cooper, 1985; Cooper & Tom, 1984; Good, 1981; Spindler & Spindler, 1982). Race also mediates perceptions of attractiveness, a factor that has been found to influence teachers' assignments of grades, along with their judgements of students' intelligence and academic potential (Ritts, Patterson & Tubbs, 1992). Finally, counselors' interactions with and subsequent treatment of students are structured by their perceptions of social class, race, and ethnicity (Schultz & Erickson, 1982).

In accordance with these findings, 27 percent of all study participants and 37 percent of youths of color perceived adults' views or treatment of students as varying along ethnic or racial lines. First, youths emphasized differences in expectations, describing the varied beliefs that teachers communicate about their students' academic or economic futures and teachers' varied expectations for student behavior. As indicated in the quotes below, negative expectations were conveyed verbally (through classroom conversation), nonverbally (through looks and glances), and finally, through rules and regulations targeted at particular social groups:

> *Marian, Filipina American:* She doesn't like anyone, she's kind of racist in a way. …. just the way she talks, you know. If she's talking about a bad neighborhood, she'll say the Black kids. The Whites are all in the good neighborhoods and stuff. She always says that. …. And then just stuff, she'll just, whenever we talk about bad people, she'll mention Blacks and gangs. All the Black people are bad. (RA34STB:317–359)

> *Rosa, Mexican American:* When he talks about people that will end up on the streets and … and then he turns around and looks at all the Mexicans. I want to get up and tell him off or just walk out. (ES40STB:823–828)

*Javier, Mexican immigrant:* There are some who don't like Hispanics. They don't like it when Hispanics speak Spanish in
class .... They're afraid we'll say bad words in Spanish and because
of that they won't let us speak Spanish. (ES38STA:520–533)

Policies which ban students from wearing particular colors and types of
clothing in an attempt to control gang activity were also effective in communicating adult expectations concerning the probability of deviance among
particular social groups. Messages were amplified by the fact that although
Vietnamese, Latino, and African American gangs were operating at low levels at two of the high schools in our study, where such policies had been
instituted they targeted colors associated only with Latino and African American groups. Thus, it was clear to members of these groups that disciplinary
rules had been constructed especially to control their activities: "A lot of the
rules they set because of them, like the rules about the colors set because of
the Black kids, and maybe the Mexicans too" (ES51STEN:1168–1171).

In addition to describing differences in expectations, youths argue
that teachers and administrators vary in their treatment of social groups.
Here, two themes emerged. First, some felt that teachers directed positive
care and attention more toward European Americans. Second, youths
described teachers as targeting and disciplining members of some groups for
infractions that went unpunished when committed by others. The comments below help illustrate these themes:

*Andrea, Vietnamese immigrant:* Some of my teachers, like I got Ds
and they don't even ask [me about it], they don't even care
because the one [for them] is Americans. I mean, they ask them
how are you doing and all. That's stupid, you know. Why don't
you ever ask me that? They just ask Americans. I don't really care
about my teachers. (ES48STEN:1492–1499)

*Maria, Mexican immigrant:* Well, the Anglos were playing football
there on the grass and she didn't say anything to them. But then
later the Mexicans went to play and she took the ball away and
didn't give it back. .... All of us should be treated with respect.
And not only them. They shouldn't have respect just for them.
No way. (ES41STB:555–586)

When speaking of targeting youth for disciplinary treatment, students were
critical of differential treatment generated by colors' policies. As Lindsey, a

European American, put it, "I mean, he could be White wearing a red hat but they don't consider him in a gang cause he's White, you know" (OR06STD:428–434).

Theories of delinquency have drawn on the concept of labeling, arguing that individuals labeled as deviant may begin to reorganize their self-conceptions and behave in accordance with the social definition placed on them by others (Gottfredson, Fink & Graham, 1994; Hawkins, Doueck & Lishner, 1988). The youths we interviewed also argue for the power of labeling, explaining that negative expectations or differential treatment may work to produce opposition by contributing to a sense of meaninglessness and powerlessness:

> *Johnnie, African American:* .... if somebody keeps telling you you're gonna' be nobody, you're going to take that in and you're going to say, 'Well damn, I'm going to be nobody. Look at my grades, they're right.' .... Strict teachers in St. Louis that's their *main* object is to tell the student that you're lower than trash, you're nothin'. ....
> *Interviewer:* How do you think that makes the students there feel toward school?
> *Johnnie:* Like 'Ahh, the hell with it.' They don't care. (RA27STB: 1400–1405; 1448–1469)

> *Maria, Mexican immigrant:* .... they hate Mexicans at this school. .... that woman from cooking [class], she pulled the students' hair. .... One of my friends, she was wearing a black dress that was short and tight. She told her first, that that was the way her husband liked them .... and then she told her that if she wore that skirt again she would send her to the office .... the Mexicans are treated badly by all of the teachers. That is also why—the Mexicans get tired of getting treated this way, and that is why we do those [bad] things too. (ES41STB:461–495; 570–575)

In turn, the youths linked manifestations of equal treatment and high expectations to improved classroom relations and student behavior:

> *Maria, Mexican immigrant:* The class where there's the most respect, from what I've seen, is the social studies class with Mr. Vargas. Because he applies an even hand to Mexicans and Anglos. And that is why no one ever says anything, bad words to him. (ES41STB:636–644)

*Marbella, Mexican immigrant:* Well, he's [that teacher] a good person. He's on very good terms with us [the Mexican students]. He tells us that he would perhaps like to be Mexican because, well we want to study, we want to be someone in this country. He tells us that many times people who are not born here and who know English don't make use of it, and that sometimes we who don't know it, we make use of it. (ES50STC:54–62)

In short, adolescents suggest that differential expectations and treatment can function as significant speech acts which encourage manifestations of opposition or engagement. In accordance with students' comments, studies indicate that teachers' expectations have a limited but significant effect on student achievement (Brophy, 1983).

### Bureaucratized Relationships and Practices

Organizational theorists concerned with the creation of engaging and effective work settings have pointed to the importance of supporting and soliciting worker input as a means to encourage affiliation with the institution. Supporting this argument, the effective schools literature indicates that teachers' satisfaction and engagement increase with a sense of control, particularly as teachers are given opportunities to participate in decisions concerning the organization and realization of their work (Corcoran, 1990; Louis, 1992).[6] There is also some evidence that increased opportunities for participation reduce teacher stress, burnout, and absenteeism (Bacharach, Bauer, & Conley, 1986; Dawson, 1985). Conversely, when teachers' voices are discounted or ignored, workplace satisfaction decreases (Corcoran, 1990).

Similar to teachers, participants in the Students' Multiple Worlds Study argue that bureaucratized relationships with adults and limited opportunities for input due to bureaucratized practices decrease their satisfaction and engagement with the academic environment. Specifically, students are critical of adults who strictly enforce status divisions by rigidly enforcing rules and regulations which they have created, by silencing youths who attempt to express their opinions about adult authority, and by distancing themselves from students. In all, 20 percent of the sample critiqued bureaucratic relationships and practices.

Study participants said first that bureaucratic relationships affect motivation and self-efficacy. The comments below are representative:

*Joey, African American:* I don't like this school, mainly because of the principal. That's why—I'm going to go to Huntington next year. .... cause he don't try to understand us. Even if you didn't do anything wrong, whatever the teacher says goes. The old principal tried to work with you. The new one is just—you come in and he just gives you something and kicks you out of his office. (ES51STD:641–675; 697–700)

*Saul, Mexican American:* Mr. Joyce, I tried to tell him what I'm feeling, what's going on, and he gets like all mad and [says] 'Don't talk to me that way.' With the old principal, he'd even agree with me, you know. If the teachers sent me to suspension then I had to go to suspension, but he at least let me say what I had to say. .... It helps out if people will listen to you. People should listen to each other, then it works out better. (ES40STD: 583–615)

Also providing evidence of the value students place on more personalized relationships, some argued that adults who reach out can help restructure students' orientation toward school. As Javier explained: "Sometimes we Mexicans or Latinos are the problem, and that is the only problem that I don't like here. .... [The principal should] try to help them, because at times, they need help. It is not that they need to be taken out [suspended]. They simply need help, so that they feel good at school" (ES38STA: 302–328).

Youths also criticized bureaucratic practices that limited their ability to direct and control their academic futures. Again, these factors had an impact on students' sense of efficacy and motivation:

*Javier, Mexican immigrant:* The administration doesn't help me do anything. .... here, I feel that no Hispanic has any control. They think they have some, but they don't. Not one, not one Hispanic has influence. (ES38STD:134–135; 213–216)

*Andrea, Vietnamese immigrant:* .... the way she teaches I know I was not going to make it. I can tell if I can do good by the teacher, too, and I wanted to transfer to the other teacher because I heard it was easier. And Miss Lane [guidance princi-pal], she wouldn't let me. So I said okay, then I'm not going to do anything. (ES48STD:1078–1086)

Studies describing the perspectives of dropouts show that youths who exit school voice strong criticisms of teachers, counselors, and administrators for their uncaring attitudes and critique school policies related to behavior, control, and suspension. In some cases, the dropouts argue that such components contributed to their ultimate decision to drop out (Stevenson & Ellsworth, 1993; Wehlage & Rutter, 1986). Consistent with this research, youths in the sample argued that distant and authoritarian relationships and bureaucratic practices create anger and may help to exacerbate manifestations of opposition: "This year, [with] our new administrator guys it's like we're in a prison or something. .... as a result, I think people are more rebellious. Because he won't trust you with anything" (ES37STD:900–917).

It is also important to note that students of African American and Latino descents were disproportionately represented among those suspended for "defiant or disruptive behavior" at two of the schools in our study. Consistent with this data, and as discussed in the previous section, youths of color at these schools perceived themselves as particular targets for adult efforts to control. (In all, 90 percent of those raising concerns about bureaucratic relationships and practices were students of color.) Further, these students theorized that differential treatment reflected adults' biases and stereotypes. Thus, bureaucratic relationships and practices may be particularly relevant for students of color, especially as they may conclude that controlling practices, failure to listen, and failure to reach out reflect the ethnic or racial biases of adults in authority.

### Barriers to Valued Information

Information can be conceptualized as a commodity. Access to knowledge about the ways and means to access college and various careers, for example, can translate into academic capital by improving students' educational and occupational life chances. For example, studies indicate that in the long term, African Americans attending desegregated schools (particularly those in the north and/or suburban communities) are more likely to attend and graduate from college and work in white-collar jobs in the private sector (Wells & Crain, 1994). Drawing on network analysis theory, Wells and Crain point out that desegregated schools, particularly when located in wealthier suburban communities, provide African American students with more access to information about desegregated institutions and employment. Similarly, about half of the difference in higher college attendance rates among non-Catholic, private school students can be accounted for in terms of socioeconomic status (Coleman, 1987). However, differences in resources devoted to the counseling and advising of college-bound students (along with differences in school curriculum, academic standards, and school staff orientation) account for much of the remaining variation (Alexander & Eckland, 1977; Falsey & Heyns, 1984).

Though the students interviewed as part of the Students' Multiple Worlds Study were generally in their sophomore year of high school, they recognized the value of information. In all, 22 percent of the sample, and 50 percent of youths of color attending two high schools where counseling services had been eliminated, expressed a desire for more information about postsecondary opportunities and spoke of worries about the future that emanated directly from the gaps they perceived in their knowledge. Further, as students overheard conversations in classrooms and conversed with ethnically and racially different peers, some became aware that members of other social groups possessed knowledge that they lacked:

> *Sonia, Mexican American:* Sometimes it's *so hard* because I think about it, about going to college you need so many requirements and I go 'What's the difference between the state and UC system?' I go 'What's the big difference?' I don't understand any of that. And it's scary too cause [I hear other students say] 'Well, I'm going to go to UC or whatever,' and I go [to myself] 'What's that?' You know, I want to know! (ES56STD:3017–3034)

Gaps in knowledge not only generated anxiety, but also contributed to a sense of cultural estrangement by highlighting differences among student groups.

Lacking a point of comparison, individuals were generally unaware that access to information can vary substantially across school environments. However, in many cases the students were aware of structural borders (Phelan, Davidson & Yu, 1993) that interfered with the flow of information within their immediate environments. Study participants referred particularly to three factors that impeded their ability to gather the information they desired: limited advertising and lack of full disclosure concerning opportunities, sporadic and infrequently scheduled contact with knowledgeable adults, and adult dismissal of their interests, concerns, or questions. These themes are illustrated in the comments of the students below:

> *Ryan, European American:* It [the structures for giving students information] could be used more. It's not fully utilized because

they change it every year it seems. They try to do announcements but the PA isn't loud enough. The daily bulletin that they print the teachers are supposed to read, and most of the teachers are good about posting it but they won't read it .... (ES37STD: 721–729)

*Donna, Mexican/European American:* It's hard to get information about college. Just little stuff that we hear around school and about colleges, but not really basic stuff about college. Maybe it's just me, maybe I don't ask people or, I don't know what it is. Cause I do have a lot of questions. I just don't have like a person to ask, you know what I mean? Like to talk to about college. I haven't actually talked to anyone about college yet. (RA52STD: 1515–1530)

*Regina, Mexican immigrant:* .... over there at Boulevard [the district continuation high school], they take their time for every student, not like at Explorer. ....
*Interviewer:* Could you go to anybody to get information at Explorer?
*Regina:* No ... yeah, but you don't. They're like, the lady there, it's like 'Well what would you want information for?' (ES54STD: 1889–1900)

For individuals with parents, siblings, or friends who attended college, barriers to information could often be managed. However, for youths without these connections, barriers had at least two implications. First, they contributed to a sense of powerlessness and meaninglessness, as students accepted the information they received from adults. ("[I feel] kind of sad because I've been wanting to be a veterinarian for a long time." [ES40STD:889–890]) In some cases, youths also concluded that there was no place for them in the larger opportunity structure: "It's hard, you know. You can quit school and go to McDonald's, but then when you come to think about it you're not going to live off McDonald's. I don't see no future there" (ES56STB:1091–1099). Second, students became frustrated and angry, expressing this in critiques of adults who students perceived as failing to reach out to youths around them:

*Johnnie, African American:* We got counselors here and they don't even counsel you. What are they here for? We have teachers here on the student councils and all these people here are supposed to help you when you have problems, they just sit up there in their office. They don't do nothing. They don't counsel you, they don't go out and see which students are having problems. And that's why so many kids are dropping out. Cause they don't care. (RA27STEN:595–610)

*Regina, Mexican immigrant:* It's totally different over at Boulevard. .... College people go over there and talk to us, we interview them. ... They told me about going to junior college. I can go to junior college. I didn't know that. I didn't know anything!! When I went over to Boulevard they opened my eyes! Over at Explorer *where* was, *where* was—they never told us anything! They never said anything. (ES54STD:1892–1893; 1973–1990)

*Rosa, Mexican American:* .... they give you a piece of paper, classes that you're going to take next year, and then they put them on the computer and they send you a schedule to your house. .... they didn't even talk to me. .... They use their computers to determine whether you're going to be another sophomore or you're going to go on to a junior .... All they do is sit on their butts and do whatever they're told. (ES40STD:812–839; 976–981)

In sum, barriers to information affected youths' sense of efficacy and appeared to contribute to their disengagement with the academic environment.


## DISCUSSION

This chapter provides a brief overview of five school-based factors that youths perceive as contributing to a sense of social isolation, cultural estrangement, meaninglessness, and powerlessness. Students suggest that both together and separately, these components contribute to manifestations of opposition and disengagement. Further, adolescents see negative expectations, differential treatment, and barriers to information as affecting some ethnic and racial groups more than others, and in some cases argue that this contributes to the varying levels of opposition expressed by groups within school settings.

The patterns that emanate from academic tracking, the tenor of adult-student relationships, and barriers to information are manipulable. This raises the question of whether schools might begin to mediate the construction of group opposition and engagement by addressing these components of the environment. This study, focused on the process of identity construction, can not answer this question. For one, the study was not designed to control for other relevant student background characteristics, such as social class and student transportation status, which might shape academic outcomes. Thus, any patterns revealed in school-level outcome data would have to be seen as tentative, potentially reflective of factors external to the school. Further, though some student outcome data was available for each of the schools in the study, the degree of overlap in the data collected by each was minimal. (For example, student grade point averages by race and ethnicity were available for one school, but not for others.) Clearly, this limits the comparisons that can be made.

Nevertheless, it is interesting to note that the limited comparable outcome data available from schools in the study is generally consistent with the arguments advanced in this chapter. To make this point, I will draw on data summarized in Table 2.2 below.

Table 2.2. Percent of Sophomores Fulfilling U.C. Entrance Requirements/ Graduating with Class Cohort by School and Race/Ethnicity

| School | African American | Latino | European American | Asian Descent |
|---|---|---|---|---|
| Explorer | 10%/60% | 4%/48% | 28%/78% | 36%/81% |
| Huntington | 5%/71% | 4%/50% | 17%/77% | 31%/94% |
| Maple | 16%/46% | 9%/57% | 24%/64% | 46%/68% |

The table summarizes, by race and ethnicity, the percentage of high school sophomores at three schools (averaged over two years) who eventually 1) completed the classes required for admission to the University of California system and 2) graduated. The schools, particularly Maple and Explorer, are similar in terms of demographic factors, including the percentage of students transported, the percentage of students qualifying for free or reduced price lunches, and the percentage of limited English-proficient students (see endnote five).[7] However, the schools differ in terms of two institutional features. First, African American and fluent English-proficient Latino youth at Maple were more likely to be enrolled in advanced courses than their peers at Explorer and Huntington (see Table 2.1). Second, barriers to information were less pronounced at Maple. At both Explorer and Huntington, counseling services had been eliminated due to budgetary restraints, and there were no mentoring programs in place to target the college enrollment of underrepresented students of color. In contrast, at Maple, youth had access to counselors and assistance from personnel working for a statewide consortium oriented toward the college recruitment and enrollment of underrepresented students.

The first important pattern to note in Table 2.2 is that African American, Latino, and Asian descent sophomores at Maple were more likely than their peers at Explorer and Huntington to graduate having completed the course work necessary to enroll in a four-year university in the state system. This cannot be accounted for in terms of socioeconomic differences or students' linguistic status, as Maple's economic and linguistic diversity were among the most extreme of the schools studied (see endnote 5). Rather, it appears likely that some other factor accounts for the fact that, in relative terms, Maple's students of color were not only more likely to enroll in, but also to complete, advanced course work.

A second pattern lending support to the arguments advanced in this chapter is that Latinos attending Maple were more likely to graduate than were their peers at Huntington and Explorer. Again, this cannot be accounted for by demographic differences. First, Maple drew many of its Latino youths from a highly mobile immigrant population. Further, while Latinos at all of the high schools were transported to attend, those attending Maple traveled from the furthest distance (forty-five minutes versus twenty minutes for those attending Explorer and Huntington). Thus, looking at the situation from a purely geographic point of view, Latino students at Maple had an added incentive to transfer to a more proximate high school. It is also interesting to note that, in general, Maple was troubled by a declining student population, characterized particularly by the flight of its wealthier neighborhood students after desegregation to nearby high schools. (Students' tendency to transfer, discussed in chapter 8, is visible in the comparatively higher attrition rate for Maple's sophomores of Asian and European American descent.) One could imagine that such flight patterns might generate a general state of discontent, carrying over to create relatively higher attrition rates for Maple's Latino population, but in fact this was not the case.

Interestingly, however, this pattern of academic persistence did not hold true for Maple's African American population; those attending were significantly less likely to graduate than were their peers at Explorer and Huntington. Though this clearly raises important questions, demographic factors are likely relevant. First, while African Americans at Maple were transported a significant distance (forty-five minutes) to attend, their peers at

Explorer and Huntington generally walked to school from adjacent neighborhoods. Second, African Americans at Explorer and Huntington came from families who demonstrated a relative degree of comfort with less segregated settings, by virtue of the fact that they settled in an area with relatively few African Americans. In contrast, African Americans at Maple arrived from ethnically and socioeconomically segregated communities.

In sum, the patterns above suggest that the construction of oppositional and engaged identities is a highly complex and multifaceted social phenomena. A carefully designed statistical investigation would offer one route for investigating such complexity, in that it would allow investigation of the relative influence of varied factors (e.g., social class, immigrant status, school characteristics) on student outcomes. Yet, a statistical study would do little to illuminate the process of identity construction nor would it inform the discussion and clarification of contradictions. In order to facilitate analysis and learning in areas that involve multiple and conflicting meanings and interactions, scholars have turned increasingly to the use of case studies (Goldenberg, 1992; Shulman, 1986). The value of case knowledge lies both in its ability to illuminate complex and multifaceted phenomena, and in its ability to generate images that generalize to novel settings (Eisner, 1991; Shulman, 1986). Taking this approach, in the chapters that follow, I turn to the specific experiences of six individuals, considering how each constructs his or her identity in relation to particular school and classroom environments.

PART II

# Disciplinary Technologies Resisted: Unconventional Identities

CHAPTER 3

# Marbella Sanchez on
# Marginalization and Silencing

*Marbella*: But ... well, a Mexican is someone who
knows how to depend on himself. And he has to
have a different character from other people.
*Interviewer:* How is that?
*Marbella:* Well, it's a ... it's a strong character. It
doesn't let itself get vanquished very easily. For
example, if someone says 'I am going to be a doctor,' and if another person, or other people say to
him 'No, don't do that because it's a very long path,
very complicated' or something, well, he mustn't
let himself be discouraged by what they said. If he
wants to study that, he has to do that. And not give
up because other people told him 'No, don't do
that.'(ES50STEN:654–672)

—Marbella Sanchez,
sophomore student,
Explorer High School

The sizzle and smell of garlic fill the air. It is "lab day" in foods class at
Explorer High School. I lean against the hard steel corner of a stove, listening to Marbella Sanchez, a sophomore Mexican immigrant, as she stirs her
darkening garlic.

Marbella's teacher approaches. "How are you doing Marbella?" "Muy
bien maestra. Me gusta la comida italiana." ("Very well teacher. I like Italian
food.") The teacher glances at me, laughs slightly, and tries again. "It looks
like that's about ready. What else are you going to put in there?" "Cebollas,

tomates, salsa de tomates . . . qué más?" ("Onions, tomatoes, tomato sauce . . . what else?") The look and laugher come again: "I don't understand a thing she's saying."

I am puzzled. While English is Marbella's second language, I know from personal experience that her English comprehension is excellent; I usually spoke to her in English, as my oral Spanish proficiency is low.[1] Moreover, though Marbella spoke to me in Spanish, I have heard her speak English to her teachers and listened to her argue that learning English is the key to success in America. While certainly more comfortable speaking Spanish, Marbella is fully capable of responding to her teacher's queries.

With cleanup approaching, Marbella approaches her teacher, asking for the worksheet each cooking group is required to complete: "Maestra? Tiene mi papel?" ("Teacher, do you have my paper?") Mrs. Everett looks at Marbella blankly. Marbella gestures to a pile of worksheets and Everett, reading Marbella's movement, hands her a paper. Now, I can't contain my curiosity. "Marbella," I laugh, "Why don't you ask her in English?" Marbella smiles and laughs back. "Tenemos una regla. Los martes y jueves, hablamos puro español." ("We have a rule. On Tuesdays and Thursdays, we speak only Spanish.")

Over the time that I came to know Marbella, I discovered that she and her small group of friends have many rules. Some, like the one above, serve to support the group as they struggle to assert their identity in a country where they feel pressure to conform. Others help them as they work to achieve academically, part of proving that being Mexican gives one the "strong character" that facilitates resilience in a new society. Marbella's conformity to these rules is reflected not only in scenes such as the one described above, but in high academic achievement. During her first three semesters at Explorer High School, Marbella earned all *A*s and *B*s, for one 3.67 and two 3.5 GPAs. During the second semester of her sophomore year, Marbella's mother was diagnosed with a tumor. As a result, Marbella missed twenty-three days of school, as she and her sister took turns staying home to provide basic health care. Still, Marbella maintained a 2.67 GPA. In short, Marbella demonstrated that, for her, part of being Mexican is having a strong, oppositional character that enables academic success. Further, Marbella manifests aspects of the ideology others have described as typical of immigrant minorities (Gibson, 1987; Ogbu, 1987). Voicing faith in the American opportunity structure, Marbella believes academic achievement will result in future economic success: "It's to learn English, that's what's necessary to triumph here. To know English. And to succeed in school" (ES50STEN:806–808).

Yet, oppositional character and manifestations of immigrant identity were not all I saw during the months I knew Marbella. Over time, Marbella revealed a fearful, sometimes resigned, and frequently silent self, equally connected both to her sense of ethnicity and immigrant status, a self that has emerged as Marbella has realized her marginalized position and encountered disciplinary technologies at her high school. This is a self that shrinks from asserting its rights, a self that fears interaction with American-born peers. This is Marbella's silent, separatist self.

## MEMORIES OF MEXICO: FOUNDATIONS FOR "STRONG CHARACTER"

Marbella, along with her younger brother and older sister, crossed the United States-Mexico border in the summer of 1989 to join her mother. The transition was radical. Marbella left behind not only a familiar language and culture, but also the rural lifestyle she'd grown accustomed to in Tecuala, a small agricultural town approximately 800 miles south of San Diego, near the Pacific coast:

> It was a small town, almost everybody in the town was friendly. .... There were about 600 people. That was as many as could be there. Almost everybody knew each other. .... Where I am from, life is calm, it is like the country. (ES50STAB:506–528)

It was during her childhood that Marbella learned that being Mexican requires strength of character. Born in 1975, Marbella is one of thousands of Mexican children who grew up during a period of economic crisis ('La Crisis'), a period in which Mexico's stagnant economy, price inflation, drastic currency devaluation, and growing national debt affected countless rural families (Macias, 1990). Marbella's autobiographical interview reflects her place in history, as she recounts her mother's struggle to support her three young children after her husband abandoned his family. (Marbella was three years old.) Marbella recalls how her mother, faced with limited and low-paying opportunities for work, moved the family first to her mother's home and then to a rented room. For four additional years, Marbella's mother struggled to make ends meet by working at night, but eventually left in search of more lucrative work in Hermosillo, a larger city 570 miles to the north. Eight-year-old Marbella and her siblings remained behind. From third to sixth grade, Marbella saw her mother only once a month.

According to Marbella, her early history is by no means unique. When asked what she and her friends talked about in elementary school, for example, she replied: ".... we would talk about our parents. Most of us just had one parent; none of us had both a father and a mother. We often talked about that. My grandma always told us that we were too young to talk about those things" (ES50STAB:327–332).

As Marbella began sixth grade in 1985, her mother's sisters joined the wave of Mexican emigrants leaving for the United States in search of work. Marbella's mother returned to Tecuala to live with her mother and children. Three years later, still unsatisfied with the level of support she could provide, Marbella's mother followed her sisters to the United States. Marbella dropped out of school to help her grandmother, working thirteen-hour days packing mangos during the harvest season. Marbella's mother worked to save the money necessary to bring Marbella and her two siblings to the United States; they joined her one year later.

Despite the difficult economic circumstances Marbella associates with her youth, she retains a positive orientation toward characteristics she perceives as representative of her culture. She emphasizes interpersonal relationships and mutual aid in her stories and descriptions:

> .... I don't act like many people here who are American; they act differently than we do. .... [for example], like at dances. Our dances and theirs are different. We like to celebrate and I know they do too. But I've gone to some American dances, and they don't dance. When a man goes and asks an American girl to dance and she says no, then it's because he is ugly or something. Well no, [we don't do that], we like to get along together at dances and at parties.
>
> Or if we go out for a day of fresh air, we go as Mexicans. We go out for the day and we like to get along together. Everybody pulls his weight, no? Well, nobody says things like 'You didn't work.' If somebody doesn't have money and he can't bring anything, well it doesn't matter that he doesn't bring anything. But he still has to be there, because he's our friend. (ES50STEN: 153–181)

Enacting these behaviors and norms, Marbella's mother, out of work herself, took two youths (Marbella's close friends) into her home when their mother left for work in another U.S. city during the 1990 recession. Marbella's descriptions and her mother's behavior are in accordance with the heavy emphasis on mutual aid and support among kin found in Mexican agrarian communities (Uribe, Levine & Levine, 1994).

Besides remembering times of economic hardship, Marbella also recollects successful, happy days in elementary school:

> Everything was easy in school. The teacher helped us. If we didn't understand, she would explain slowly. .... I had her for three years, so I thought everything was easy. .... I liked school a lot. If I couldn't go to school I would stay home very sad. I really liked going to school because I had fun.
>
> Another thing I remember is when I was seven. We were going to go on parade and I was going to carry the school's banner. It was very nice because all the people were there seeing us and I was at the front of the parade. ... It feels very nice to carry the flag because they choose the most intelligent student. It's a very pretty feeling because when they choose you everyone says 'So, you're smart!' (ES50STAB:454–474, 30–46)

Marbella's descriptions also suggest that her mother (who graduated from high school) and grandmother place a high priority on Marbella's education. For example, because of Marbella's exceptional performance during her elementary years, the family pooled its resources to enroll her in a secondary private school, usually restricted to the elite. The family believed this would provide Marbella with a better education. Marbella recalls the decision:

> There were only two schools there [in Tecuala]. I wanted to go to the federal [public] one, and my grandmother didn't want me to. She put me in the school that I didn't like. That school was only for rich people. It was a school you had to pay for, only for those who had money. .... because she had some land, she was going to sell it so I could go to that school. .... my aunts who were working here [in the United States] sent money so I could go. (ES50STAB:604–628)

Marbella also describes her mother's continued efforts to support her children's transition to their U.S. high school, despite her long days doing janitorial work:

.... sometimes when we have bad grades she says to us, 'What happened?' and 'What went wrong?' and we tell her and she helps us with that. And she talks to the teacher, and she tells him that we need him to give us the work again to see if we can do it well. ....

My mom really likes to be informed about how we're doing. Sometimes, well, if we are doing poorly in school, perhaps she can help us with something. ... She studied, she studied a lot in Mexico. Sometimes neither I nor my sister understand algebra and well she—very rarely—but she helps us. Sometimes she can't help us because like she's working. She works from six in the morning to four or five in the afternoon; she arrives at five, takes a bath, and she's gone at seven at night and she goes out [to work] until two or three in the morning and she doesn't have time. (ES50STC:1189–1247)

Like her daughter, Marbella's mother believes that learning English and graduating from high school are essential first steps to "become someone."

Marbella's memories of economic struggle, her successful elementary and middle school history, and her mother's support are relevant to understanding Marbella's drive to succeed and her readiness to challenge those who doubt her intelligence. At the same time, her positive memories of Mexico and positive orientation toward norms and values she associates with Mexican culture are relevant to her desire to resist pressures to assimilate. I turn now to consider these aspects of Marbella's persona.


MARBELLA'S GAMBLE: AN OPPOSITIONAL SELF

It's like a bet to be here. It's like a bet that we ought to win because we need to demonstrate to other people that we indeed can make it. That it's not because we are Hispanic we can't make it. At times they [Americans] are treating you badly, right? Then you say to yourself, 'I am going to demonstrate to those people that I indeed can be something, and that I have the capability to be something. It's not because I'm Hispanic that I can't make it.' At these times, they give you desire to study more and

become someone more quickly, so as to demon-
strate to all the world that it is not because you are
Mexican you are going to stop below.
(ES50STEN:441–463)

—Marbella Sanchez

Gambling on academic success, Marbella manifests a public ethnic
identity that is both pro-academic and oppositional. In a one-hour interview
focusing on the meaning of her ethnicity, Marbella speaks of "becoming
someone" ('llegar hacer alguien') three times, "being something" twice,
and "succeeding" four times. Marbella's drive appears to stem as much
from her desire to make a public political statement about her Mexican
origin ("to demonstrate to those people") as to advance her self-interests.
Further, while willing to work hard to succeed in school, Marbella resists
pressures to conform, asserting the linguistic aspects of her ethnic identity.

The pro-academic aspect of Marbella's public identity reveals itself in
the strategies she has adopted to achieve, in her readiness to assist fellow
immigrants with academic work, and in her stubborn attacks on institutional
roadblocks that impede her educational progress. It was reflected, for example, in the rules Marbella and her peers created to maintain high standards
for the group: holding parties at six-week grading periods and allowing
only those with *A*s and *B*s to attend, and going to the library at lunch to
study as a group when a test was approaching.

It showed in physical science class, when Marbella yanked a desk from
under the feet of two male immigrant peers, ignoring their yells of protest
and chastising them for their boisterous classroom behavior: "Quiet! I can't
hear anything."

It was revealed during Marbella's freshman year, as she resisted her
school's efforts to channel her into low-level mathematics. Approaching
her school's vice principal of guidance, Marbella argued for recognition of
her academic abilities: "She wanted to leave me in basic math, but I talked
a lot with her until she let me go to pre-algebra. The only thing you do in
basic math is what little kids do: addition, division, and multiplication"
(ES50STD:458–466).

The premium that Marbella places on her education can also be seen
in the severe critiques she reserves for teachers that she perceives as failing to
respect the intelligence of her and her peers:

Now we have not advanced in the book. We haven't done very
much, the teacher uses up all the time explaining and we don't

do anything. Sometimes he spends one whole week on one page. We don't feel comfortable because he treats us like if we were kindergarten kids. We feel bad, the teacher feels that we don't understand even the simpler concepts. I don't like the teacher treating us like little kids. We understand, the problem is that he is not consistent in his explanations. (ES50STD:831–850)

Among her teachers, Marbella is recognized for her academic efforts and friendly, almost radiant, persona:

*Social studies teacher:* If I were to have an image of what I thought a nun [was like]. .... Goodness just comes out of her. And she would be like, she would be an excellent teacher. She would be an excellent teacher for children. ....

In my social studies class, she did *well*. She didn't do barely passing. She *did* well .... the writings that she submitted to me, the sentence structures were well written. In Spanish, of course. The structures were good. Her thoughts were good. When we had to construct thought to go beyond, [like answer] OK, why. The why question was answered, completely. Some kids might do one sentence, she would do a full paragraph on the why questions. (ES044ST1:143–177)

*Science teacher:* Sparkly Marbella .... real concerned about her grades, starting off the beginning of the year. And wanted to be sure she had everything done right, that all the points were there. (ES040ST1:393–402)

*Computer literacy teacher:* She's an excellent student. She knew her keyboard when she came in and she always does her work. Sometimes when she finishes her assignments she will go back and do some more practice work. (ES50STO1:p. 12)

Marbella is perceived as both cooperative and hardworking, "excellent," "concerned," and thoughtful.

While clearly conforming to academic behavioral norms, Marbella simultaneously resists pressures to assimilate. It is clear, for example, that the majority of her teachers want and expect Marbella to speak English. Yet, as previously mentioned, Marbella resists by choosing to speak Spanish on particular days of the week. Marbella and her friends have also worked together to engage in more public forms of protest against such pressures:

*Interviewer:* You said that the woman who drives the bus now is very nice. Was there another person before?
*Marbella:* Yes, before there was a woman who spoke Spanish. It seemed like she didn't like us speaking Spanish. She said that we were not civilized, and all kinds of things. She said that we should speak English, since we were in this country we shouldn't speak Spanish. We came to talk to the office to say that we didn't like her anymore. (ES50STD:218–240)

Marbella also demonstrates resistance to assimilationist pressures by insisting that her American-born acquaintances make some effort to cross into her social world. When, for example, Marbella spied an advertisement for study in Mexico during a visit to a university, she ripped it from the wall and urged me to enroll so I could improve my Spanish.

Marbella describes herself as having carefully selected friends who support both the pro-academic and oppositional aspects of her identity: "Well, you know, I don't have a lot of friends because I am selective. Because I won't hang out with a person who doesn't like to study" (ES50STA:507–511). Like her, Marbella believes that her peers are oriented toward "becoming someone" and behaving in a serious, rather formal, manner:

.... my friends, they think that a Mexican is someone who goes forward, someone who becomes someone, who has a career and who can triumph in a country that is not his own. And also, they think that speaking—or perhaps character— that speaking correctly is one of the most important things. Because if you speak like, I don't know, like a 'cholo' [a person linked to a local gang structure] or something like that, well, that is not good. If you speak correctly you can get a better job than someone who does not speak correctly. (ES50STEN: 578–595)

Marbella compares her orientation and behavior to that of her fellow immigrants, whom she describes as oriented toward socializing rather than academic achievement:

Well, I only have a few friends, only a few true friends, five only. We are always together because we share the same ideas. For example, we don't use bad words when we talk like the other girls here. Also, they [other Latina immigrants] invite us to leave school early [cut class] with them. That is why we don't have many friends. We come to school to study, not to go out. Also, they don't like us because our grades are better than theirs [are] .... we usually fight. They said I am crazy. And not too many talk to me anymore. (ES50STB:270–284, 300–302)

Confirming Marbella's description, the school's English as a Second Language (ESL) resource teacher describes a general trend toward academic disengagement among Explorer's immigrant students. He points out that while many youths enter with a desire to succeed, their desire dampens over time:

.... the students that come here tend to be just arriving from Mexico, and they still have a lot of high expectations that you can build on. When students have been here a few years, that rubs off. And they kind of lose their enthusiasm, and their spirit, and their hope. .... Some of them had unrealistic dreams, and so when you first come here you think you can do it, and then you realize 'Well, maybe I can't.' (ES090ST1:438–461, 744–761)

In the context of the description above, Marbella appears both resilient and somewhat unusual, resisting a more general trend towards disengagement with the educational process.

In sum, Marbella presents herself as highly motivated, eager to attain bilingual skills, and determined to maintain and assert her ethnic identity. For Marbella, being Mexican means having the strength of character to succeed academically. Marbella believes that such success, through enabling her to "become somebody," will allow her to mount an effective challenge to negative stereotypes.


## A SECOND LOOK: MARBELLA'S SILENT, SEPARATIST SELF

*Interviewer:* Is there tension between the Hispanics and Americans?
*Marbella:* No, the groups don't mix.
*Interviewer:* The groups don't mix?
*Marbella:* No, because they try to humiliate us .... to many of us, including me, they call us things.
(ES50STA:407–414)

> *Marbella:* I avoid fighting in the school, because I
> know I am the Mexican, and in a fight between a
> Mexican girl and a White girl, the Mexican cannot
> win. (ES50STA: 444–449)

Ironically, Marbella is at once determined to challenge and infil-
trate, yet resigned to her marginalization and segregation, hopeful about
her future chances, yet pessimistic about near-term prospects. These seeming contradictions are manifested most clearly in Marbella's interview
transcripts, as her optimistic statements are paralleled by an emphasis on
the importance of remaining silent in the face of discriminatory actions,
an affinity for some segregationist practices that shield and protect, and
expressions of skepticism about the reality of her immigrant voice being
heard. Thus, coexisting with Marbella's opposition is a passive, silent, and
separatist self, far different than the persona described in the preceding
section.

This is the self who, having been hit by a group of American peers,
fell silent and turned away: "I have a P.E. class, and there are some Americans with me, and so, it was my turn, it was my turn to play basketball.
Then—well because in Mexico they gave us some basketball classes so I
know a lot and I always beat them—they got mad …. Later they stopped
me, and one of them hit me. …. I paid no attention to them. …. My classmates asked me, 'Why are you afraid of them?' …. 'Why bother? [I said]. It
is not worth the trouble'"(ES50STA:434–449).

This is the self who rationalized her isolation in P.E. class during her
sophomore year. (Ninety percent of the students in Marbella's class are
Latino, most of them immigrants.) "It's probably better that way. Because
they [Americans] treat us badly."

This is the self whose English voice falls silent because of a European
American peer: "I want to talk to her [my teacher] in English, but there is
always a gringo named John there, and he is very mean. …. That's why I
don't speak in English with Mrs. Bryant anymore. Since she understands
Spanish, I talk to her in Spanish" (ES50STD:991–1006).

This is the self who expresses futility about bringing actions she perceives as discriminatory or disrespectful to the attention of powerful adults in
her environment:

> We go to Mr. Acevedo [principal]. Then, because none of us
> can communicate well with him, and they [European American
> peers] can, they tell him what they want to. And so it sounds like

we are the ones who don't respect them. 'How can that be?' I ask. 'If they don't respect us, how are we going to respect them?' (ES50STA:490–498)

Marbella believes the silent, separatist aspects of her persona are the product of her location in a social system in which she and her peers are viewed and treated as inferior. Concluding that European American youth do not respect her, Marbella shrinks from social interaction:

They think that they are better than us. They think that because we are in their country, we are underneath them. That makes us afraid to talk to them in English because we think they will laugh at us. .... If we are talking in English, they look at us like they disapprove of our speaking English. They look at us funny and giggle. (ES50STD:939–971)

These meanings structure Marbella's behavior in ways that are somewhat antithetical to the goals and beliefs she expresses. For example, Marbella emphasized her conviction that mastering English was essential to her future: "It's to learn English, that's what's necessary to triumph here. To know English. And to succeed in school" (ES50STEN: 795–808). Yet Marbella often falls silent in integrated settings, not speaking unless spoken to. During the days I spent with Marbella at school she spoke to just two culturally different peers: the first, a Filipina immigrant, the second, a Spanish-speaking European American who volunteers as a tutor in Explorer's ESL classrooms. Marbella explains:

.... in the [one] class where I have contact with Americans well, I simply don't speak to them. The only one where I'm around them is "Link" period and [there] I apply myself to my homework and don't pay attention to them. But, if they speak to me politely, I speak to them. But if not, well I just ignore them and do my homework. (ES50STEN:866–875)

Marbella describes herself as profoundly hesitant to engage in the casual, everyday conversation necessary to achieve English mastery, to engage in linguistic activity that would enable her to begin to "demonstrate to other people that we indeed can make it" (ES50STEN:442–443).

For Marbella, being Mexican necessitates a certain resignation to actions and procedures meant to silence or degrade, a certain degree of distancing behavior in order to protect herself from psychological harm. In the quote which opens this chapter, she speaks of the importance of struggling against efforts to vanquish. Yet, at a basic level, Marbella expresses a feeling of powerlessness relative to her European American-born peers and succumbs to their efforts to silence.

I turn now to Marbella's school experiences, identifying and naming practices that enable the "structuring of silence" (Weis & Fine, 1993). First, I consider school-based factors, which discipline Marbella and those around her to a set of beliefs about what it means to be Mexican, marginalizing immigrant Latinos and removing much of the force from their achievements and voice. To understand Marbella's hesitancy to demonstrate her bilingual and academic competencies, one must consider the value placed on such competencies by those around her. Second, I consider disciplinary policies and relationships that act upon and constrain Marbella's ability to critique and resist. The latter provide additional insight into Marbella's tendency to remain silent in the face of insult or acts of discrimination.

## SORTING MECHANISMS:
## THE MARGINALIZATION OF MARBELLA

*Marbella:* Later we will be in the medium classes, but since we don't speak English, we are in the lowest classes. (ES50STA:149–152)

*Huberto, ESL aide:* .... most of the things Explorer is doing, they never think, you know, they never talk to [immigrant] students, 'Hey, Explorer is doing a tutoring program, an awards program.' We're the last to know. They never call us, they never tell us about what the school is doing for the students, you know. .... They seem—they don't care about us. That's why they—most of the students want to quit school. Because they feel discriminated [against] or isolated. And it's really sad when someone doesn't care for you. (ES105ST1:196–224)

The first set of practices that work effectively to silence Marbella can be located in disciplinary mechanisms that marginalize youth based on linguistic status and delegitimate immigrants' academic accomplishments. Marbella, like her fellow 355 Latino students in need of language assistance

(25.3 percent of the student body), was placed in the ESL track as soon as she arrived at Explorer. Here, Marbella was effectively segregated from the remainder of the school population for the academic day. During her sophomore year, for example, Marbella attended English/Reading ESL, algebra, P.E., physical science, computer literacy, and foods classes. Of these six classes, five (foods being the exception) were composed almost entirely of immigrants (almost all of them Latino). Marbella's only other consistent opportunity for contact with language-proficient students occurred during five-minute passing periods, the lunch hour, and a thirty-minute "Link" period (homeroom) following lunch.

Segregation ostensibly enables students to receive academic content in their native language. However, Marbella had only one teacher during her first two years of high school who spoke Spanish. In reality, for many second-language learners, segregation has at best allowed for reduced class size (twenty-five to thirty youth versus thirty-five), bilingual aides, and slowed speech on the part of European American teachers, with little or no training in second-language instruction.

At times, it was difficult to find any justification for Marbella's segregation. For example, in Marbella's computer literacy course, thirty immigrant students learned word processing and typing skills. When asked what made this an ESL class, the teacher explained that, in reality, the only difference was that she did not test the students for speed. Though initially planning to integrate ESL vocabulary into students' work, the teacher said she had received little cooperation from teachers in the form of vocabulary lists.

Likewise, though P.E. is officially integrated, Marbella had just two European American classmates out of a group of approximately thirty in her class. This goes against school policy. However, according to the vice principal of curriculum, grouping policies at the departmental level (along with "scheduling difficulties") permit resegregation to occur: "It's not purposeful. .... now what may have happened, they may have regrouped the kids out there. You get a hundred kids, and half of them may be Hispanic. They may regroup those kids. .... And they are supposed to be regrouping by skill level" (ES072ST2:688–701). In Marbella's case, "skill level" correlated with linguistic and ethnic status, a relationship that went unquestioned by those around her.

Policies both amplify and attach status to Explorer's academic differentiation. Most importantly, high-achieving ESL students are shut out of the honor society because they cannot take the classes that qualify them for admission. Though students like Marbella were recognized at a year-end awards banquet, the banquet was held in the evening and only ESL students and their parents attended. The achievements of immigrants were thus not made part of the public school discourse, keeping evidence of their existence hidden from European American and English-speaking Latino peers.

Academic segregation is augmented by policies that distance and separate youths, fostering social segregation by socioeconomic (and thus linguistic) status. For example, students like Marbella, who qualify for free or reduced-price lunches, must line up inside the school cafeteria for hot meals. Lunch lines for students who buy hamburgers, pizza, and other popular fare are located in the outside courtyard. As a result, youths of color dominate the dimly lit cafeteria, while clumps of European Americans dominate the area outside. (During the ten days I ate lunch in the cafeteria, I and a group of special education students were the only European Americans present.) Because of the strong relationship between immigrant status and income, many of the students hidden from public view are second-language speakers. Marbella feels academic and social segregation combine to contribute to her isolation: "Most of the students I've met are Chicanos, not Americans, because there are no Americans in my classes, only Chicanos. .... Since last year almost all the Mexicans get together in the cafeteria and the gringos meet outside .... since the very beginning (ES50STD: 1058–1076).

The necessity of English comprehension for social participation is also communicated in a daily speech event: the posting (and occasional reading) of the school bulletin. The bulletin advertises school activities and scholarship opportunities. It is read and posted in English, despite the complaints of the school registrar:

> *Registrar:* I fight like crazy to get a lot of things in Spanish. It's very hard to make sure that a lot of these flyers that go out, for instance, for the kids—I feel that the kids are being left out of student activities. The Hispanic kids. Because like all of the announcements are always in English ... aren't they? Every day, have you ever heard them? Yeah, they're in English. The daily bulletin is in English. How are they going to hear anything? And I don't know, maybe in their classrooms the teachers are translating them but I seriously doubt that. You know, telling them about information.
> *Interviewer:* What is it that makes it hard to do that [get things translated]?

*Registrar:* I don't know. We've got the personnel here who speak Spanish. There shouldn't be any reason why the daily bulletin should not be translated into Spanish, every single day. .... I've asked. I've said, 'Why don't we tell them in Spanish? I think it's a good idea.' I don't know, maybe they are trying to encourage the kids to learn English. (ES117ST1:164–197)

The regular posting of the daily bulletin becomes a speech act that structures access to information by linguistic status.

In the context of this social system, Marbella has become increasingly aware of her marginalization. The quote which opens this section indicates that she knows ESL classes are not looked upon in the same way as are other classes at her high school. Marbella's perception of her marginalization is also reflected in her descriptions of academic expectations for immigrant youth:

*Interviewer:* The teachers or other people at this school, do they think that Mexicans as a group are going to do something? Do they have expectations for Mexicans?
*Marbella:* I think so. Because some think that because you are Mexican, you can't do anything. Or that because you are Mexican you can't succeed in this country. .... I have seen some who, because they see that you are Mexican, they don't give you something that ... something difficult that really you can do. They make it very easy for you. And for the Americans they make it a little bit more difficult. Because they think that, I don't know, that you can't do it ... that you are not intelligent, or maybe, I don't know.
*Interviewer:* How many think like that?
*Marbella:* There are *many* teachers here who think like that. (ES50STEN:1035–1076)

At the same time, Marbella feels relatively powerless to challenge the school's efforts to channel her into courses characterized by low expectations: "I guess the only area in which I have control is in my understanding of the subjects. But not in the manner of choosing them" (ES50STD:606–610). According to Marbella, no one interviewed her about her prior school history upon her arrival at Explorer. Rather, she was given a schedule and told what she would take after being tested for English and Spanish language comprehension. Though she successfully resisted her placement in basic math, Marbella found herself in a clothing class during her freshman year, and was placed in a foods class rather than continuing computer literacy as a second-semester sophomore: "I liked computers better, but I had to take cooking. .... I wrote down two choices, first computers and then cooking. But in computers there wasn't room for anybody else, so they had to put me in cooking" (ES50STD:285–293).

## DISCIPLINARY POLICIES AND BUREAUCRATIZED RELATIONS: THE SILENCING OF MARBELLA

To me, the biggest problem that I see at this school, [is] that the kids aren't listened to. I mean, they're crying for help, and no one is out there. (ES106ST1:125–130)

—Dave Santos, ESL aide

References to fears going unheard and the futility of protest run through much of Marbella's discourse. In three of our five interviews, Marbella describes incidents in which she felt immigrant students were first mistreated, and then their protests were ignored or discounted. Typically, as in the incident below, Marbella perceives linguistic and ethnic differences as being relevant to the eventual outcome of these conflicts:

I don't like that class because the teacher is very racist. We have Hispanics, or actually Mexicans [immigrants], and there are some Americans there. Sometimes he chides us a lot and he doesn't say anything to them. Like sometimes we have to wear a blue-and-white shirt. If you wear a sweater, you have to wear the sweater underneath and the shirt on top.

Yesterday this—I have a friend named Bernardino. He was wearing his white shirt underneath a black sweater. And there were two Americans who were also dressed like that. Then the teacher said a lot of things to the Mexican, Bernardino. And he made him take it off and put it on top of the sweater. And he didn't say anything to the two Americans. Because of that, we all got mad because he didn't say anything to them. And he has to be equal with everyone.

He told him that he was going to throw him out of that class, because he didn't like stupid people who don't follow the rules in his class. Like he [Bernardino] knows English well, so he [the teacher] asked him 'Why is it like that with you?'

> [Bernardino asked] 'Why didn't you say anything to the rest of the students? ... Because the rest of them are American?' And he [the teacher] told him 'That has nothing to do with it. Here it has nothing to do with Mexican or American. Here, it has to do with how we come dressed. You are nobody to tell me anything. I am the teacher and you are the student.' (ES50STC: 406–449)

The school's disciplinarian would most logically assist Marbella and her immigrant peers in the clarification and resolution of such student–teacher conflicts. However, the vice principal of discipline (Mr. Joyce) describes himself as a "traditionalist." This, he explains, means that he is likely to support a teacher before a student and does not believe in giving second chances. Explaining further, Joyce adds:

> I'll sit here, and I'll listen, and I'll point out what I think the school's position is on their particular behavior, what I think their parent's position is, and then I'll drop the bomb on 'em. And a lot of kids think, well he's listening, he's explaining, I'm going to get off. And then boom! I'll put them on the hook. It's a surprise but they've accepted it. I guess that's a sort of a traditionalist approach. (ES100ST1:127–184)

Six of the fifteen Explorer students interviewed compared Joyce unfavorably to the previous vice principal of discipline. Most often, students complained that Joyce refused to trust or listen to youths: "Mr. Joyce, whatever the teacher said, that must be right, cause teachers don't lie, so ..." (African American male); "He must fancy himself like a Stalin figure because he'll see you and come up to you and [ask] 'Where are you going?' He is so much more disciplinary than the guy last year, and as a result I think people are more rebellious. He won't trust you with anything" (European American male).

Many of the incidents Marbella would protest are located at the peer, rather than student–teacher, level. However, based on her observations, Marbella doubts whether Joyce is impartial when weighing the testimony from members of different ethnic groups:

> *Interviewer:* Can you talk a little bit about Mr. Joyce's discipline?
> *Marbella:* Well, I remember mentioning [before] that sometimes he is not so good. He can be a little bit racist with us, the Mexican students. For instance, about a week ago we had a pep rally here in the gym. .... A gringo and the Mexican had a fight out-

side the gym. Mr. Joyce didn't tell him anything, he didn't say anything to the gringo or the Mexican. Later on, inside, the Mexican was making noise over where the seniors were. The gringo was where the juniors were and shouted 'Fuck your mother' at him. Of course the Mexican got mad and went over to where the gringo was. Mr. Joyce grabbed him, took him outside and threw him out of school for three days, but he said nothing to the gringo. All the Mexicans there were very upset, so we started shouting and he got mad. Most of us went outside the gym. .... I think most of the Mexicans now purposely don't behave because they don't like Mr. Joyce. (ES50STD:750–791)

Statistics lend insight into Marbella's belief that Joyce focuses on the behavior of Latinos. During Marbella's sophomore year, 55.8 percent of those suspended were Latino, though they made up just 40.6 percent of the total school population; during her junior year, Latinos were 67.7 percent of those suspended, but 38.4 percent of the total school population then. Suspension rate data is also consistent with Marbella's argument that authoritarian systems create manifestations of oppositional behavior. The absolute number of students suspended after Joyce arrived at Explorer increased by 50 percent. Almost all of this increase came about due to increases in the number of youths of color who were suspended.

Though situated in a disciplinary system revolving around efficiency and control, Marbella could speak to other adults in the environment. However, Marbella's descriptions suggest she does not have the types of relationships that would facilitate voicing her concerns, and it appears that the responsibility for reaching out has been placed on her shoulders. For example, Marbella's homeroom teacher is responsible for monitoring her students' academic progress and conferring with students about their course selections. (There are no counselors at Marbella's high school, due to budget cuts.) This teacher speaks Spanish and Marbella describes their relationship as "good." However, though she attended this class daily, Marbella did not have a serious conversation with her teacher about her courses. As Marbella sees it, "She is always busy, she doesn't seem to have time" (ES50STD:481–483). Likewise, Marbella knows that the guidance principal has information about colleges and careers. She, too, appears busy: "I went once and she was busy that day. She is always busy giving tests" (ES50STD:553–554). When Marbella's pattern of attendance changed substantially during the second semester of her sophomore year, due to her mother's illness, those charged with monitoring attendance did not ask Marbella where she had been. Finally, despite her "sparkly" personality and model behavior, Marbella does not draw attention; neither the principal of discipline nor the guidance principal recognized her name. The latter spoke fluent Spanish and monitored the cafeteria where Marbella ate every day during the lunch hour.

Ironically, it appears that model behavior may be partially responsible for Marbella's invisibility. She describes her younger brother, who does poorly and causes problems in school, as relatively well-known:

> .... we have a brother here. My brother is very lazy. Every once in awhile they [the school] are punishing him and .... well they hardly say anything about us [Marbella and her sister], except that we have never had to go to study hall or any of that. But about my brother, yes. And my mother has to call every week, because they told my brother that if he doesn't act better that he was going to have to return to Mexico. And because of that she has to call each week to ask about my brother's education. ....
>
> Sometimes Mr. Casper (ESL resource teacher) answers and she speaks with him. But like Mr. Casper doesn't know us, neither me nor my sister. He looks us up in his dispatches and he says that we have nothing, neither study hall nor anything else. (ES50STC:1173–1187, 1222–1229)

In sum, from Marbella's vantage point, there is no one in the environment inviting her or other immigrants to voice their concerns. Further, because the emphasis appears to be on managing and controlling conflict, it could be risky for Marbella to confront a teacher or a peer. At some level, Marbella appears to recognize and act upon this. ("I avoid fighting in the school, because I know I am the Mexican, and in a fight between a Mexican girl and a White girl, the Mexican cannot win.") Thus, silence and separatism are eminently practical strategies.

## CONSTRAINTS ON DEVELOPMENT: MARBELLA'S SOPHOMORE CLASSROOM EXPERIENCES

> I think my teachers should learn another method of teaching, because the one they use is not very effective. I also would like them to realize we are intelligent, that we can do things, would like them

not to discriminate against us, to treat us like civilized persons, not like some sort of objects.
(ES50STC: written protocol)

> —Marbella Sanchez

The statement above, written by Marbella in response to a written
prompt when she was a sophomore, clearly reveals that she feels her education is not what it could be. In addition to the need for access to challenging
material, pedagogical method and the need for respect and personalization in
day-to-day interactions emerge as concerns.

In this section, I illustrate resource constraints that may be significant to
Marbella's academic development and relevant to the concerns she expresses
above, considering her classroom experiences in courses where content is
meant to parallel that found in courses taken by English speakers. Also, by
considering the standards and criteria Marbella applies when evaluating her
experiences across these classes, we gain additional insight into her sensitivity toward practices that silence and marginalize. In fact, Marbella was willing to forgive significant deficits in course content when she perceived the
teacher to be operating in a manner consistent with her oppositional pro-
academic identity. To illustrate resource constraints and Marbella's orientation,
I describe two courses: physical science and algebra.

Marbella described science as her favorite class. During the periods I
observed, students focused primarily on the acquisition of scientific vocabulary. For example, on one of the days that I attended class, students were
learning the properties of light (reflection, refraction, polarization, diffusion,
interference, diffraction). They watched a movie, taking notes when directed,
and saw a simple in-class demonstration of refraction. (To demonstrate refraction the teacher fired a laser beam through a chalk cloud.) On other days, students worked out of English language textbooks, answering questions at the
end of the chapter and defining words. Marbella's teacher, Mr. Snyder, has
received no training in teaching linguistic minority students and spends most
of his day teaching chemistry. Hands-on laboratories are rare. Despite the
fact that twenty-two out of Snyder's twenty-five students are non-English
speaking Latino immigrants, his aide speaks Vietnamese rather than Spanish.

Science was dominated by a group of males Marbella describes as "students that don't like to work, like to be shouting in class," as "little kids" that
sometimes "behave quite badly" (ES50STD:322–328, ES50ST03:p.7). These
students often bellowed at one another or at their classmates, sometimes
disrupting their teacher's explanations:

[Lots of loud talking between students, as Snyder comes forward to start class.]

*Snyder:* Alright, today we're going to see a movie to help you distinguish between [said slowly, as Snyder writes on board] *reflection* and *refraction.*

[Snyder looks toward a student who sits near the light switch, and snaps his finger. The light snaps off almost instantaneously. Another student pulls down the shade.]

*Male student:* [bellowing] Mr. Snyder, no tengo lápiz! (Mr. Snyder, I don't have a pencil!)

*Peers:* [screaming loudly] No tengo lápiz! No tengo pluma! Mr. Snyder! Mr. Snyder! (I don't have a pencil! I don't have a pen!)

*Other peers:* Ey cabrón!! Dónde está su lápiz?! (Hey bastard!![2] Where's your pencil?!) (ES50ST03:p.6)

Marbella, who frowns on this behavior, believes her peers take advantage of her teacher's lack of Spanish: "The students know very well that Mr. Snyder doesn't understand when they speak Spanish. If Mr. Snyder had a T.A. who knew Spanish, they would behave better" (ES50STD:819–823).

Snyder describes himself as directing a substantial part of his efforts toward building positive relationships with students such as those described above. As he explains, "Whatever strong suit I have, which is questionable, is probably getting along with students you know. And sometimes, if I can't teach them, I just try to be friends with them" (ES040ST1:37–42). Marbella agrees with one aspect of Snyder's self-assessment, arguing that he is well-liked by his students. For example, she emphasized that her classmates become quiet when they were asked to take notes and that they planned to bring Snyder a gift at the end of the year. Nevertheless, popularity aside, Snyder feels he shortchanges his students with his curricular and pedagogical decisions. He makes them because of time constraints and a lack of surety about what to do otherwise:

.... this class is extremely difficult for me for a number of reasons. Ah, I have—most of the other teachers have had some type of a, ahm. ... ESL training of some type, if nothing but workshops or something like that. Somehow, I ended up this year coming to school and having an ESL class, and really, feeling a little uncomfortable ....

And, you know, there are [other] reasons why this class is hard for me. Teaching only one section of it for one thing. I've got four sections of chemistry, and then toward the end of the day, I face—I have this class. It's too easy to concentrate on getting ready for chemistry classes, and save this one until right before lunch, and figure out before lunch what I'm going to do. I really, I really don't feel good about it. I should be doing a better job. So, I don't know. It's a—but after many, many years of—it's unfortunate. Because there are some kids in here that really are smart. ....

Ideally I'd like, I need to put more hands-on stuff in. You know, I'm thinking that way. I'm just going to have to spend more time preparing for this class, which I haven't done. That would be a way to make it better. The few labs that I've done in here—which are a few, but I've done some—I came away feeling like I got to have another one. But again, having just the one class, and other time restraints, trying to run chemistry class at the same time and in the same room makes it difficult. (ESO40ST1:44–56, 199–223, 640–653)

To cope with linguistic differences, Snyder acts intuitively, depending often on humor and using physical as well as verbal explanations to make his points. "To observe is to do this," says Snyder, as he raises cupped hands to his eyes to focus on a point on the desk. "No estan en vacaciones, quiete por favor" ("We're not on vacation, be quiet please"), he adds later (ES50ST01:p.11).

The pedagogical situation in Marbella's algebra class is similar in many respects. Like Snyder, Marbella's teacher (Mr. Uldine) is a middle-aged male who came to his immigrant students with no ESL training. He arrived mid-year, from a job in business, after Marbella's first teacher left for another position. This was Uldine's first teaching position, and he was working hard simply to keep abreast of his students. Uldine was well aware that the level and degree of his preparation were far from ideal. "I'm flying by the seat of my pants," he commented, the first day I came to class with Marbella.

To cope with the language differences between himself and his students, Uldine made extensive use of a Spanish-speaking tutor, who recently graduated from Explorer, and took advantage of his students' willingness to help one another. Students spent the period volunteering to come forward to the blackboard to demonstrate and explain how they worked out individual problems. During these demonstrations, Uldine and his tutor circulated throughout the classroom, stopping at various desks to offer words of encouragement or to urge students to work. Some students yelled encouragement as their friends explained problems, while others worked alone or in small groups on their homework assignment or sat listlessly at their desks. Uldine, who came up with this pedagogical technique with the aide of his tutor, revealed its purpose on two occasions, once praising his students for "taking responsibility for their work," and later reminding them "you're all teachers" (ES50ST01: p.6, ES50ST02: p.4).

Yet, teachers must also provide explanations and introduce students to new content. Over the course of three months, the work in algebra became steadily more difficult. For example, in January, students solved simple equations (e.g., $6 = 2/a$). In April, on their six-week examination, they were asked to simplify and solve more complex problems (e.g., simplify $(4a - 1)(2a + 3)$, solve $6y^2 = 22y + 40$). From the perspective of Marbella (and her friends), Uldine's attempts to explain the concepts and strategies necessary to solve complex problems were inconsistent and highly confusing:

> I don't understand the teacher. He explains very fast; but also it seems like he doesn't know how to explain. One day he does something one way and the next day he does it in a different way. That's what makes it difficult for us. When the test comes we don't know how we are supposed to do it. That's difficult. (ES50STD:130–146)

To provide evidence of students' lack of understanding, Marbella cited the six-week grades. According to her, no student received an *A*. Only one youth, a Vietnamese male, received a *B*. The remaining students, including Marbella and her sister, received *C*s. In contrast, Marbella earned straight *A*s in algebra throughout the first semester.

In both science and math, Marbella encounters certain resource constraints. In science, she works with a teacher who has no ESL experience and there is no aide to provide language assistance. Further, she encounters a curriculum that has been stripped of authentic scientific activity. In math, she encounters a teacher who is himself learning how to teach, brought in mid-year on an emergency credential. Further, he holds students responsible for concepts that he has failed to clearly explain, threatening Marbella's academic success.

Interestingly, however, Marbella praised science. While puzzling, Marbella's response can be interpreted in light of her desire to achieve academically and her orientation toward strategies she perceives as inclusive. When explaining why science was her favorite class, Marbella first cited Snyder's ability to provide accessible explanations:

*Marbella:* I like it [physical science] because we come to know the world more closely and how people are and how many things are made that sometimes we didn't know [about]. And the teacher explains the class [well].
*Interviewer:* How does he explain the class? What does he do?
*Marbella:* What does he do? Well, he speaks to us completely in English, but he explains his class very well. He might use the blackboard to show us what each thing means, or he might rouse our interest in what we are doing, so that we follow better. (ES50STD:19–37)

Marbella also referred to Snyder's patient attempts to negotiate with youths as evidence of his faith in and affection for students. Finally, she explained:

Well, he's a good person. He's on very good terms with us. He tells us that he would perhaps like to be Mexican because, well we want to study, we want to be someone in this country. He tells us that many times people who are not born here and who know English don't make use of it, and that sometimes we who don't know it, we make use of it. (ES50STC:54–62)

Snyder's comments are explicitly supportive of beliefs and values integral to Marbella's pro-academic identity. His curriculum and explanations are accessible. Thus, Snyder appears to be a "good person," one who seems to understand and find ways to support Marbella's goals and agenda.

In contrast, Uldine provides instruction that threatens to academically marginalize Marbella. Further, and equally important, Marbella felt that Uldine was manipulative in the way he negotiated for attention and that he was prone to inappropriate displays of power over his students. When comparing Uldine to Snyder, Marbella emphasized his lack of patience and his readiness to yell at students when there were no observers in the room (ES50ST02:pp.2–3). She (and her friends) told me, again and again, that any displays of affection and encouragement he showed while I was in class were not genuine, but put on for my benefit: "If someone comes to the class to observe, the teacher acts differently. We don't like that either. On those occasions he tries to be nicer, to explain better. We don't like that" (ES50STD:850–855). Marbella was also incensed by Uldine's decision to send her best friend (also an excellent student) to in-school suspension because she failed to bring her book to class. Though the friend explained that the book had been taken from the locker room, Uldine did not relent until another teacher intervened on her behalf. What appears to be relevant in this situation is that in an attempt to discipline and control, Uldine replicates the more general pattern of the school. This creates the fear and frustration conducive to the emergence of Marbella's silent self and perhaps triggers the feeling she describes earlier of being "treated like some sort of object."

## SUPPORT FOR OPPOSITIONAL IDENTITY: FRESHMAN SOCIAL STUDIES

Marbella's awareness and sensitivity to practices that threaten to further marginalize can be seen in her evaluation of individual classrooms. Marbella appears highly attuned to the degree of academic support provided and the ways in which teachers use power and handle relationships. Both combine to convey meanings relevant to her faith in the possibility of maintaining an identity that is both pro-academic and pro-Mexican.

In this section, I change course, describing a classroom that Marbella praised throughout her freshman and sophomore years. Marbella frequently referred to the empowering messages, worthwhile content, and valuable information she encountered in social studies; all factors relevant to the construction of her oppositional identity. In this class, an examination of cultural diversity, Mexican culture and history, and aspects of the American opportunity structure were explicit parts of the curriculum.

Marbella's teacher, Mr. Vargas, is a fluent Spanish speaker and a bilingual specialist who chose to return to the classroom after spending seven years in the district office. There, he worked as an ESL resource person, training teachers "how to deal with a tough subject like biology without watering it down ... and being able to one, have that kid succeed, two, not be frustrated when you're doing it, and number three, make that kid a part of the school" (ES04401X:177–185). Vargas believes low expectations for language minority students, reflected in an unchallenging curriculum, are a major impediment to students' advancement. Based on this belief, he has created a curriculum that asks students to go beyond memorizing names and places to analyzing how and why historical events occurred. In addition, students are given major assignments that require research outside the classroom. For example, as a freshman, Marbella worked in a group to prepare a five-minute oral report about an ancient culture of her choice. Students were required to prepare visual aides and to offer both information and opinions about their chosen cultures.

Many of Vargas' assignments parallel those found in Explorer's other English language freshman social studies classrooms. However, Vargas' students also consider American cultural processes and their implications. Vargas explains:

> .... I tell them, 'You cannot make it if you don't understand something.' They need to understand where they are. And where they are has different values, and different norms, and different situations. And, to do this, then we have to look inside ourselves. And we do this, I have them look inside of themselves. Who am I? And where are we going?
>
> And we looked at rules and regulations, and where did they come from? And can we make a difference in our lives if we had rules and regulations that guided us, ourselves? (ES044ST1:487–516, 543–551)

Vargas also discusses the existence of racism, not only in America as a whole but within his high school as well: "I talk to them about racism, and how it exists, and how it affects everybody, and the Black experience. .... And I told them, you know, to expect it. They [the faculty] will tolerate skin color, they will tolerate everything except the language. I tell them, you've got to learn English" (ES044ST1:561–568).

According to Marbella, this is the only class where she has been given the opportunity to explore her own as well as others' heritages. When asked how teachers speak of her heritage, Marbella replied:

> It's not spoken about very well—the Mexican heritage—here in the United States. .... Mr. Vargas is the only one that talks of the Mexican heritage, or that has us look up things in libraries, about Mexican culture and other things. ....
>
> Last year I was in his class. He asked us to discover how Mexico really was. He asked us to examine Mexican culture; he gave us books bought in Mexico. And he told us that our culture was very grand, and that we mustn't lose it, our culture ... and that it is marvelous, that culture, no? And also we examined the Chinese culture. And he also asked us to examine the Indians of the past, to explore how they were living and all that. And how they arrived in Mexico, and all that. (ES50STEN:692–716, 774–787)

Marbella also says Vargas is the only adult who has helped make the norms and values in her new environment more explicit:

*Interviewer:* Has there been someone or something that has helped you in your transition after moving to the United States?
*Marbella:* Yes. Mr Vargas talked to us about the American culture and the Mexican culture. .... I learned a little bit. For instance, about some presidents, about the natives who first got here. .... we also talked about how Americans are, the way they behaved. Mr. Vargas asked a Mexican and an American to stand in front of the class and behave the way they really were, that way we could see.
*Interviewer:* For example?
*Marbella:* Mr. Vargas had the same conversation with the Mexican and with the American, but the answers [to the questions he asked] were different. (ES50STD:1300–1343)

As part of his effort to educate his students about the new social system in which they find themselves, Vargas also provides students with basic information about the ways and means to access various colleges and careers. For example, he organizes Saturday trips to local universities so students can learn about higher education opportunities. According to Marbella, Vargas is also adamant in encouraging his students to take courses that have academic content. For example, after lobbying for an ESL science class, Mr. Vargas "told us a lot about that class, he told us that we needed that class. Maybe not exactly as a prerequisite for graduation, but to understand many things about life" (ES50STD:271–275). Further, Vargas urges his students to avoid classes like clothing and foods, because electives such as computers better their chances of college acceptance. Marbella also indicated that Vargas was the only person in her environment who has provided her with information about various career options:

*Interviewer:* You mentioned receiving information about careers in Mexico but not here. Have they given you information about different classes here?
*Marbella:* Mr. Vargas is the one who has given us some information about careers. He talked to us about salaries, about the requirements to enter that field, and about what college we have to go to for that major.
*Interviewer:* When did he tell you that? Was it during class time?
*Marbella:* It was in class. He gave us all a book, and he spent about three days talking about careers and colleges. That was last year. (ES50STD:393–406)

As Marbella sees it, Mr. Vargas "talks to us about life, about what we should do, that we should succeed, and he helps us a lot in our subjects so that we can move forward" (ES50STA:145–148).

At the institutional level, Vargas has made some moves to counter the disabling messages emanating from Explorer's disciplinary technologies. For example, as a group, his students formed a ballet folklórico dance group to assert their cultural presence in the school. This later became an elective:

> [In class we brainstormed] What is one way we can have an impact on this school? So we made up a club, the folkloric [dance] class, that's what came from [the discussion] last year. From them! And now, you know, it's taught as a class. But it came from them. (ES044ST1:516–536)

Vargas also intervened in an incident involving Marbella's best friend, helping Concha to resist a disciplinary action both she and he viewed as inappropriate:

> .... he [Concha's teacher] gave a rule, or he said something, that, 'If you don't bring your book to class tomorrow, you will be sent to SIS (in-school suspension).' Which, in this case, if you had two SISs, you would go to Saturday school. And Concha, accidentally, or by design by someone else, her book was lost in the locker room. The girls' locker room. Didn't have the book the next day. So that *edict* [Vargas' voice is edged with anger] which Mr., which that gentleman said, you know, 'This is an edict and you follow it.' She comes in, no book, he knew it, she knew it, boom! SIS. Saturday school. You're dead, right where you are. She came to the only person that I guess she could find, you know, I just happened to be there. Actually no, she did look for me. (laughs) That's right. She found me, and she said, 'I'm going to in-school suspension. For no fault.' In Spanish. 'Can you help me?' And then she explained what happened.
>
> So I took that explanation to the gentlemen, and I asked him 'Would you *not* do this? Would you *believe* her? Because I believe her, and I believe what she's saying is true.' And he said, you know he said that because [I told him that], sure. .... But I'm not sure that he did [believe her]. *I* believed her. When a kid tells me that, when a kid sensitive like Concha would tell me or anyone, 'This is what happened,' you know, I *do*, because I've been

in those shoes before. I've been in those shoes before. I've looked
at people and I've said, 'Please believe me, I really did the work,'
you know. But he didn't believe her. He didn't believe her.
(ES044ST1:295–349)

Because Vargas provides a curriculum in which students have the opportunity to explore cultural diversity, social systems, and racism, because he
helps his students gain a better understanding of the ways and means to
attend college and to pursue various careers, and because he serves as a
resource to assist in fights against attempts to discipline, Marbella views
him as a significant and meaningful source of support.


## REFLECTION

Marbella is, on the one hand, a youth buoyed and strengthened by her ethnic self-conceptions, while at the same time aware and fearful of forces that
constrain her movement. While Marbella's ethnicity serves as a source of
force and power, it also becomes an eddy she retreats to for protection.
Marbella's ability to maintain her particular brand of opposition is impressive, given the array of constraining disciplinary technologies aligned against
her. In many ways, she manifests an ability to resist constraints on her academic development—an ability described as characteristic of immigrant
minorities (Suarez-Orozco, 1989). A culturalist perspective would emphasize the pro-academic aspects of Marbella's ideology, linking them to her
immigrant status. Yet, the silent, separatist aspects of Marbella's persona also
exist. These aspects of her behavior not only slow Marbella's acquisition of
the cultural and linguistic skills necessary to assert her rights, but also suggest
a certain resignation to disciplinary practices and procedures.

While Marbella believes educational achievement will result in
improved economic opportunities, she is also highly aware that her chances
are structured and limited by inequitable academic opportunities. I have
linked the silent and resigned aspects of Marbella's persona to her growing
recognition of structured inequality, a recognition that has been enabled
only with two years' experience in an American high school. In particular,
Marbella is aware of and responsive to practices in the environment that
work to marginalize immigrant minorities and pacify youths. With regard to
marginalization, academic and social segregation, buttressed by policies and
practices that both support its existence and preference the achievements of

English speakers, work effectively to delegitimate Marbella's accomplishments. Importantly, in failing to find ways to incorporate the language and culture of 40 percent of the student body into the official school discourse, in failing to provide public recognition to its high-achieving ESL students, Explorer misses a prime opportunity to challenge conceptions of Latino students' academic abilities, and conveys the message that the knowledge and skills from students' ESL world is less highly valued and somehow different than that of the world of their European American classmates.

Disciplinary practices and technologized relations work to control and pacify Explorer students, thereby structuring the silent, separatist aspects of Marbella's persona. Easy to overlook, these features of the environment are extremely circumscribing. Without a place for voice, and with an efficient disciplinarian quick to assess and dispose, Explorer's immigrant students are effectively silenced. One ESL aide believes the level of frustration among the students with whom he works is reflected in their self-defeating screams of frustration: ".... you hear a lot of La Raza always shouting and screaming, and you try to talk to them and they're real defensive. And I think that's part of the—you get here, you sit down, everyone's talking, no one's really paying attention to you, you don't understand" (ES106ST3:284–291).

Resource constraints, limiting the ability of so many public schools to respond to diversity, are also relevant to Marbella's situation. With one exception, Marbella has had no bilingual teachers and few teachers with ESL training, despite the fact that she attends the district school designated as the receiving ground for newly arrived immigrants. On the whole, according to one bilingual teacher, the situation for immigrants has improved: "They [the faculty] have accepted the growth of ESL from the way it was when I first walked in, where there were ten students and no materials. Nothing, nothing, nothing. To now, where ESL is a big department, big budget by the books. And then people have acknowledged that ESL is not bogus. That was a key operating word four years ago. Bogus" (ES044ST1:605–614).

Yet, Marbella's teachers described themselves as caught: underprepared, inexperienced, and uncertain about how to handle their classroom situations. There were villains in Marbella's descriptions—a clothing teacher who pulled hair to gain the attention of Spanish speakers, the P.E. teacher who would not let Bernardino wear his sweater over his T-shirt. Nevertheless, the majority of Marbella's teachers appeared to be well-meaning, yet not sure how best to be of assistance. As Marbella put it, "They understand that we are Mexican, and we cannot exactly do everything. They help us as much as they can, the teachers do" (ES50STEN:957–961). The problem, as Marbella points out, is that adults so often underestimate, so often downscale their expectations, rather than provide scaffolding appropriate to high-level cognitive engagement. Marbella is left marginalized, fighting harder to prevent others from structuring her into a category she recognizes as a false social construction.

# CHAPTER 4

# Carla Chávez on Masking and Isolation

> *Carla:* I feel that, you know, that Latins aren't
> stupid. I'd like to be one of them that could achieve
> something. Cause most people think that Latins
> aren't—you know, that they can't do nothing, that
> they're just going to become like in the lower class.
> And, I think that that's not true. I think that every-
> body's the same. You can do anything you want to.
> *Interviewer:* When did you start thinking about these
> things?
> *Carla:* A long time ago. Probably in elementary
> school. (RA28STEN:125–144)
> —Carla Chávez, sophomore student,
> Huntington High School

It's been a long morning in the accelerated track at Huntington High School. Through geometry and advanced English, I talked to few people. Neither did Carla Chávez, in her rush to keep up with the quick classroom pace. Even in chemistry, where students sit together in groups of four, there was little rest from the push to keep up and play well in the academic game. As Carla and her table mates worked on crossword puzzles designed to help them master chemistry vocabulary, I recorded their questions and casual conversation: "Is neutral with a 'eu' or a 'ue'?" "What did you get for number fifteen? I got a really big number." "Can you guys show me how you did this?" "When is our *To Kill a Mockingbird* assignment due?" "Hey, I found out how to get on Mr. Sugimoto's good side." For Carla, who has been in advanced classes since eighth grade, such behavior is part of the necessary daily routine. She works hard to challenge others' stereotypes, viewing academic achievement as a means to teach others about Latino capabilities.

Now, at lunchtime, I am ready for the break and eager for a change in conversation. While many of Carla's class friends continue their rush toward college acceptance by spending their lunch hour at extracurricular meetings, Carla has told me that she prefers to spend social time with friends from her community, all of them Latina. None of her close friends attend her advanced classes; according to Carla, the majority earn Cs.

Carla and I bump through milling groups of students, making our way to the locker room. Three women stand in front of a large mirror. One leans against the wall and two busily apply hair spray and wield combs in an effort to coax their bangs to stand high. All wear makeup and all are dressed up. Carla, whose bangs fall in her un-madeup face and white sweat-shirt falls casually over black jeans, seems to stand out in a way that she did not in her classrooms.

Yet, despite surface-level differences, Carla quickly fits in. Her classroom persona disappears as the conversation moves easily from talk of the weekend and a concert to talk of friends, boyfriends, and family. Carla's use of language shifts as she pushes her ethnicity to the fore: "Que quieres comer?" "I ain't eatin'. Why you eatin' yogurt? It's sick!!" There is no talk of grades and assignments on the days I eat lunch with these young women. Rather, they express interest in and concern for the more personal aspects of life.

Over the fifteen months I knew Carla, lunchtime was the only time when she revealed the linguistic aspects of her cultural background or talked about her home life and personal concerns. Carla's drive to succeed was linked to her desire to challenge stereotypes and alter statistics; time spent with friends from home offered an indication of her commitment to her community and evidence of her expressed desire to do well without hiding her background. Yet, during most of the school day, I would watch Carla leave her ethnic self outside the classroom door, adapting to northern European American middle-class norms of classroom interaction and topics of conversation while with her classmates. On a day-to-day basis in the classroom, Carla conformed even as she resisted messages and meanings from others about her ethnicity.

## "IT'S A DIFFERENT LIFE THAT WE LIVE": ETHNICITY OUTSIDE THE CLASSROOM

.... with my classroom friends, they like different things, they're into probably different music, they

have like a different life than I do. .... I don't know,
I guess how our parents, you know, had brought
you up. ... It's different and stuff. It's a different life
that we live. (RA28STC:879–883, 905–906,
935–936)

—Carla Chávez

Carla, one of more than 100 Latino students who ride the bus to her high school, spends her time out of school in a Latino working-class neighborhood. Whether relaxing with friends and family at her father's large home in downtown Mostaza, working weekends selling 'churros' at the local flea market, or sleeping and eating at her mother's apartment (Carla's parents were divorced when she was in middle school), Carla is surrounded by people who are familiar with her heritage and supportive of her ethnic self.

Carla's mother, who works weekdays as an inspector in a paper factory and weekends at a local taqueria, is the daughter of Cuban immigrants who fled their home when Fidel Castro triumphed in the early 1960s. Her family left behind a successful small retail store and a comfortable lifestyle to struggle to make a living in the United States. Carla's mother did not finish high school, but eventually earned her GED at night school. Carla's father immigrated to the United States from Mexico in his early twenties to find work. While he dropped out of school at an early age to work and speaks little English, he has succeeded in establishing his living as a welder.

While immigrants, in some respects, Carla's parents are casual and flexible about maintaining the most obvious markers of their heritages. Carla's father speaks little English, but Carla is allowed to respond to him in both English and Spanish. Carla's mother spoke to Carla in Spanish when she was a child, but now speaks both English and Spanish to her daughter. Carla's father takes trips to Mexico to attend festivals during the summer, but Carla has never been to Mexico and knows little about these activities. Carla's fifteenth birthday was treated as an occasion for lavish celebration, but she was allowed to choose a trip to Hawaii over celebrating a quinceañera, the traditional celebration for a Latina woman coming of age.

When it comes to the matter of familial roles, however, Carla's parents are more strident about enforcing cultural expectations. For one, Carla describes a set of restrictions that she connects to her parents' expectations for teenage Latina females. She wishes that she could go cruising, for example, but her parents feel this is inappropriate; further, Carla resents when her father and brothers ask her to cook for them. Second, in their words and actions, Carla's parents teach her that commitments to the extended family should be placed above self-interest. (Marcelo and Carola Suarez-Orozco (1993) have identified the emphasis on extended family as a cultural norm that cuts across Latino ethnic groups.) When asked what her family values in their heritage, for example, Carla responded:

> Family, probably family. Well my mom's always—cause right now my grandmother's in debt. She ain't doing that good. So, she don't have a job and she's taking care of her. And, you know, she's always sending money over there. She—my mom paid almost $5,000 to her last year. And then my dad, he always sends money. He always tries to help his family in Mexico. ... I guess being Hispanic, the family is like really important. Really important to them. More than jobs, house, money. (RA28STEN:491–515)

When Carla's uncle, struggling to make a living in the recession, had to commute to work in the area from his home fifty miles away, he, his wife, and his child were invited to stay in Carla's family home during the week so they could save money on gas. When Carla's eighteen-year-old brother impregnated his girlfriend, she and the child came to live with Carla's family. When this same brother quit his job, Carla's father continued to support the new family. Carla's readiness to sacrifice for the sake of the family can be seen in her decision to live with her mother after her parents' divorce. The only one of four children to make this choice, Carla did so out of concern for her mother's welfare. In fact, she prefers being with her large extended family in her father's home.

In selecting friends, Carla has searched for peers who have similar values. All of Carla's close friends are Latina. As in her family, group cohesiveness is central. For example, Carla describes willingness to organize activities and behavior around others' needs as a behavior of primary importance:

> *Carla:* .... friendships, trust [matter]. It don't matter the money you have, it doesn't matter. .... If nobody has money, we try to find—we have things to do. Or else, if somebody does have money, and somebody else doesn't, we just buy it, buy something for them, like that.
> *Interviewer:* You share.
> *Carla:* Yeah, share. And then nobody asks for it back, 'No, you keep it.' (RA28STB:280–295)

Mutual support is also critical: "My close friends, they're special because we always talk about our problems together and when one cries everybody cries," Carla explains. When asked about responsibilities to her friends, Carla replied, "Well, it's just that—the only thing I can say is that you're always there for them. You talk to them (RA28STEN:653–659)."

Carla's friendships are based in conversation, facilitated by similar experiences:

> They talk to me, about their problems, we talk about things. We have a lot of things in common. And there are some things in common that we have. We have a lot of things in common, but we're also different. And we just talk. We talk to each other without being uncomfortable. We're comfortable with each other so we talk to each other about things. (RA28STB:118–127)

Talk revolves around activities, relationships, and personal feelings, rather than school:

> *Interviewer:* What kinds of things do you like to talk about with your friends?
> *Carla:* The things that happen that day, or rumors or what's happening, what's going on with other people, different things.
> *Interviewer:* School?
> *Carla:* School? No, not really. We really don't talk about school much. We're here enough. If we have like, homework, we talk, 'Ohh, I have so much homework!' or if we have a test, 'Did you study for the test?' (RA28STB:43–49, 63–70)

> I don't talk to them about school and all that. I talk to them more about my personal life and how I feel. It's different. (RA28STD:1267–1270)

Conversations range from banter to serious discussions about relationships and friends: "You shouldn't eat that. I read that it has 500 calories." "How are you and Carlos doing?" "I just got used to the idea of her being pregnant and now she's getting married!" With friends, Carla can talk about her problems and frustrations, which during sophomore year included her family's divorce and familial restrictions. "I feel so lonely at my mom's house," and "Even if I took karate lessons, they [my parents] probably still wouldn't let me go out. They don't trust me!" Further, while grades and school are generally not discussed, and her three closest friends have left high school, Carla describes her friends as being supportive of her academic achievement:

"All of my friends expect me to get high, like good grades. They expect more from me than other people. They're 'Yeah, Carla's going to become a doctor. We're going to get free [health care],' you know, like that. When I get bad grades they're all like 'Uught-uh!'" (RA28STEN:602–614).

Carla finds that her friends' interests and values set her at ease in a way that those of her friends from her classes do not. As Carla explains, "I feel more comfortable with them. That I don't feel with my friends from class" (RA28STC:858–860). She has no desire or intention to give up her identity: "Hey, I'm Mexican, right? I ain't going to try to be something I ain't. I couldn't, you know, everybody would know it's an act. You can work among White people without being White" (RA28STEN:810–815). Consistent with this description, while with friends, Carla speaks English, but inserts Spanish words and phrases when appropriate: "We sometimes put in Mexican words, if Spanish goes real well" (RA28STEN:572–574). Carla moves from mainstream American standard English to employ other grammatical constructions in her casual conversations, particularly when making an emphatic point: "No it ain't! You tell me how it's different!" "It don't say that here!" Most noticeably, Carla relaxes, letting her interests and concerns move to the fore.

## THE DRIVEN CARLA

> Ever since I was little I guess, in third or fourth
> grade, I decided to get better grades. And then,
> when I see my brother drop out, I said, 'I'm not
> going to be like him.' I want to be something in
> life. Do something to help others.
> (RA28STA:222–228)
>
> —Carla Chávez

Achievement-conscious and oriented toward college and a career, Carla's driven self is visible throughout her interview discourse and revealed in her achievement data. She is fixated with "becoming," a phrase that she used on fourteen separate occasions during our interviews. She is determined to resist the economic forces which she sees as constraining her older brother and friends. And Carla is focussed, doing as much or more than her teachers ask of her, while working twenty hours per week and volunteering at a local hospital.

Carla's drive is manifested first in her soaring scores on the California Test of Basic Skills (CTBS). Classified as fluent English-proficient in the third grade, Carla ranked in the 67th percentile in math, the 59th percentile in language, and the 51st percentile in reading. By the fifth grade, Carla's scores had climbed to the 76th percentile in math, the 70th percentile in language, and the 63rd percentile in reading. By the eighth grade, her scores had jumped again: to the 99th percentile in math, the 95th percentile in language, and the 83rd percentile in reading. By her sophomore year, after four years of accelerated English, Carla's reading scores had climbed again to the 93rd percentile.

Carla's drive is also apparent in her desire to maintain her excellent academic record. In middle school, Carla earned straight *A*s, for a 4.0 GPA overall; during her freshman year of high school she repeated this performance. As a sophomore, Carla's grades dipped just slightly to a 3.5. Carla's response was renewed effort and concern: "It gets you. It gets you seeing those grades. I want to get higher. .... it gets me upset" (RA28STD:126–131).

Carla's drive is reflected in her steady attendance, completion of homework, and attentiveness in class. On the one occasion when her homework was not complete, Carla was visibly distraught. "He's checking homework?! I haven't finished two of our assignments," she gasped. As the teacher called for the work, Carla pleaded for time: "Wait! I'm getting my stuff together."

Finally, Carla's drive can be perceived in the joy she expresses when she realizes she is working as well or better than her classmates. While Carla says she does not discuss grades with her classroom friends, she is attuned to where she stands relative to classmates when it comes to general understanding: "The chapter that we're on is hard. I understand it though. Yesterday we had a worksheet? I guess a lot of them couldn't understand it. But I went home and I did it. And it was easy. (laughs happily) I just did it" (RA28STC:405–411).

Teachers are quite aware of Carla's determination. As early as fourth grade, she was earning accolades: "What a fantastic student! She shows so much effort!" Of eighteen middle school teachers who commented, all noted Carla's excellent conduct, and thirteen noted that her "preparation shows a high degree of responsibility." In high school, Carla's effort and care continue to stand out. Even among highly motivated classmates, she appears to be conscientious and diligent. "She comes in and sits down and does her work. Her writing is almost like she used the head of a pin to write. Very unusual. But she does volumes and volumes of written work (social studies teacher)"; "She has good study habits, her homework is always in. She seems very academically motivated (chemistry teacher)"; "She does all of her work very carefully (English teacher)."

Carla's drive for academic success appears to stem from at least three factors: her desire to challenge low expectations for Latinos, her fear of facing the economic difficulties and limited occupational opportunities friends and family members have experienced, and her familial expectations. First, Carla is conscious of the political significance of academic achievement. She speaks often of others' low expectations for Latino adolescents:

> I think Mr. Perry, my teacher, I think he didn't expect much from me because I was Hispanic, I was like the only [one in the class]. But then I was like the first one to get the best score in the class, so he was really surprised! And I got it like a couple of times, and we got a champion's chair. You could choose where you sat. .... It made me feel good. (RA28STAB:1593–1625)

Carla's hope is that she might help to challenge negative predictions: "I feel that, you know, that Latins aren't stupid. I'd like to be one of them that could achieve something. Cause most people think that Latins aren't—you know, that they can't do nothing, that they're just going to become like in the lower class."

Second, Carla is keenly aware of the difficulties her friends and family members have experienced in the job market. She attributes these difficulties to limited education. For example, when asked what type of family she would expect her friends to have, Carla replied:

> The type of family they would have? I can't imagine them having family. Cause it's hard for them. It's really hard to find jobs when you're a high school dropout and everything. Cause, it's hard. (RA28STEN:676–683)

Carla is interested in professional, white-collar careers that will enable her to "help others":

> Hopefully I'll be a doctor. Be a pediatrician or gynecologist, hopefully help other people. .... I really want to be helpful somewhere in that area .... If I don't become that I want to help teenagers. Do social work. Try to help if they have problems, help them in some way. (RA28STD:689–691, 723–735)

Because she is aware that the career goals she expresses require postsecondary education, Carla is thus driven partially by her desire to "do something in life."

Finally, though she does not mention this explicitly, Carla's drive may reflect familial socialization. According to Carla, her mother "thinks that Hispanic people could do it. You know, they're just as good as any other. They could do what they want. They could achieve anything" (RA28STEN:422–459). Carla's parents also voice the belief that success in school is the key to social and economic advancement:

> *Interviewer:* Did he [your dad] go to high school?
> *Carla:* No. He said that he never did well in school. That's why he wants us to stay in school and get a job. .... It will be better for us, for a better life. (RA28STA:497–507)

> *Interviewer:* In thinking about your family, what would you say is really, really important to them?
> *Carla:* That we don't get in trouble—that we won't become messed up when we grow up. That we find—that we'll get a job, and not be in poverty. Like they did when they were young, so that we won't have to face up to so many hardships as they have. And that we not follow their footsteps. .... Because they tell us 'We don't want you to be poor, and have such a hard life.' They want us to be happy, in doing what we want, and having a family, whatever we want, just be happy with that. And that we won't be sad and miserable. .... They don't want us to work as hard. We know they want us to get an education, cause they didn't, you know, finish school. (RA28STB: 730–761)

While neither parent can help with homework or provide information about college, their beliefs translate into pride and support for Carla's academic accomplishments. Carla's achievements are especially important because of the academic difficulties her siblings have experienced. (Carla's eighteen-year-old brother dropped out of high school, was sent briefly to juvenile hall after attempting to steal a car, and is currently unemployed. Her seventeen-year-old brother is in the vocational program at a neighboring high school and is a below-average student.)

> You know, they show—like when my grades are good, they go telling people .... telling their friends, 'Yeah, I think she's gonna become what she wants to. She's the only one in our family who can achieve what she wants.' (RA28STB:559–565)

For Carla, such encouragement is a source of emotional support: "I like the thought, cause it just gives me more hope that I could become what I want.

So it's a little bit easier on me, instead of having parents who are always putting me down, all 'You're no good' and things like that" (RA28STB: 593–599).

## CARLA'S CONTROLLED SELF

> *Interviewer:* Do you ever feel that you can't share things that are going on at home with kids in your high-track classes?
> *Carla:* Oh yeah!! You don't really share your personal life with them, cause you really aren't, you know, the culture isn't quite [the same]. We don't talk about that. We just talk about school or school things. We just talk about school.
> (RA28STD:1248–1259)

> *Freshman English teacher:* She is a very controlled girl. …. Not in an obnoxious way. But she has mapped out her life and she knows what she has to do and she has decided, at least in English, I don't know about her other classes, but she is going to be a good student and she does all of her work, very carefully. (RA003ST1:p.1)

Private and often silent, Carla's controlled self emerges before and after the lunch hour, when she is away from her Latina friends. Carla's controlled self is alert, straining to discern what is and what is not important to succeed in the academic race. This self is quiet, concerned about making mistakes. Carla's controlled self does not discuss her home life, her or her friends' worries, and does not use constructions like "ain't" in casual conversation.

Carla's controlled self is present in what she talks about in chemistry, the only course where she has an opportunity to chat with class friends because she sits in a group. "I finished the rough draft of my essay for English." "How much did you write down for the first one?" "Mrs. Cook, she's messed up. She tests different classes on different days!" Non-academic conversations with these friends are light and non-personal, despite the fact that Carla identifies an Asian American woman in her work group as one of her best classroom friends. "I had toast and orange juice for breakfast."

"Your hair looks good like that Carla." "I hate my feet." The closest a conversation came to home was when Carla displayed photos of her Latina friends after I, spying the pictures in her wallet, asked to see them.

Carla's controlled self is present in her private struggle to stay abreast of a crowd that often seems to know things she does not, such as when Carla tells her Spanish teacher that she needs a pass to go to the bathroom and then goes to the office to get a PSAT practice booklet. Not only had she just learned this booklet existed during a casual passing period conversation with a classroom friend, but also learned this friend was already practicing and doing well on a test on which Carla worries about doing poorly. Carla appeared nonchalant during the conversation, casual when she asked where she might find the booklet. Yet, immediately upon arriving at her next period, she found a way to depart for the office.

Finally, Carla's controlled self is present in her silence in all of her classes. Of the five teachers interviewed about Carla, three noted her tendency to disappear quietly in the crowd: "She'll raise her hand, but not very often. .... I don't see her as a leader" (RA031ST1:27–28,34). "She's the type that teachers will overlook because she doesn't stand out—either as a nuisance or as a top student. So she'll get overlooked because of the sheer number of students that teachers deal with" (RA076ST1:38–43). "She'd get a little bit more attention if she'd turn around and raise a fuss. She's kind of a model student. *Too* much so, I would say" (RA28ST08:p.8).

Carla's teachers' comments indicate that she has been extremely successful in masking the ethnic aspects of her persona, pushing them to the background. None of the teachers we interviewed could tell us anything about Carla's friends. Her advanced world history and advanced English teachers' descriptions are typical:

*World history teacher:* I don't see her palling around with anybody. Not in here. She talks—who is next to her? Marian is right in front of her. Valerie is behind her. She is right between them. And she doesn't have much to say to anybody.
*Interviewer:* She is pretty alone?
*Teacher:* Well she may have other friends—maybe from another group—I don't know. It's hard to tell. But I'll keep an eye out. It seems like someone else may meet her at the door. (RA036ST1:p.6)

*English teacher:* .... I don't see her out of class so I don't know what's going on there. I don't see her in the halls. I don't see her as a leader. (RA031ST1:21–34)

Similarly, no one recognized Carla's altruistic side or knew her well enough to realize that she worked and volunteered. Nor did any teacher comment on Carla's desire to become a physician.

Carla has adopted a persona that enables her to blend, even disappear, into the classroom crowd. Special in the eyes of family and neighborhood friends, Carla is perceived as quintessentially ordinary by classroom teachers. Adults also are entirely unaware of Carla's commitment to her community. In practice, Carla's classroom behavior thus appears to work against the political desires she expresses, for she masks both out-of-school achievements and the political aspects of her ambitions in silent and controlled behavior.

When asked explicitly about the silence and masking that mark her controlled classroom persona, Carla spoke only but often of the fact that she felt "uncomfortable." Over the course of two years, it became increasingly evident that Carla's discomfort was not related to some personal particularity but rather to the workings of sorting mechanisms in her environment as well to her perceptions of others' low expectations. I turn now to consider the meanings Carla discerns from the workings of disciplinary technologies at Huntington High School.

## CONTROLLING CARLA: DISCIPLINARY TECHNOLOGY AT HUNTINGTON HIGH SCHOOL

> *Interviewer:* How was the transition to the accelerated classes?
> *Carla:* It was different. It was, yeah—cause it was like more challenging. Different people. Mostly White people. (RA28STAB:1627–1633)
> —Carla Chávez

As a student in advanced courses, Carla is part of a segregated contingent. As Carla indicates in the quote that opens this section, her placement in this track as an eighth grader was "different." Having attended diverse classrooms during her first two years of middle school, she suddenly found herself surrounded by a sea of White faces.

There has been little change in high school. On most mornings, Carla boards a school bus with other Latino students. However, upon arrival in the wealthier section of town, Carla moves into classes dominated by European American- and Asian-descent peers, moving from geometry to chemistry to advanced English to advanced world history. Though most Latino students at Huntington are English-speaking and share classes with their European American- and Asian-descent classmates, there is a sharp separation between general and advanced courses. For example, during Carla's sophomore year, European American- and Asian-descent youths made up 87.5 percent of the population in the advanced English track. Latino students, who made up 19.2 percent of Huntington's fluent English-speaking population, comprised just 10.6 percent of these classes (see Table 2.1). This pattern repeated itself in the math and science departments, where Latino students were far more likely to take consumer math than calculus, far more likely to take physical science than physics. School statistics do not indicate how many Latinos in the advanced track are transported. However, during her sophomore year, Carla was usually the *only* transported Latina female in the advanced courses she attended. Differential rates of academic preparation are also reflected in statistics concerning college preparation. The vast majority of Huntington's Latinos who do graduate do not meet attendance requirements for the state college system. During Carla's sophomore year, for example, only 6.8 percent of graduating Latino seniors completed the University of California's A–F requirements. This compares to 34.5 percent of Asian-descent and 19.4 percent of European American-descent youth. When attrition rates are taken into account, just 4 percent of Latino sophomores in the two class cohorts preceding Carla's eventually completed these requirements (see Table 2.2).

The patterns in Huntington's environment are both a continuation and extension of the academic segregation initially established in middle school. The majority of Carla's classmates have been in advanced classes since the seventh grade. (Carla was recommended to these courses as an eighth grader, based on her past year's performance.) As students from feeder middle schools arrive at Huntington, those previously enrolled in advanced track courses continue in the accelerated track. At the same time, youths scoring in the lowest quartile on eighth grade national achievement tests are separated from their classmates, placed in remedial English, social studies, and mathematics courses. Such sorting mechanisms generate further academic differentiation along ethnic lines. For example, Latino and African American students comprised 40 percent of those in remedial math courses (consumer math and pre-algebra), but made up just 25 percent of the student body.

The majority of teachers with whom I spoke did not discuss or question these sorting practices; there were also no academic enrichment programs in place designed to affect the social patterns that emanate from practices designed to divide and separate. Rather, one of the more contentious debates among faculty emanated from district pressure to integrate remedial and general courses. Math teachers expressed anger over the pressure to eliminate a system they perceived as being highly efficient and appropriate: "[If we detrack] we will not have any options for them [lower-scoring students] because nobody wants to admit that [if] we bring in 600 ninth graders there's going to be a huge amount that aren't ready for this level of attention to detail. So I don't know what's going to happen, aside from the fact that they're just going to have a miserable year and fail, I'll have a miserable year, the kids that are OK will have a miserable year, everything's miserable because folks won't admit that they should be more attentive to where [the students] are at" (RA046ST1:310–325).

Similarly, the social studies faculty argued forcefully for the continuation of remedial courses. As the principal of curriculum notes, this worked effectively to silence those among the faculty who wished to eliminate the existing system: "Social studies is still sitting there saying 'Nope, we need the remedial classes.' We've talked about it. .... They're still pretty set. Peter Ulman [a social studies teacher], he has come in to talk to me [to argue for heterogenous grouping]. And he says, you know, 'Don't tell anybody I've talked to you'" (RA110ST1:290–296; 310–313).

The academic differentiation between Latinos and European Americans is complemented by the curriculum Carla encounters. By the end of her sophomore year, for example, Carla had taken three quarters of world history. As Carla notes below, the emphasis in these courses was on Western Europe and Asia:

> *Interviewer:* In terms of your teachers, how is your heritage talked about, if at all.
> *Carla:* I don't think it's talked about. I mean, all my classes, there are no Mexicans in my classes, they're in other classes.
> *Interviewer:* What about in world history? Does your teacher ever discuss the relationship between Mexico and the United States? Or immigration? Or about anything that might be related?
> *Carla:* No. [It was] like China's, and Britain's and all that. Except when they're doing the expansion of Spain. And they settled in Florida. (RA28STEN:766–688)

Carla's encounter with the Huntington staff also reinforces the implicit curricular message that scholarship is the domain of non-Latino citizens. By the end of her sophomore year, Carla had had ten European American and three Asian American teachers. Her two Latino teachers taught Spanish, not an advanced course.

Carla is not only aware of the differentiation that exists in her environment (during four separate interviews, she refers to the fact that there are few Latino students in her classes), but draws meaning from its existence. First, though Carla has attended advanced courses for several years, she still views them as the property of European Americans:

> You know [in middle school] the White people were separate from the Mexicans. .... I was in all White classes. I knew the White people, because I was in their classes. Like right now in Huntington too .... (RA28STAB:1703–1714)

In Carla's mind, serious academic endeavor appears to be primarily the domain of European American adolescents.

Second, Carla operates with the assumption that teachers "expect a lot of us to drop out, not to graduate" and that classmates "probably have this view that most Hispanics are dumb or something." Her perceptions, combined with her isolation, generate the feeling of discomfort which Carla describes as relevant to understanding the silence and masking that typify her controlled classroom persona:

> *Interviewer:* Can you talk a little bit about how you feel about being in the accelerated track?
> *Carla:* Well, I kind of feel uncomfortable. Not many Mexicans and Hispanics are in those classes. And so it kind of makes me feel uncomfortable.
> *Interviewer:* What about that makes you feel uncomfortable?
> *Carla:* Because ... they probably think of me as weird, because they think Hispanics, probably they have this view that most Hispanics are dumb or something. Have that opinion, you know, get bad grades. So, I don't know why I feel uncomfortable, I just ... means you're not really with any other ... many people. (RA28STD:540–570)

Isolated in her advanced courses, Carla feels both vulnerable and alone. Various scholars have argued that stigmatized individuals who become aware of the prejudice of others may avoid aggressive participation in group discussions (Hiltz & Turoff, 1993). Social categories pervade social interactions, with solo individuals from stigmatized groups more likely to be evaluated extremely by majority individuals (Fiske & Taylor, 1978; Kanter, 1977; Taylor, Fiske, Etcoff & Ruderman, 1978). Long a part of the advanced student contingent, Carla may avoid conversations about home because of her awareness that these could generate further awareness of her stigmatized social status. Similarly, Carla may remain silent in order to avoid mistakes that will place her in the evaluative spotlight. Regardless, it is clear that Carla's isolation makes her feel different, rendering her uncomfortable and uneasy even among peers she has known for several years.

## REVEALING KNOWLEDGE GAPS: BARRIERS TO INFORMATION AND THE CONSTRUCTION OF SOCIAL DIFFERENCE

> .... Lisa, my gosh, she knows all those things about tests and all that. .... She's a good source of information. Like they [classroom friends] know all these things about college, what tests you're supposed to take, and I'm all, 'How'd you find that out?' (RA28STD:1009–1021)
>
> —Carla Chávez

As discussed in chapter 2, numerous studies indicate that students' chances for crossing social borders improve with access to information that helps them make intelligent decisions about course selection, college application, and careers (Alexander & Eckland, 1977; Falsey & Heyns, 1984). Due to her participation in advanced classes, Carla has become increasingly aware that every bit of information she can glean about colleges and achievement tests may be valuable. Frequently, she is reminded of the reputations of various universities. Daily, she hears her classroom peers discuss the importance of maintaining high grades in advanced classes. Carla is also aware of the powerful sorting effects of societal disciplinary technologies, such as the SAT and other achievement tests: "I'm worried about those achievement tests. When I'm going to take them. They're all relating to the future, which college" (RA28STD:453–463). Yet, as indicated in the quote in the beginning of this chapter, even when she is among classmates with comparable grades and test scores, Carla often feels out of the loop. She lacks basic insights into the workings of the college application process, a factor that not only constrains her ability to challenge social categories, but also reveals a knowledge gap between herself and her classroom peers, thereby contributing to her sense of difference.

Carla faces a specific barrier in her quest for information. Most notably, she has no structured relationship with a knowledgeable adult who might help her access information. Due to cuts in funding, Huntington does not have academic or personal counseling. To compensate, Huntington has developed the Assist program, which assigns twenty to thirty students to one teacher for four years of high school. Assist teachers meet with their students on a weekly basis. During this period, they are expected to communicate information about courses and alert students to information about colleges and scholarships. In addition, teachers are expected to meet with their advisees once or more per semester to discuss and plan students' class schedules. However, some teachers resent the work this system requires, while others feel unprepared to provide their students with the necessary information. As a result, some do not provide the intended instruction. In Carla's case, Assist has provided no information of consequence. At the end of her sophomore year, her Assist teacher still barely knew her:

> *Carla:* I [had] already made my schedule. He just looked at my stuff, 'Oh, accelerated!' They were surprised, I guess.
> *Interviewer:* Really?
> *Carla:* Yeah, I guess, I guess he didn't know I was in accelerated classes.
> *Interviewer:* You mean you've had this person all year for [the] Assist [program] and he didn't know?
> *Carla:* Yeah, and last year also. And he didn't know I was accelerated.
> *Interviewer:* You're kidding!
> *Carla:* Yeah, he looked on my list and my mom was supposed to come for a meeting, and she wasn't able to. And he saw the list that I had and he saw accelerated and he goes, 'Oh that's good.' And that was that. (RA28STD:834–851)

By the end of her sophomore year, Carla had had no conversation with any school adult about scholarships, financial aid, or the college admissions process.

For youths with parents who have attended a university, such information deficits are manageable. They and their parents know ways and means to gather necessary information on their own. For Carla, however, this is not feasible; recall that neither of her immigrant parents has experience with postsecondary education, nor does she have close friends or relatives who have attended college. Thus, as a strategy for gathering information, Carla relies on casual conversations with European American and Asian-descent peers and on information she picks up while listening to adults in class.

While often benefitting from this, Carla's strategy carries three hidden costs. First, even as Carla gathers information she finds herself dependent on culturally different peers. Second, as illustrated in a segment of the classroom dialogue below, Carla subjects herself to added messages about being different and to increasing and unnecessary pressure to conform:

> Carla is sitting in chemistry, at a table with three Asian American classmates. Another researcher, accompanying these students, is at the table as well.
> *Researcher:* Carla, I hear you may be interested in applying to Stanford.
> *Carla:* Yeah. I think so.
> *Lisa:* What was it like?
> *Carla:* It was *nice.* Lots of bikes! (laughs)
> *Lisa:* Well, you have to have lots of extracurriculars.

Lisa is well aware that Carla does not participate in school government or related school activities. She casts doubts on Carla's chances even as she communicates interest. What Lisa fails to mention, perhaps because she does not know, is that Carla's work activities, both paid and unpaid, are relevant to college admission.

Third and finally, when adults make pronouncements that are misleading or incomplete, Carla may accept the information they deliver with little questioning:

> *Carla:* People ask questions, you know, what would be—like Denise? She wants to go to Stanford also. And she already has her tuition paid and everything, her parents already have the money? .... I'm all 'Whoa!' .... And then Mr. Quincy found this out, and [he said], 'Of course she's going to get into Stanford if her parents pay, you know, up front.' If they paid like before time. Is that true?
> *Interviewer:* No.
> *Carla:* No? He was telling us that, I don't know if it's true or not. He was telling us other things about which school would be good for certain things to go afterward, which schools would be good for that. .... And he was telling about that it's better to go to a two-year junior college and then switch to a regular college because they teach you the same things. He was telling us our parents probably think—they don't like this because they think

the people up there don't know. 'Oh, your child goes to a junior college?' They think that's not as good as a regular college, and you know it's the same thing. (RA28STD: 894–957)

It is apparent that Carla is unaware that a degree from a junior college, equivalent education or not, does not ensure that she will be admitted to a four-year college of the quality she desires (e.g., Stanford).

The barriers to information Carla encounters, combined with the strategies she adopts to augment her knowledge base, create a situation where knowledge differences between herself and her classmates are rendered apparent. This factor contributes to her ever-growing sense of cultural estrangement and marginalization.

## REFLECTION

Carla is a student driven to succeed, with this orientation stemming both from a politically based desire to prove Latina capability as well as a fear of finding herself in a situation like that of her friends and brother. She is a youth oriented toward her community and her heritage, loyal to her Latina friends and committed to a set of interests and values she sees as different from those of friends brought up in cultures other than her own. Carla manifests this loyalty quietly but publicly, as she chooses to spend free time at school with friends from her community. At the same time, within her classes she appears as virtually invisible, hardworking but otherwise unremarkable. She is generally silent, save when discussing academic matters with her friends. Thus, both the personal and political significance of Carla's efforts are muted by self-control and silence. Ironically, though Carla is highly aware of her isolation and fears others view her as an outsider, it appears teachers see little. Carla's invisibility has implications, for it will likely affect the type of recommendations she will receive when applying to college, the advice she will receive about her chances for admission and, perhaps, her long-run chances of becoming a physician.

I have linked Carla's self-control to discomfort, a feeling she attributes to her presence in a segregated academic environment. Together, aspects of this environment combine to convey the message that achievement and advanced scholarship are the domains of non–Latinos. Advanced classrooms dominated by European and Asian faces, a traditional curriculum, and lopsided staffing patterns are among the factors relevant to understanding

Carla's continuing doubts about the validity of her presence in advanced courses. Failure to provide Carla with basic information about routes to postsecondary education also contributes to her feelings of being different. Though academic content is accessible to Carla, "cultural capital" (Bourdieu & Passeron, 1977), by which I mean knowledge that enables individuals to maintain status and privilege, remains elusive. As Carla relies on peers for information about college and careers, a knowledge gap between herself and her classroom friends becomes apparent. Together, isolation and this knowledge gap contribute to Carla's sense of discomfort, creating conditions conducive to the emergence of her controlled classroom persona. Carla is left silent, struggling against statistics, even as she disappears into the crowd.

PART III

# Dominant Discourses Accepted: Conformist Identities

# CHAPTER 5

# Sonia Gonzales on Craziness

And it's like—I don't know but Mexicans are more
crazier than White people. It's—we have like different kinds of thinking I guess, I don't know. Like we
want to do everything—it's like they [Whites] take
everything slowly you know. You know they take
everything slow, and I don't know it's just that they
think about the future more and stuff. And us, you
know what happens, happens. And it's just meant
to happen. And it's like we do crazy things, and we
never think about the consequences that might
happen. .... it's like more Mexican and Black people
are the ones that come out pregnant. And you don't
see like White people screwing around. And when
you go to juvenile, you never see like a White person in there, cause they have their act together and
Mexicans, they just tend to screw around all the
time. (ES56STB:964–979, 1009–1017)

—Sonia Gonzales,
sophomore student,
Explorer High School

It is a warm spring day, and I wait, worrying and wondering as a current of
young men and women move without comment around my adult body. It
is passing period at Explorer High School. I look around. The center of the
campus is normally eerie, quiet, the silence punctuated only by the echoing
steps of students scurrying to and from the administrative building and the
squawks of walkie-talkies on the belts of campus security people. Now, it is

flooded with almost 1,400 young bodies moving between classes. I see the standard clumps: groups of Mexican immigrants, speaking Spanish. Groups of neighborhood youth—mostly European American. Fewer students of Asian descent—mostly Vietnamese immigrants. I do not see the body for which I am looking.

I have an appointment to see Sonia Gonzales, a popular sophomore student of Mexican descent, whose comments open this chapter. I first met Sonia in April 1990, when I was recruiting Latino students for this study. I was interested in Sonia's experience at Explorer, for her academic performance plummeted upon entering this environment. During middle school, Sonia earned mostly *B*s and *C*s, finishing with 2.33 and 2.17 GPAs respectively during her seventh- and eighth-grade years. During her freshman year, she failed six of the twelve courses she took (for a 0.58 GPA overall). While Sonia's eighth-grade CTBS scores were not high (49th percentile in mathematics, 43rd percentile in language, 29th percentile in reading), they were not so low that they made me wonder if she could do her academic work.

Over the next fourteen months, the markers of Sonia's engagement were not to improve. During the first semester of her sophomore year, she failed five out of six classes, passing only driver's education with a *D*–. Her absences during the same ninety-day period ranged from a high of thirty days missed in English, her least favorite class, to a low of twelve days missed in life science, her favorite course. Yet these official markers of disengagement hide another peculiarity. During the period I spent with Sonia, I would see her academic performance and verbal self-presentation fluctuate. Indeed, during the ten hours I spent interviewing Sonia and the approximately forty hours I spent with her in classrooms, I was to see two selves emerge. The first, and most dominant, was a "crazy" self who believes in spontaneity and defiance of parental and school authority, a self who equates being Mexican with social and academic failure and sees the sociocultural borders between her community and school worlds as insurmountable. The second, and nearly submerged, was a "schoolgirl" self who worries about her grades, speaks of attending college, and believes that Mexican-descent youths can follow a difficult but navigable path to academic and professional success.

I continue to wait, hopeful but worried, in our prearranged meeting place. I had planned to meet Sonia after her first-period algebra class, where her teacher informed me with a question in his voice that she failed to show up for class. As the warning bell rings, Sonia arrives from the wrong direction, her notebook clutched in front of her chin, her body pressed close to the side of her female companion, her brown eyes, rimmed with dark eyeliner, watchful. She is smiling. "We went out for breakfast," she laughs. Sonia's "crazy" self has arrived.


## WHERE IS SONIA COMING FROM?

Sonia, one of over 300 Latino students who ride a bus from downtown barrios to Explorer, leaves her well-kept, working-class neighborhood around 7 A.M. every school day. At home, Sonia lives with her father, mother, younger sister (five years Sonia's junior), uncle, and grandparents (mother's parents). Sonia's father, a production worker, and her mother, a cannery worker, arrived as a married couple in the United States from Guadalajara, Mexico, in their teens. While both of Sonia's parents were raised in Mexico, her mother's family has been connected to Mostaza since the early 1940s, when Sonia's grandfather moved there at age seventeen to support his then-young bride and children. Sonia was born in the United States when her mother was sixteen.

While Sonia and her parents are U.S. citizens, much of the family's heart remains in Mexico:

> Our family, it's like, all of our family is like always into Mexican stuff. Like we're always talking about going to Mexico, we're always talking about going to Mexican parties, everything, all, everything. Any free chance that we get, any vacations, we want to go to Mexico. ....
>
> It's like for Christmas time usually we like, the whole family gets together. So like all my cousins, all my aunts, everybody, we all make like tamales, anything Mexican you know. Hot chocolate or whatever, Mexican style. And we listen to Mexican music, and it's fun. It's like, it gets everybody happy. (ES56STEN: 59–67, 142–150)

At home, Sonia speaks Spanish exclusively. Family vacations revolve around trips to Guadalajara, particularly at holiday time. In all, Sonia has been to Mexico five times.

Like her parents, Sonia has maintained a strong emotional commitment to her Mexican identity. She sums this up succinctly in her comparison of American and Mexican cultures:

Right here it's like totally different, it's a totally different culture.
Right here, you know, everything's like, very sad looking. I
don't know, it's sad. Over there [in Mexico] out in the streets
you can see everybody happy, being friends, just talking to one
another. Just talking to everybody, it's like really fun. It's like
very ... everybody talks to everybody over there. .... everybody
respects one another over there in Mexico. Over here it's like,
nobody gives a damn about nobody else, it's just like they're
only looking to themselves. Over there it's like everybody takes
care of everybody else. (ES56STEN:90–100, 124–130)

Sonia's current friends, mostly Mexican immigrant and first-generation
Mexican Americans, share her pro-Mexico orientation. They prefer to
speak Spanish, prefer Mexican music, prefer dancing at mostly Mexican
parties, and are fiercely critical of Mexican-descent students who hide their
ability to speak Spanish or who otherwise appear to deny their culture.
Sonia sums up this viewpoint below:

*Sonia:* You know, like some people if you ask them if they're
Mexican, you know, like they're Mexican American, they'll go,
'Oh no, I'm not Mexican.'
*Interviewer:* Really!?
*Sonia:* Yeah! That's what I hate. It's like, some people, they're
Mexican, they have Mexican blood inside of them, but they were
born here. That doesn't make a difference, they're still Mexican,
I think. And like they say, 'No, I'm not Mexican.' And like, they
know how to speak Spanish and everything and they try to tell
you, 'Oh, I don't speak Spanish.' And you try to talk to them in
Spanish and they go, 'I don't understand what you're saying.'
They try to deny their culture. (ES56STEN:21–38)

According to Sonia, she and her friends also express their pro-Mexican orientation through affiliation and friendship with "Sureño" gang members. Sureños
embrace several neighborhood gangs, oriented, among other things, toward the
assertion and preservation of the Spanish language and Mexican culture.

Sonia's place in history is reflected in the lessons her parents teach her
about the economic situation in the United States, as compared to Mexico.
Arriving in the area during a manufacturing boom, Sonia's father succeeded in
establishing himself as a production worker, eventually purchasing the family
home. Consistent with this, Sonia's interviews suggest that her parents manifest

what Carola and Marcelo Suarez-Orozco (1993) term "the immigrants' dual frame of reference," in which "immigrants are constantly comparing and contrasting their current lot in the host society against their previous experiences and expectations in the country of origin."

> .... my parents said that they prefer to be poor here, than being poor in Mexico. Cause the poverty over there is scary. It's different. Right here, being poor here, over there it's like being rich. And it's like, over there, it's really ugly, you know, it's scary. You see these little kids out in the street, you know, no clothes whatsoever, you know, all dirty. They're small begging out in the streets because there's nothing, there's no money. And there's people dying. (ES56STEN:3206–3219)

Sonia's mother also appears to manifest classic immigrant beliefs about education. (According to Sonia, her father has little involvement in her education.) For example, according to Sonia, her mother believes education is the key to professional and economic success in America:

> *Interviewer:* Can you tell me a little bit about your mom and how you talk to her about your school and how she's involved?
> *Sonia:* My mom, she's always trying to encourage me. She's always telling me, 'Go to school, try to be someone in life. Get a good education cause if you get a good education you get a good job, a good paying job' and everything. And she's always encouraging me to come to school and try my best. (ES56STC:883–897)

Sonia's mother's beliefs concerning schooling are reflected in the ways and means in which she has attempted to support Sonia's education. For example, based on the recommendations of middle school teachers, she made Sonia attend Explorer. Sonia also describes her mother as constantly asking if Sonia has completed her homework and consistently encouraging her to graduate from high school. At the same time, because Sonia's mother did not graduate, she cannot offer assistance with homework. Further, she has not contacted the school about Sonia's declining performance, perhaps because of fears related to cross-cultural communication. (Sonia's mother does not speak English.) As Sonia's grades have plummeted, Sonia says her mother has alternated between pleading with Sonia to do her homework, yelling at Sonia for destroying her future, and throwing her hands up in despair. She has not shown Sonia's father Sonia's high school report cards, because she is afraid of his possibly violent reaction.

In light of Sonia's academic history, Sonia says her current educational performance is particularly upsetting and incomprehensible for her mother. As an elementary student, Sonia attended a bilingual school near her home. Her elementary school record indicates steady progress. For example, her teachers cite her excellent conduct and study habits, with her third-grade teacher commenting "very good student" and her fifth-grade teacher "Sonia is a student with a lot of ability" and "I want great things for her." She earned *A*s and *B*s in all subject areas, with the exception of handwriting. Entering as a Spanish speaker, Sonia was classified as being fluent English-proficient in the fourth grade. Sonia's CTBS scores also reflect progress. In the fourth grade, she scored in the 46th percentile in reading, the 36th percentile in language, and the 37th percentile in math. By the fifth grade, while her reading score fell to the 34th percentile, Sonia scored in the 53rd percentile in language and the 79th percentile in math.

During her first year of middle school—sixth grade—Sonia continued to excel, earning *A*s and *B*s. Her grades fell slightly (to *B*s and *C*s) in the seventh and eighth grades, because, according to Sonia, she became involved with a peer group which was not academically oriented. Nevertheless, most of her teachers (twenty-one out of twenty-four) continued to cite her excellent conduct and six (out of the ten who commented) of her teachers mentioned her acceptable preparation. During her three years in middle school, only three teachers mentioned incomplete assignments, and four cited inadequate preparation. Again, Sonia's CTBS scores indicate competence. She scored in the 38th percentile in reading, the 55th percentile in language, and the 61st percentile in math during her seventh-grade year.

In sum, Sonia comes to school with a pro-Mexico orientation, supported by both friends and family. She also remembers a successful early school history. In addition, according to Sonia, her family is not critical of the American opportunity structure; rather, they compare and contrast the economic situations in Mexico and the United States and encourage Sonia to apply herself to her education.

## SONIA'S "CRAZY" SELF

It's like we all have these—I mean we're young, and
we have all these crazy ideas you know. All of a
sudden we come to school, we come to school,

come to study and everything, and then all of a
sudden we have this great idea .... (ES56STD:
349–355)

—Sonia Gonzales

Sonia's "crazy" self—the self who values spontaneity, fun, and danger,
the self who cuts, drinks, and parties, sometimes with gang members—is
Sonia's public identity, a persona linked intimately with Sonia's sense of her
ethnicity. In four interviews, Sonia used the word "crazy" seven times to
describe herself, sixteen times to characterize individual friends, sixteen times
to refer to herself and her peers ("we"), and six times to characterize Mexicans
as a group. Sonia's crazy self skipped twenty-three out of 180 school days
over the year and missed sixty-two periods of English over the same time
period. Sonia's crazy self also became increasingly dominant during her first
two years of high school, with her grades falling steadily and her absences
increasing until the end of the first semester of her sophomore year.

While with me, Sonia did her best to keep her crazy self under control. She attended school. She arrived on time for classes. Yet, Sonia's crazy
self revealed itself, raising its head during social interactions and evidencing
itself in uncompleted homework, borrowed pencils and paper, and friendly
teasing from peers.

It revealed itself during passing period when Sonia laughed as her
best friend Maria informed us, "I have to go, I'll be late to class." Sonia
commented, "I don't know what's wrong with her, all of a sudden worrying about being late."

Sonia's crazy self was also revealed during lunchtime, when her friends
opened her fat white notebook, overflowing with papers. A pile of uncompleted worksheets, tucked haphazardly into a back pocket, spilled onto the
table. "Look at all this work Sonia hasn't done!"

It was manifested during English class, when Sonia asked her Latina
girlfriend to borrow a piece of paper. Hearing this, a male friend yelled,
"Oh, you're such a good example. No paper, no pens." In return, Sonia
quipped, "Shut up!! You're blowing my cover! I've been trying so hard all
day to be a schoolgirl!"

Sonia's crazy self was also displayed through the steady decline in her
academic performance. Sonia's highest semester grade at the end of her
sophomore year was a *C+* in physical education (P.E.). She had earned a
total of fifty credits of the 225 required to graduate by the end of her
sophomore year.

Finally, Sonia's crazy self was revealed in the bravado with which she speaks of defying authority, of throwing caution to the wind:

> White girls, they're like, 'Oh my mom's going to do this' and they're all scared, and you know they don't like cut and everything. .... I mean, my parents are the same way and everything, but it's like, I don't listen to them. Cause sometimes I go 'Well, if they're gonna beat me up or something, I might as well have fun!' Cause sometimes my mom goes 'Well, be home by 7.' And I'm not here, I'll be like a half an hour late. And I go, 'Oh well, I might as well just have fun, and stay here like 'til 1 in the morning.' .... And like us, we just let ourselves have fun while we're here. (ES56STEN:219–245)

In explaining craziness, Sonia speaks in terms of psychological factors. She perceives craziness as a powerful state of being, as a characteristic which reflects cultural differences. For her, craziness differentiates Mexican-descent adolescents (and African Americans) from their European American peers. Thus, for Sonia, European Americans are "calm" and "careful" while Mexicans "don't care about what we do" because "us Mexicans are more daring." Mexicans are also more spontaneous: "We never plan like one day ahead or something, we just do it," and "We are always looking for action." This translates into behaviors that preclude academic success, most notably skipping class and failing to complete assignments: ". . . . us Mexicans, we like, 'Oh, we don't care if we do our homework' or whatever" (ES56STC:1443–1444). For Sonia, these differences are significant and immutable. Thus, attempts to blur the social borders between ethnic groups are futile:

> *Sonia:* But to fit in it's just like—for them [Whites] to fit in it's so hard. I think it's very hard for them because like us Mexicans think of their people—they're like more at calm, they're careful. And it's like us, we don't care, we don't care about what we do or whatever, and White people it's like they're more cautious of what they do, what people might think.
> *Interviewer:* How about if you wanted to hang out with White people, what would be the barriers for you?
> *Sonia:* Oh my gosh, I just couldn't do that because they're just much too quiet, too calm, two different cultures, personalities, different. I just couldn't. (ES56STD:3258–3267, 3322–3330)

Interestingly, Sonia's crazy behavior is not noticeably different than that of many European American teens. In general, for Sonia, craziness in practice consists of a variety of experimental behaviors in which adolescents of all backgrounds tend to engage: sneaking out at night, partying, drinking, and cutting classes. Although Sonia occasionally sees a gun, goes along with friends as they steal alcohol, and knows gang members, her involvement in these sorts of activities are the exception rather than the rule. Nevertheless, Sonia is emphatic in her belief that European Americans cannot fit into her social world: "It's not so much that we wouldn't accept you guys, it's just so much that I don't think—they won't, White people wouldn't be willing to do what us Mexicans do, you know? Like we do all kinds of crazy things. It's just they'd say, 'That's too much for me' or something like that" (ES56STD:3392–3400).

In trying to understand Sonia's craziness, I considered a variety of factors. First, and most obvious, it was possible that Sonia no longer had the ability to do her academic work. However, her academic performance and behavior during one period indicated that this was not the case. For six weeks during the second semester, Sonia was involved in a fight with her two best friends. During this period, she attended class regularly, receiving the second highest grade (*A*–) in life science, and passing five out of six classes with an overall GPA of 2.06.

Second, it was possible that Sonia did not believe schoolwork would pay off. Again, however, this explanation was unsatisfactory in light of Sonia's interview data. First, during our interviews Sonia equated education with a good job on three separate occasions and also said this belief keeps her in school: "Well, sometimes I just feel like dropping out and forgetting everything. But then I think about it and I go, 'Nope, not worth it.' Because at the long run I have to, you know, stay here, I have to come to school so I can get a good education and if I want to get a good job. So that's what keeps me going, my future" (ES56STD:141–150). Second, Sonia gave profoundly ideological responses when asked about her perceptions of the American social structure:

> *Interviewer:* Last year I was talking to both a Black and a Mexican woman. They felt that, like a doctor or a lawyer, some professions that tend to be higher paid, that only White people could do those things.
> *Sonia:* Well yeah. But nowadays I mean, we have to see the truth too. When you—let's put it this way. When you give it all you

got, and you try, it's like, whatever culture you are, whatever color you are, it doesn't matter. Cause there's always a lot of opportunities. You could take that person down to court if they're prejudiced. So that's nothing that could get in your way, so much [as] what you want to do.

*Interviewer:* So you think that those people are not seeing the truth?

*Sonia:* Not seeing the truth. Not really trying! .... Cause you have to try, you know, it's not like, you know. Cause if I tried and be something in my life, I'm not going to let, you know, somebody, just because they're White or something, tell me that I can't do this you know. You could. You know, there's laws that protect you. That's what I think. (ES56STEN:3393–3428)

Further, Sonia did not criticize or tease her Latina friends who were relatively successful in school, and expressed admiration for the students some call "schoolgirls": "Some girls and boys that are really good at school, they call them schoolboys, schoolgirls, stuff like that. I don't see no reason to be embarrassed because I think it's good, I mean, I'd like to be a schoolgirl myself, you know, I want good grades. I mean they're showing that they know more than the person that's putting them down" (ES56STB: 636–647).

✓     Third, it was possible Sonia simply did not care about school performance. This explanation, however, also seemed too simplistic in light of Sonia's interview data and behavior. For one, Sonia expressed interest in college during three different interviews. Second, Sonia spoke often of her worries about her grades, high school graduation, and future economic opportunities. This was particularly true during Sonia's ninth-grade year. The statements below are representative:

.... I try and try. Sometimes you know it's just like—I'm lazy, I'm a lazy person, so I think if I would try better I would get good grades and it's like when I—I'm really concerned about my grades, even though people don't really notice that I've got—I'm really always concerned about my grades. Most of my friends think that, you know, I don't care about my grades, I don't care about—and I do, I care a lot about my grades. (ES56STC:1374–1385)

My mom was talking to me the other day and she got mad at me because I got my report card and I got 'Fs.' And she sits

> down and she talks to me and she goes, 'If you don't want to go
> to school, just quit.' I know it hurts her but you know. I don't
> want to quit yet. I don't want to quit, 'cause one thing I want to
> get more education. And I want to get a good job. And then
> later on get a family, you know. (ES56STB:2243–2261)

There were also moments when Sonia revealed a schoolgirl self, demonstrating the concern for academic performance she claims in her comments above. In life science, for example, Sonia was once the last student to finish a test on vertebrates, working in great concentration and occasionally muttering, "I don't know what he's trying to do here." In foods class, Sonia asked a tablemate completing their "management sheet," a worksheet which asks students to detail how they will divide, manage, and carry out cooking tasks, to "try to make it better so we can get twenty points this time," and then added, "We got all the points for the last sheet." In English class, Sonia smiled as she turned in her assignment, smiled when her close friend said "congratulations." Perhaps most significant, when Sonia was counseled out of Explorer at the end of her junior year, she enrolled in independent study, completing her work and continuing on to her senior year.

In the end, it appeared Sonia's craziness most reflected the ideology of a peer group to which she had pledged her allegiance. While Sonia described craziness as a psychological and cultural characteristic, in practice it was quintessentially social. First, craziness was one factor Sonia perceived as being integral to her popularity:

> *Sonia:* I think Mexicans become more popular.
> *Interviewer:* You do?
> *Sonia:* Yeah. Because like, right now it's like, I'm popular. Not to
> be bragging about it but I am. .... Cause everywhere I walk
> around campus it's like, 'Ey, what are you doing? What's up?' ....
> I have all kinds of friends, cause they know I'm crazy and every-
> thing, but I always listen to people and everything so, I have all
> kinds of friends. (ES56STEN:2377–2408)

Second, from Sonia's perspective, it was essential to have friends present in order for craziness to occur: "If I wouldn't have any friends here, I think there'd be nothing else better to do than just do my work. But since my friends are here it's like, OK, let's go over here and cut" (ES56STC:1212–1217). As mentioned previously, Sonia's grades and attendance improved markedly during a period where she was fighting with her two best friends. Thus, Sonia's behavioral data support her verbal assertions, providing further indication of the powerful role her friends play in structuring her behavior.

However, to say simply that Sonia's ideology emanates from social connections is to ignore the context in which she operates. It is critical to consider how Sonia and her closest friends have come to internalize a set of powerful and constraining definitions about what it means to be Mexican. To some extent, as Sonia notes in the quote that opens this chapter, these beliefs reflect county statistics: As Sonia notes, Latinos and African Americans are disproportionately represented among teenagers giving birth and Latinos are overrepresented among juvenile referrals. Yet, things are clearly not so segmented as Sonia asserts. For one, European Americans are well-represented among juvenile referrals and teenagers giving birth in the county, comprising 27.5 percent and 22 percent of these populations, respectively. Further, there are numerous Latinos in the region who demonstrate that they have their "act together" in a variety of ways.

In the sections that follow, I will argue that the convictions of Sonia and her peers must be considered in relation to categorical meanings present in their school environment. Over a two-year period, Sonia referred to various school practices and policies that actually work to confirm, rather than challenge, her convictions that Mexicans are destined to "screw up." Further, there was nothing in Sonia's environment to validate the more pedagogically positive aspects of her ideology. Spontaneity, risk-taking, and a willingness to question authority, highly relevant to learning, were not appropriate behaviors in her academic classrooms. Thus, rather than challenge Sonia's ideology, in practice Sonia's school experience communicates the meanings she herself asserts: Latino youths are irredeemable and destined for academic and societal marginalization. At the same time, classroom experiences suggest that academic success is contingent on the ability to adhere to rules and follow directions, behaviors Sonia has come to perceive as characteristic of European Americans.

## CONSTRUCTING CRAZINESS AT EXPLORER HIGH SCHOOL

> And so teachers are always more into watching us.
> They're always aware of what we're doing, you
> know? It's like they're always more concerned about

us. It's like, we can't even do nothing wrong cause
we're already—first of all cause of all the reputation
Mexicans and Blacks built up already. And so, they
always let that reputation—they think all of them
are the same, you know? And they're not all the
same! Cause there's some Mexicans that are really
schoolgirls and everything. And they look at them
and they're going to think that they're going to do
bad. (ES56STEN:2725–2741)

—Sonia Gonzales

As a freshman student, Sonia moved into an environment that was
caught up in significant social change. Prior to court-ordered desegregation
in the mid-1980s, Explorer's student body was 81.8 percent European
American, with the majority of these students being middle- and upper
middle-class. By 1990, when Sonia was a sophomore, enrollment for youths
of color had jumped from 18.2 percent to 57.8 percent; of these students,
30.6 percent qualified for free or reduced price lunches. The majority of
Explorer's new students were of Mexican descent; in all, Latino students
made up 40.6 percent of Explorer's student body in 1990.

Increasing concern and anxiety about these new students have paralleled diversification. According to the principal, fear, doubt, and outright
skepticism about the feasibility of working productively with these youths
have been clearly expressed:

The faculty feel, 'We had a perfectly good school, look what
they've done to us.' .... The faculty frustration level has risen by
leaps and bounds. .... Teachers who've been here for years and
now have different kids ... a lot are old and have no capacity to
change. Teachers have been used to lecturing and leading the lesson. They aren't getting satisfaction from kids' achievement now,
because they aren't achieving. (ES06801:257–261, 164–175)

Teachers' worries reached their height soon after Sonia's arrival at Explorer,
when a stabbing incident occurred. Though the event involved an off-
campus Latino adolescent who came to the school in search of a rival gang
member, the happening was perceived as further evidence that the school
was out of control. Worries about low skills, student hostility, parental
investment, and immaturity are themes that run through the interviews
carried out with thirty faculty members at Explorer, and nearly 60 percent

of them listed "disrespect for authority" as their primary concern, in a survey that was carried out by the administration in the months following the stabbing incident.

In the context of this situation, adults in the environment have responded with seemingly contradictory yet complementary responses. On the one hand, those in the disciplinary branch of the administration have implemented a set of practices designed to control and manage the student body. Meant to ensure safety, the primary thrusts of this plan also work effectively to support the idea that Explorer's Latino students are dangerous and irredeemable. On the other hand, adults have ignored the achievement gap between Maple's European American and Latino students. Even as outward manifestations of craziness are silenced, quiet manifestations of craziness are ignored and tacitly accepted. The end result is an environment that works effectively to support and further the formation of the theories and beliefs that undergird Sonia's crazy identity.

## MAKING CRAZINESS: SURVEILLANCE AND SUSPENSION

Increased reconnaissance and surveillance, organized around monitoring student activity during passing periods and lunchtime, and identifying students operating as "key players" in the environment, were the first steps taken to control the student body. Carried out by the principal of discipline and two campus assistants, students' movements around the campus are closely monitored and strictly controlled. The campus is patrolled by assistants, who communicate by walkie-talkie. Adults in these roles generally do not communicate with youths during the lunch hour and passing period, but rather watch and monitor student movement. Students seen on campus during classroom hours are subject to immediate referral to Saturday school. Describing the atmosphere, one high-achieving European American student observed, "It's like a police state really sometimes. All these guys buzzing around with walkie-talkies. .... This year I tried to walk from the library to the locker room in the middle of eighth period to change [for track]. Two people tried to give me Saturday school" (ES37STD:922–937).

Though these tactics affect all students, certain policies make it clear that the administration is particularly concerned about the activities of Latinos. Soon after the stabbing incident, certain colors associated with Latino gangs were banned from campus. Students wearing two or more pieces of red or blue—the colors associated with rival Latino gangs—were called into the discipline office and given one warning. According to the disciplinary principal, this "colors campaign" was integral in an effort to identify "major players" on campus. Based on the students who visited his office, the disciplinary principal compiled a list of names. Those students seen as defiant were quickly expelled; the remainder of students were watched carefully.

Explorer's system of school-level surveillance has been complemented by classroom disciplinary mechanisms that ensure quick classroom removal of youths who are perceived as disobedient. First, teachers have been given the prerogative to remove any student from the classroom at any time, sending them to "in-school suspension." Second, according to the principal of discipline, students sent to his office due to classroom conflict face certain reprisal, typically Saturday school or, in severe instances, suspension: "I support teachers. That's very, very important to me. And I've remained consistent. .... I'm one of those guys that thinks that schools or institutions of any kind run better when there's a hatchet man" (ES100ST1:508–510; 1288–1298). Again, these aspects of Explorer's environment affect all individuals. However, informal tabulations and official statistics indicate that Latinos are more commonly subject to these efforts to control. For example, over one two-week period a reading of the surnames of youths referred to Saturday school indicated that forty out of sixty were Latinos. According to the curriculum principal, these figures are consistent with a more general pattern:

> It's been brought up—I noticed it but I didn't say anything. It's been brought up several times. 'How come there's so many Hispanic kids sitting down here in front of Joyce's door?' He's disciplinarian. I have a letter from a teacher saying, 'Look at all these kids and the poor grades they're getting and note that they're all Hispanic.' .... Maybe that has a connection to how they [teachers] deal with kids, particularly the Hispanic kids. Because see anything that you tell a kid to do and they don't do, you can interpret that as disrespect for authority. (ES070ST1: 1253–1278

As indicated in chapter 3, data on out-of-school suspensions confirm that Latinos at Explorer are disproportionately subject to disciplinary action. Further, Latinos comprised 92.3 percent of those who were suspended for "defiant or disruptive behavior," the second most commonly cited reason for student suspension (after threatening or causing physical injury).

Though frequently absent, Sonia does not wander around the campus during passing period, does not wear colors, and has not been subject to disciplinary actions due to conflicts with peers or misbehavior in class. Nevertheless, Sonia is keenly aware of Explorer's surveillance system; she referred to the feeling of "being watched" on three occasions. If Sonia's descriptions are accurate, than the disciplinary staff develops its sense of who to watch not only by noting who wears colors, but also through knowledge of a youth's friends and associates:

> Mr. Joyce [discipline principal]? He's an asshole. He used to be at Brookvale High. He knows Ralph [Sonia's friend's boyfriend] really good, he used to be like a real troublemaker and that's why they kicked him out of Brookvale. Ralph, like when he used to come pick us up at the beginning of the school year, he [the principal] came up to us and then he goes—he came to our table during lunch-time—he goes, 'Hmm, I can see you guys are really popular around here, you guys are really known.' And he goes, 'Erica, I've heard a lot about you. Sonia, I heard a lot about you.' Mr. Joyce, it's like he'd be watching .... he's always keeping an eye on us. (ES56STEN:2812–2829; 2883–2889)

Though Sonia had no significant discipline record, she views this surveillance as an indication that she has been predefined as crazy: "Cause you know how we build up our reputation since last year, cause they always look at the people who behave bad. They're always watching them, cause they always follow in their same footsteps" (ES56STEN:2883–2889).

## ACCEPTING CRAZINESS:
## BUREAUCRATIZED RELATIONSHIPS AND THE
## SIGNALING OF ADULT RESIGNATION

The notions that differences between Latinos and European Americans create unbridgeable social borders, and that such differences also work to generate differences in academic achievement are critical to Sonia's belief system. Sonia's day-to-day experiences over two years of high school have supported this aspect of her ideology. First, as described in chapter 3, a set of practices in Explorer's environment work to isolate and marginalize non-English-speaking youths, separating 64 percent of the Latino population from their European American peers. Second, academic and social divisions are repeated in the English-speaking environment. Advanced courses are dominated by European Americans, while fluent English-speaking (FEP) Latinos are concentrated in general and remedial classes. (As indicated in Table 2.1, Latinos make up 22.8 percent of Explorer's FEP population, but comprise only 7.6 percent of the accelerated English track.) Explorer's staff is also overwhelmingly European American; during Sonia's first two years of high school, all of her teachers were European American. Finally, school activities are also the province of European Americans; during Sonia's sophomore year, there were no Latinos in student government or on the cheerleading squad.

According to Explorer's principal, the school's explicit mission is to integrate its new students into the student body. Given this mission in light of the situation above, one might expect a set of concentrated and targeted efforts to address both academic and social differentiation. However, even as adults verbalize concerns about student behavior and express the desire for integration, there is a notable absence of efforts directed toward academic empowerment or social inclusion. In both their general approach to Explorer's Latino population as a whole, and in their specific response to Sonia's craziness in particular, adults communicate their tacit acceptance of the divisions which permeate Explorer's environment.

First, for example, despite the fact that 58 percent of the students at Explorer are students of color, and many come from families where neither parent has attended college, there are no mentoring or targeted college recruitment efforts in place. Latinos and African Americans at local universities and businesses have no formal connections with Explorer students, nor do youths from Explorer visit colleges with diverse populations. Thus, Sonia and her classmates are not made aware of the many Latinos in the area who have succeeded both academically and professionally. Further, Explorer is not connected to national programs targeted toward the college enrollment of youths of color, such as Upward Bound. Rather, individuals are expected to research these and other opportunities on their own. (Limited information about college scholarships can be obtained by going to a career center tucked in the back corner of the library.) High-achieving Latino students who have successfully infiltrated Explorer classrooms note this deficit:

> Like Upward Bound, I just decided to investigate it myself. The answers the principal of guidance gave me were always too simple. It was 'No.' I could have had so much scholarship money. I

only have $1,500 in scholarships. I don't understand it. There's so much money around here and she told me I didn't qualify. ....
And I see these kids going through the same struggle I did. (ES106ST1:272–289; 305–308)

Sonia is keenly aware that she lacks information relative to her European American classmates: "Some times it's so hard because I think about it, about going to college, you need so many requirements and I go, 'What's the big difference between the state and UC system?' I don't understand any of that. And it's scary too cause I hear other students say, 'Well, I'm going to UC' or whatever, and I go [to myself] 'What's that?'' You know, I want to know!" (EC56STD:3017–3034). In not providing information relevant to accessing higher-education opportunities, Explorer provides Sonia with one more reason to believe that European Americans "have their act together," while Latinos do not.

A second factor relevant to communicating tacit acceptance of the idea that European Americans and Latinos are differentially suited for academic endeavor is Explorer's traditional curriculum, which emphasizes European history and literature. At no time during the twenty days I spent in classrooms at Explorer were cultural or economic diversity referred to or discussed. Consistent with these observations, I explicitly asked four students (two Latina, one Vietnamese, and one African American) whether they had encountered curriculum relevant to their heritage during their first two years of high school. All students said that their exposure to such content had been minimal to nonexistent. According to Sonia, for example, just one teacher presented content relevant to her ethnicity. Further, from her perspective, this teacher emphasized negative social statistics (e.g., the correlations between ethnic background and poverty, ethnic background and teen pregnancy):

> *Sonia:* Like last year, Mr. Kula. .... It's like he used to say all this and that. But he was always, everything bad was Hispanics, Blacks. All of us Latino. Us, you know. I mean, I understand cause there's a big majority of Hispanics and Blacks that are not doing that good? But there's a lot of them that. .... So we felt right there that he was discriminating us, you know, he's prejudiced. ....
> *Interviewer:* Have you ever had a teacher that talked about really amazing things in Mexican culture? Or talked about things that would make you proud?
> *Sonia:* Um-um, never. (ES56STEN:1933–1964)

In her first two years of high school, despite enrollment in a world history course both years, Sonia has not considered the works or accomplishments of people of color, nor has she engaged in serious discussions of the mechanisms that work to generate social divisions.

Third and finally, tacit acceptance of academic divisions between Latino and European American youths has been personalized for Sonia in the sense that adults have paid little attention to her academic decline. Despite the fact that Sonia entered Explorer as a relatively successful middle-school student, she has had no conversation with any school official about her rate of academic progress. Further, according to Sonia, just one teacher "got on my case," during her sophomore year, telling her she was capable of more. This same individual, her favorite teacher, was the sole teacher who noted and praised Sonia's added academic effort when her grades rose for the six-week period referred to previously.

Consistent with the above, Sonia feels that in general Explorer's adults operate and act upon lowered expectations for Latinos. In her experience, such expectations are communicated in two primary ways. First, as she indicates in her quote that opens this section, as well as in her statement below, to Sonia, teachers appear to watch and to fear Latino students. Adults keep their distance from youths like Sonia, who signal allegiance to Latino culture through their dress and makeup:

> *Interviewer:* Do you see teachers as having certain expectations of Mexicans?
> *Sonia:* Well yeah, it's like once they see a Mexican right away, you know, especially when they dressed like this [like me], you know. Sometimes when I wear my Pendletons or I wear a lot of eyeliner or something, you know, we look scary looking sometimes, you know? I guess that's the way teachers are, you know. The first impression has a lot to say about a person, you know. But, they should always look at what a person has. They have to talk to that person, get to know that person. (ES56STEN:2680–2721)

Second, though Sonia feels the majority of her teachers treat her with respect, some communicate that they have given up on her as well as her Latina friends:

> *Sonia:* .... most teachers, you know, White teachers, some of them are kind of prejudiced. Kind of prejudiced.
> *Interviewer:* What makes you know that?

*Sonia:* It's probably the way they look at you, the way they talk, you know, when they're talking about something like when they talk about the people who are going to drop out. .... And then Mr. Kula, when he's talking about teenage pregnancy or something like that. He turns around and he looked at us. It's like, he tries to look around the whole room so we won't notice but like he mostly tries to get it through our heads, you know. Sometimes I think he's prejudiced. (ES56STB:1883–1911)

In sum, though adults appear to ignore Sonia's academic performance they nevertheless convince her, through looks and glances, that they view her as dangerous and destined for academic failure.

Together, an emphasis on controlling and removing youths perceived as disobedient or dangerous and the seeming acceptance of the academic and social divisions that permeate Explorer's environment work together to communicate the idea that Latinos are different and irredeemable. Sonia sees many Latinos thrown out of school because they are perceived as troublemakers; furthermore, no Mexican-descent individuals are presented as role models, either by the school or in the curriculum. Sonia's disengagement from school, along with that of her close friends, goes generally unnoticed and unremarked. Given this set of conditions, there are no reasons for Sonia to question her conclusion that youths of Mexican and European American descent are fundamentally different.

## CLASSROOM LESSONS: CONSTRUCTING WHITENESS

Like White people, they really think about what
they're going to do, they're like more serious, more
shy. You know, they're more serious about what
they're going to do. (ES56STB:984–988)

Most White people tend to [be] more school active
you know, always more involved with school ....
(ES56STC:1440–1442)

—Sonia Gonzales

In a previous section, I described Sonia's conviction that youths of Mexican descent are "crazy." As indicated in the quotes above, Sonia is equally emphatic when voicing ideas about "White" psychology and behavior. For Sonia, European Americans are, by nature, quiet, calm, careful, and cautious.

As Sonia has no close friends of European American descent, and has little contact with European Americans after returning to her home, her primary source of information about White psychology comes from day-to-day experiences in high school. However, it is not likely that Sonia draws her conclusions from interactions. During lunch and passing period, Sonia spends her time exclusively with Latinos and African Americans. During class, the conversations she holds with European Americans are brief and revolve around the task at hand. As Sonia explains, "I mean, I talk to them and say, 'What are you doing?' or, you know, talk about school, talk about the class. But it's not like we're talking about our friends or anything like that" (ES56STD:3521–3526). In sum, Sonia knows few European Americans, and the relationships she does have do not lend themselves to the degree of knowledge she asserts above.

However, Sonia's conclusions about White psychology are completely consistent with observations of behaviors necessary for success in the academic classrooms she attends. During her sophomore year, Sonia attended six classes; of these, four were academic. (These included algebra, English, life science, and world history; Sonia also took P.E. and a foods class.) Here, interaction patterns and tasks combined to corroborate Sonia's belief that calm, quiet, care, and caution are essential to academic success.

First, in three of four academic classrooms, Sonia spent the majority of her time in virtual silence, her only interactions consisting of brief comments or asides to peers. In English and life science, for example, Sonia engaged in seat work, completing worksheets, and answering short-answer questions from her textbook. While students in science could collaborate, in English class they were threatened with in-school suspension for speaking during silent reading or seat work. In math and world history, Sonia spent most of the period listening silently as a teacher demonstrated, lectured, and posed questions. Students either took notes or remained silent unless they were called upon. Those who did not were quickly reprimanded: "Alright, we're going to play a third-grade game. I hear your voice, and you're out" (ES56ST06:p. 1). On six out of the seven days I attended Sonia's world history course, for example, students took notes. At times, they were free to write what they pleased; at other times, even note taking was highly directed, with the teacher stopping at key points to tell students what to write down: "Here is another term to note. Pugachev. He started a peasant uprising. Write down that the peasants hated their masters." And: "This is what you need to know. Catherine the Great was not Russian, she was German. She expanded the empire and power. She didn't solve the domestic problems."

Second, in all of Sonia's academic classrooms, activities conveyed the idea that care and caution, critical for the memorization of detail, are essential to successful academic work. While the content in Sonia's classrooms varied significantly, in general, the emphasis was on learning facts, definitions, specific answers, and prescribed problem-solving procedures. In world history, for example, on a test on the medieval period, students were expected to name the predominant architectural style and to define terms such as *nave*, *buttress*, and *gargoyle*. Students were also asked to define social categories, including the terms *king*, *knight*, *vassal*, *serf*, *peasant*, and *lord*. In life science, students regularly completed long worksheets which focused on intricate biological detail. During one period, for example, Sonia worked halfheartedly answering thirty-nine questions about algae. Here, she perused her text for answers to questions such as "What can be the smallest size of algae? What are the large algae plants called? List four things that all algae have in common."

Sophomore English provides the most vivid illustration of the emphasis on calm, quiet, care, and caution that Sonia encountered during her school day. There, students did four things: 1) memorized vocabulary 2) completed grammar exercises, 3) read quietly/answered questions from a book of annotated stories and 4) took tests. As in other courses, attention to detail was critical for academic success:

> *Teacher:* Get out your blue grammar books. Let's get going on the homework from last Thursday. We're doing prepositional phrases, which are a group of words that work like some thing. Verbal, what's a verbal? Verbs that do what?
> *Students:* Modify.
> *Teacher:* What are three kinds?
> *Student:* Gerund, infinitive.
> *Teacher:* For example, what does a gerund work like?
> *Student:* An adjective.
> *Teacher:* OK, the first verb here is what?
> [The teacher continues the exercise, asking students to identify what functions as what in particular sentences, then moves to an exercise that asks students to distinguish between complements and appositives.]
> *Teacher:* The dog is a collie. Collie, what's that?
> *Student:* Predicate nominative.
> *Teacher:* The dog, a collie, is barking. What is 'a collie'?

*Student:* An appositive.
*Teacher:* It's called an appositive. The difference is what it comes after, the verb or the noun. (ES56ST01:p.15)

Interaction during English was confined to brief, fifteen-minute drill sessions such as the one described above. Other forms of interaction during the period were actively discouraged by the teacher. Two students who violated this norm were promptly chastised: "We have a pretty good class here and I'm not going to let you ruin it. I suggest that you look at how the other people behave and adjust to that." "Regina, you get by most days without coming. Now sit down." As Sonia notes, the class is structured to keep talking—either between students or between students and teacher—to a minimum:

> You can't talk in there cause if you talk you go to in-school sus-
> pension. .... It's strict and there's hardly ever group work in
> there, so nobody's talking in there, just we read, read, read, and
> that's all we do. (ES56STC:232–242)

During the days I spent with Sonia, she had no personal interaction with her teacher. As she sees it, "It's just like—he just tells you what to do and that's it" (ES56STC:301–303). Confirming Sonia's description, her teacher describes himself as having made a conscious decision to organize his curriculum around seat work and basic forms of recitation pedagogy in order to maintain and ensure control: "The discipline is at such a volatile state—that in order to maintain the discipline, there must be—you must have something for them to do each moment. And not something that lasts, that requires too long of an attention span, and then changes along the way. .... Unfortunately this gets misconstrued as a laziness on the part of the teachers, but this is not the case. I think it's a question of pragmatism. You're doing what you can with the clientele you have" (ES031ST1:138–163).

In sum, no class that I attended with Sonia on a regular basis mounted a significant challenge to her conclusions about the type of mind-set that characterizes those who succeed academically in an American public high school. Indeed, in the majority of instances, my observations supported what she had to say about the behavior of the more school-oriented peers enrolled in her general track courses. In order to meet the behavioral expectations in most of these classrooms, they did have to stay "calm." They did have to stay "quiet." They did have to be "careful." Noting that European American peers conform to these norms, and being aware that European

Americans earn better grades than do Sonia and her Latino peers, it is not surprising Sonia concludes that European Americans are more psychologically suited for constrained situations.

## REFLECTION

> I'd walk into the counselor's office for whatever
> reason and looks of disdain greeted me—one meant
> for a criminal, alien, to be feared. It was harder to
> defy this expectation than just accept it and fall into
> the trapping. It was a jacket I could try to take off,
> but they kept putting it back on. The first hint of
> trouble and the preconceptions proved true. So why
> not be proud? Why not be an outlaw? Why not
> make it our own? (1993:84)
> —Luis Rodríguez, author

Enrolled in the general track of her high school, Sonia has become increasingly involved in "crazy" behavior, which she defines as characteristic of what it means to be Mexican. Part of a highly social peer group whose members spend significant periods of time away from school, Sonia skips classes, does not do homework, and consequently fails the majority of her classes. At the same time, Sonia reveals some interest in the very "school-girl" behaviors her crazy self rejects, as well as faith in the American opportunity structure. Thus, Sonia is not clearly and consistently oppositional. Rather, she appears to embrace stereotypes, making them her own even as she questions their generalizability.

I have argued that Sonia's crazy self cannot be fully examined without consideration of the definitions and meanings which permeate her school environment. Situated in a school where disciplinary practices are in accordance with Sonia's view that Mexican-descent youths are psychologically prone to "screwing up," navigating an environment where adults appear to keep a safe distance from Latino students, even as they attempt to watch and circumscribe their behavior, there is no discourse present to challenge the meanings Sonia and her peers accept and reproduce. It is notable, for example, that Sonia can practice the most academically harmful aspects of her "crazy" ethnic identity relatively unfettered. Her truancy and academic failure are ignored. Sonia thus discovers that the school officials with whom she most often has contact make many efforts to watch and identify behavioral weaknesses in Latinos, and little effort to identify or nurture academic capabilities.

It is important to note that some features of Sonia's ideology and behavior are not inconsistent with learning and education, but rather with proper academic comportment as defined by the school. Sonia shows a preference for activities that require risk-taking and spontaneity, for example. Both are behaviors integral to work requiring creative thinking. Sonia also shows a capacity for analysis, as she notices patterns in her environment and seeks to construct and assert theories which enable her to make sense of what she sees. Finally, Sonia orients toward collaborative activites, demonstrating an ability to work with others to plan and organize social activities. However, within the classroom, Sonia encounters a narrow conception of learning; here, neither creativity nor analysis nor collaborative skills are relevant. This reinforces Sonia's idea that academically successful European American classmates must be different than herself. Otherwise, Sonia reasons, they would not be able to endure the behaviors and activities required for school success.

In sum, the conclusions Sonia draws and her behavior are consistent with meanings conveyed by the environment in which she operates. There are simply no good reasons why Sonia should question her beliefs about the psychological differences she perceives. For Sonia, therefore, craziness remains an immutable social characteristic, integral to her sense of ethnicity and synonymous with academic failure.

# CHAPTER 6

# Ryan Moore on Fitting In

.... I don't want to sound derogatory because I don't mean to—but it's kind of like the people who come here for the pick [to work in the fields] and they're transferring out they just don't identify with the American culture. ...

[My one Spanish-speaking friend] ran hurdles with me, that's where I got to know him, and then we got close because we both were new at it. And the fact that he spoke English made it easier and then I practiced my Spanish on him. .... In fact he's got a will to fit in. It's like the classic people coming to America, the classic thing you read about. It's the same kind of will which I don't see in these people who come across in a bus, or a boxcar, or in the back of a truck. I think they're here for our welfare sometimes. He wants to succeed, he wants to grow and get better and fit in and become a better person, so it's so easy because he shares the same ... when he wants to succeed and go farther and not just take it easy, then it is great. (ES37STD:1155–1161; 1364–1391)

—Ryan Moore,
sophomore student,
Explorer High School

Walking through the courtyard at Explorer High School, Ryan Moore sees a group of five Latino males. Speaking loudly in Spanish, laughing, hit-

135

ting, and jumping on one another, the group moves forward. Ryan gauges the distance between himself and the throng, then alters his walking angle. Cutting across the courtyard, Ryan avoids the group.

Ryan's movement—purposeful, careful and strategic—can be viewed as one of the many efforts he has made during high school to orient himself toward environments where the sociocultural components match his vision of what it means to be an American. Oriented toward the future and confident in an equation between academic and professional success, Ryan is a European American Protestant committed to notions of hard work and deferred gratification in exchange for economic and professional opportunities. For Ryan, such beliefs have been channeled into a series of efforts to match a student ideal that combines academic achievement with school involvement. During his freshman year, Ryan earned a 4.0 grade point average and this pattern continued into his sophomore year, when he maintained a 3.7 average. Concurrent with this, Ryan played soccer, ran track, volunteered his assistance for the school play, and participated in his school's academic honor society. Finally, Ryan served as treasurer of his sophomore class and secretary of his junior class. For Ryan, involvement in such activities provides evidence of his own efforts to "grow" and "get better," and he has earned accolades from the adults who surround him. Friendly, polite, and unassuming, Ryan is also well-liked. Ryan is described by school personnel as being "really good," "responsible," and "self-directed."

As time went on, however, it became clear that the all-American persona Ryan presents is not entirely self-directed. As Ryan spoke of his efforts to grow and get better, it was increasingly apparent that he had developed a conformist ideology. Predicated on the necessity of adapting, in order to access opportunity, Ryan has come to expect evidence of efforts to "fit in" to ideals defined by more powerful others, both from himself and from his peers. Reflecting this ideology, Ryan has come to believe that those who do not work hard to assimilate, those who manifest preferences for language, behaviors, and activities different than his own, are not only less classically American, but also to be avoided: "... the Hispanics, they tend to hang around in gangs. Not formal gangs, just—they're kind of like a group that goes around and you see that you realize okay, they're here, I want to be there, when they're there I want to be here" (ES37STA:495–503).

This chapter considers Ryan's all-American persona and the ideology of conformity that underlies it. It explores how a youth, eager to grow, has learned that it is important to look compliant. We will see that in relation to disciplinary technologies, classroom expectations, and discursive practices at his high school, the conformist aspects of Ryan's persona can be viewed as "sensible."

## GENESIS OF AN ALL-AMERICAN PERSONA

Well, you know, he comes from very caring parents .... his parents are very active here in the school. Father's the head of the booster club. Mother's in the office. Anyway, so just lovely people. And he reflects that. (ES072ST1:1734–1735; 1819–1823)

—Guidance principal,
Explorer High School

Arriving at school from an upper-middle-class residential neighborhood, Ryan is described by administrators and teachers as coming from an ideal environment critical to fostering his academic success and school involvement. Ryan's father, an engineer, grew up in the community, attended a high school close to Explorer, and then graduated from a prestigious engineering program at a state university. His mother, also a college graduate, suspended her career in interior design when Ryan was born. Committed to "being at home with her children," she has only recently resumed part-time employment. Completing the family are Ryan's sister, three years his junior, and a dog.

When speaking of his family, Ryan depicts an environment that has nurtured and supported many of the values and behaviors praised and supported by school authorities. For example, Ryan and his mother's descriptions indicate the family has worked since preschool to orient Ryan and his younger sister toward academic effort, self-directed learning, and school involvement. During preschool, Ryan's mother recounts spending hours with Ryan and his younger sister reading out loud. In high school, Ryan says his parents have talked to him regularly about school, encouraging his academic performance: "They ask me what's up in my classes, usually just to see if everything's alright. And my dad talks to me about algebra, and he kind of pushes me, but not bad or anything" (ES37STC:1349–1353). Ryan has also gathered information about college from his father, who discusses and describes his experiences at the university he attended. For Ryan, it is clear that his parents expect college attendance: "That's no doubt. It's always been talked about and everything, that I'm going to college so it's pretty— we don't even talk about it because they just know" (ES37STB:631–635).

Familial emphases on self-directed learning have paralleled this socialization to academic effort. Again, beginning in preschool, Ryan's mother worked with her children on art projects, took them on outings to nearby parks and museums, and encouraged individual hobbies her children could pursue on their own. For example, at age three, Ryan became fascinated with ships. Over the years, his parents helped him obtain books and models and taught him the skills needed to gather historical information. As he grew older, the family visited shipyards and ports and the garage was organized to accommodate a large model shipyard. In high school, interest in this activity has continued, with Ryan exploring different boat designs and the factors which affect flotation.

Concurrent with this, Ryan's parents involve themselves in the schools Ryan and his sister attend. Ryan's mother has volunteered in the classroom, and both parents have and continue to be involved in the parent-teacher association (PTA) and supporting activities. During Ryan's high school years, his father has served as president of the school's booster club, while his mother continues her involvement with the PTA and volunteers at Ryan's younger sister's middle school. Through regular communication with the high school, Ryan's parents have also established a relationship with various administrators, as exemplified by comments from personnel such as the administrator who speaks below:

> .... he'd worked out his schedule, and so the mother called me and she said, 'You know, we've left every thing up to Ryan. But maybe we shouldn't leave that much up to him.' And so she said, 'What does he need to take as far as college and university?' And so we talked. And she said, 'Well that's what he's done!' I said, 'That's Ryan.' (ES072ST1:1738–1747)

In addition to promoting some of the behaviors school personnel value, Ryan's descriptions suggest his parents socialize their children to some of the values that underlie the ideology Ryan espouses. Most notably, Ryan's parents emphasize deferred gratification and an orientation toward the future. For example, as a sophomore, Ryan struggled with his parents over the issue of whether to purchase a Mustang as his first car. His parents discouraged what they viewed as a foolhardy investment, but at the same time urged Ryan to look forward to making such purchases in the future:

[My mom] she's trying I guess to save face and I'm trying to sell my point about a Mustang so we talked for like three hours. When then it came out, all of this stuff about, 'Well it's not in the financial plan that you were going to get a car right now and don't think that we are strapped or anything but it just wasn't in the plan. And then for you to get a Mustang we don't know how much money we are going to have to put into it.' ....

So last night we talked for like three hours and my dad gives me all of these horror stories about his car and says how he wanted some car when he was a kid and his parents didn't let him get it and so he understands but it's just not going to work right now because he needs something you don't have to work on. .... And he goes, 'But don't give up your dream. Just postpone it.' And all this baloney and just—three hours worth of this. .... he starts trying to convince me that I shouldn't give up. (ES37STAB:743–803)

Similarly, when Ryan expressed frustration with one of his courses, his father advised him to sit tight until he knew how this class might affect his academic future: "... my dad, well I always tell him stuff about it and he says, 'Well, if it gets to the point where you can't do well in the class because of it, then let me know.' I'm getting an *A* in the class so you can't really say [anything]. 'Well, you're getting an *A*, what's wrong with him?' (ES37STC:225–232).

According to Ryan, his parents value demonstrations of academic effort as much as the actual grades he accrues: "My parents are like, 'As long as you did your best, that's fine.' .... I'm not really pressured to do well. They want me to do well ...." (ES37STD:226–230; 465–468)." However, Ryan's parents have little reason to doubt that that effort will translate into indicators of superior academic achievement. With little exception, Ryan's elementary school report cards contain the highest marks possible. These patterns continued into middle school, when Ryan's grade point average ranged from 3.83 to 4.0. Similarly, Ryan's test scores are consistently impressive. On the CTBS, administered twice in the first grade and every year thereafter, his scores range from the 87th percentile to the 98th percentile. By eighth grade, all of his scores were in the 99th percentile. In second grade, Ryan was identified to participate in GATE (Gifted and Talented Program), with testing indicating a full-scale IQ of 141 (verbal, 142; nonverbal, 130).

Paralleling these indicators of achievement are consistently laudatory comments by Ryan's elementary school teachers. "A delightful child" and "an outstanding student" are qualities mentioned again and again.

*First grade:* Good student, great ideas, able to express vocabulary above grade level. Interested in all academic areas. Very responsible. He is a delightful child.

*Second grade:* Extremely capable young man who is able to deal in the abstract areas. Ryan is an outstanding student.

*Third grade:* Ryan is performing at a high level. He always puts his best foot forward. Ryan can be counted on to keep up on his studies. He seems to enjoy research projects. He's an outstanding student.

*Fourth grade:* Ryan, you're a wonderful person. Your enthusiasm added much to our class.

*Fifth grade:* Ryan is a mature, well-rounded leader. Great to have in class. Students like Ryan make teaching a very rewarding experience.

Similarly, in every class during middle school, teachers indicate Ryan's "excellent conduct and attitude."

Just as Ryan has continued to maintain his record of academic achievement upon entering high school, so have teachers' and administrators' perceptions remained consistently laudatory. To adults, Ryan manifests an all-American persona, which is perceived as "responsible," future-oriented, and involved. He is described not just as an excellent student, but as a cultural ideal:

*Guidance principal:* .... he was selected for this prestigious Leadership Training Program. So, and before I selected him, I went to different people. Now see, because he's an officer and that type of thing. And I went to different people [including varied teachers and the principal of activities] and I said, 'OK, these are the ones, what do you think?' 'Ryan Moore' [they said unanimously] .... [He's] self-motivated, self-directed. Very responsible, leadership skills, uhm, people like him. You know, and much respected by his teachers also. He's just that kind of a student. (ES072ST1:1763–1790).

Ryan is the boy teachers want in the neighborhood as well as in the corporate board room. He is described by his biology teacher as "very nice. He's out for sports and seems to come from a nice family. I don't know his parents personally but they are involved with the Boosters Club and taking him to sports. So seems like a nice family and a nice person .... [the] type you would like to have—wouldn't mind in the neighborhood type. He would be ideal." Ryan's English teacher adds: "He comes from an area where the kids are really good. .... I have no doubt he will do fine in life. He'll have three secretaries to take care of him."

In the eyes of school adults, Ryan and his family appear to represent the image of all that is considered desirable in American middle-class culture. Criteria for this designation include success and achievement, parental involvement, and manifestations of "responsibility" and "self-direction." Their criteria for excellence are consistent with those described in other studies concerned with mainstream European American teachers' expectations for ideal student behavior (Spindler, 1987).

## RYAN'S CONFORMIST PERSONA

.... for now it's what I have to do. I have to fit in,
really to make it, at least to make it and be happy.
Because it doesn't bother me to go out and drive
aggressively because that is what everybody else is
doing. It would bother me to drive on some road
that a whole bunch of people are driving nice and
cut everybody off. But for now, until it changes,
you have to fit in. You have to kinda go with the
flow. (ES37STAB:1783–1793)

—Ryan Moore

For Ryan, "fitting in," manifested by participating well in a mainstream cultural game where the rules are set by more powerful others, has come to be of critical importance. Thus, the all-American persona Ryan has learned to project is more than "responsible," more than "focused." While adults describe Ryan as self-directed, he is also highly aware of others' expectations and structures his behavior accordingly. Ryan has been taught that he must adjust even to situations he finds disturbing and unpleasant if he is to succeed. Thus, he is often cautious and conservative when raising concerns, aware of the ways in which power and rewards are distributed and couching his critiques accordingly. He is sometimes judgmental, critical of peers who appear less interested in participating in the game others have defined as necessary for success. Because Ryan has been taught to equate "growing" and "getting better" with an ability to compete well in the mainstream cultural game, Ryan's all-American persona can thus also appear conformist and oriented toward, as he puts it, "looking out for yourself."

The conformist aspects of Ryan's persona could be seen first in his efforts to adapt to social studies, a classroom he viewed as both highly biased and unfair. Though Ryan described himself as both bored and uncomfortable in class, he attended daily and consistently completed his academic work. Further, Ryan described himself as endeavoring to read and adapt to his teacher's demands. For example, when his teacher presented a model for essay writing quite different than that encountered in English, Ryan was skeptical: ".... they tried to pass it off as this is a social studies paragraph, an English paragraph is a different sort .... in social studies you'd get an *A*, [they'd write] 'All this is beautiful.' In English, you'd be 'Lacking any originality, the words are dull'" (ES37STB:886–896). Rather than raising questions or investigating this further, however, Ryan adapted: "So some people [like me] I guess adjusted to the fact that there was different ways, but a lot of people that were maybe not really understanding from the start, it affected them" (ES37STB:880–910).

Conformity could also be seen in the careful and cautious manner in which Ryan learned to voice concerns to school officials. For example, after a year of dissatisfaction in social studies, Ryan decided to register a protest. However, rather than rallying other students to support him, Ryan couched his criticisms in terms acceptable to the institution. He went first to the principal, listing his complaints. He made certain to focus on course content rather than on the personality of the teacher involved, highlighting strengths and weaknesses in the course. When Ryan's critique was discounted and he was again assigned to this teacher for his sophomore year, Ryan reacted eventually with equanimity and resignation: ".... if I got my class changed to another teacher, the other teachers from what I hear aren't much better in the way they treat people and stuff. At least this way I know what he does. .... I know his system" (ES37STC:208–217). Further, Ryan channeled his efforts into adjusting to his teacher's expectations, consoling himself with the grade he earned at the end of the academic year: "When I got my *A* last year it's like, 'Yeah, that's cool. At least I got my *A*'" (ES37STAB:466–471).

An orientation toward conformity could also be seen in the way Ryan spoke of his one friendship with a Latino immigrant, Fernando. Ryan praised Fernando not just because of his personal qualities, but because he seemed to fit a cultural stereotype: "He's got a will to fit in. It's like the classic people coming to America, the classic thing you read about." Further, despite the fact that he had taken two years of Spanish, Ryan did not attempt to interact with Fernando's friends and expected Fernando to make the effort to move into his social world: "He still hangs around with his Hispanic friends .... he can, like at lunch he'll come over to talk to us" (ES37STD:1351–1355).

Finally, Ryan's orientation toward conformity is revealed in the critiques he leveled and the assumptions he made about youth he perceived as failing to "fit in" to the system:

> It seems like they don't want to be bussed here. So they're going to make our lives miserable here and bring with them the way they hang downtown .... these are the same people that will mess up our chances—like this school has something that's special. Like these are the kind of people that—I know in middle school we had outdoor lockers at one time, but people kept blowing them up, through the vents, they'd put something in there and they'd blow the door off. (ES37STA:489–532; 602–610)

Ryan purposely distanced himself from youths who appeared to him dangerous and different: "I guess it tends to alleviate some of the tension because we don't want to mess with them and I'm sure they probably don't want to get into anything with us" (ES37STD:1235–1239). His closest friends attended his academic classes and participated also in student government or school-based activities. Ryan says all of his friends want to get good grades and plan to go to college: "Everybody wants to get good grades because I mean now, everybody sees their future. And they realize that you can't mess around in school—you can mess around after school but you got to be serious while you're here" (ES37STA:421–459). He describes himself as having searched for youths with similar ideals and values: "It works better that way because they all—and the people that don't really get good grades in our group, they want to get good grades and they're always working. It's not like they're just here because the state says they have to be" (ES37STA:426–432).

Over ten years of schooling, Ryan has increasingly come to believe that in order to make it it is not only necessary to do well academically but also to adopt a "harder," competitive persona, which enables success in a game that valorizes "survival of the fittest":

> Just about any place outside your family, outside your close group of friends, you are going to have to be harder. I think especially in this area as opposed to anyplace else. Because like, here everybody is out to get you it seems. There is always a fast pace. It's like a little war going on. You know, everybody for themselves, you just—survival of the fittest really. And when you get back to your family that's great. You know, cause I'm kinda two people anyway—with my close friends and my family it's like yeah. But after that nobody is going to come and pick you up if you're knocked down really after awhile. So you just gotta look out for yourself. (ES37STAB: 1713–1731)

Ryan says he is not entirely comfortable with this all-out emphasis on competition: "I think it would be nice if everybody could—well, for where we live I don't think it would happen. But it would be nice if everybody could just relax and be less competitive and more friendly" (ES37STAB: 1713–1749). However, at the same time Ryan's comments indicate he has, over time, adapted to and to some extent internalized the competitive ethos. For example, when speaking of less academically successful peers who teased him in middle school, Ryan commented:

> [In middle school] I didn't forget about my grades. I kept those up because I could beat the people there. You know what I mean. I could—that was a place where, yeah, I was better. Even if they didn't realize it then. I developed my, my, it was like a philosophy of, 'You can come, you can come talk to me while I'm running the country and you're working in Mickey D's for the rest of your life.' (ES37STAB:1389–1399)

Though those who know Ryan would not describe him as self-centered, there are moments when Ryan reveals an orientation toward "looking out for yourself." For example, though it is clear Ryan both respects and likes his immigrant friend Fernando, Ryan sometimes assesses the friendship in instrumental terms. When Fernando was elected vice president of Ryan's class, for example, Ryan seemed happy for Fernando but at the same time also focused on how this might better Ryan's ability to compete for student body president during his senior year:

> *Ryan:* It's gonna be great .... there is a large majority of ESL people—you know, students who don't vote typically so they voted for Fernando. So that was it.
> *Interviewer:* So you feel really good about that?
> *Ryan:* Yeah. And also I see it as another way because I plan on running for ASB president this year and so if all of the Spanish speakers are involved coming to our meetings, I'll be more visible to them. .... So that will be like synonymous—so they'll vote for me I think when I run. (ES37STAB:342–370)

Ryan, focused on his own agenda, does not key into the fact that Fernando, in seeking election, was motivated primarily by his desire to increase the visibility and to voice the needs of the immigrant constituency.

Ryan recognizes that those in power are not always right, and he is not against modifications in the basic existing system. Further, Ryan believes it is important to protest when one is treated unfairly. This is particularly true in areas of academic endeavor: "If I got a *B* in the class it's like I lost. And I want to change that, or let it be known that it was unfair .... school, that affects me directly and everything. So I don't care if it intimidates me, [if I'm mistreated] I want to change it" (ES37STAB:585–603). In the end, however, Ryan has come to believe that when reasonable protests are silenced or ignored by authorities, it is necessary to channel one's anger and frustration into further efforts to compete well within the system, rather than to mobilize support for resistance:

> Basically, I go on and I'm nice and cordial and if you're nice to me then that's fine. And if you're not, if you're like closed to what I have to say then it just makes me want to go more to win. I guess I'm highly competitive. I know that from my sports and stuff. And so, it's kind of like a competition I guess I view it. (ES37STAB: 554–584)

Ryan is willing to do what is necessary to succeed, provided it does not violate his more basic principles: "You have to be strong enough to be able to change yourself but not compromise yourself. Like a lot of times I'm at school, and I change the way I act. I don't compromise what I believe in ...." (ES37STAB:1798–1805).

For Ryan, conformity to a model defined and sanctioned by more powerful others has inadvertently become part of the behavior necessary to fulfilling his American dream. Ryan has learned that growth and getting better are contingent on competing well and finding power within the context of the given system. Ryan's melting pot philosophy, expressed in the quote that opens this chapter, can also be understood in this light. At some level, Ryan perceives deviance from mainstream patterns and rules to be a rejection of what it means to be American.

In considering Ryan's experiences over his ninth- and tenth-grade years, it is apparent the conformist aspects of his persona have been not just supported but been structured by his time in high school. In the section that follows, I consider aspects of Explorer's environment that have contributed to the conformist ideology Ryan applies both to himself and to others. To do so, I consider factors that work to teach Ryan that a willingness to conform is critical for accessing opportunities for growing and getting better within his academic environment.

## CONSTRUCTING A CONFORMIST IDEOLOGY: LESSONS ON "FITTING IN"

> I mean there's two Explorer's, the Explorer that is
> seen or presented by the administration, and the
> Explorer in reality. And Explorer's divided into
> White people Explorer, college-bound students—
> you know [from] Cloverbrook—and the students
> that are bussed in. This is a divided school. There
> are two schools here. That's what you're seeing here.
> You're seeing two schools. (ES106ST1:993–1004)
> —Jaime Garcia,
> ESL aide/Explorer graduate

Since entering Explorer, Ryan has been immersed in a system that actively works to encourage adherence to a rather conventional model of social advancement. Though today Explorer is characterized by both economic and social diversity, historically it has and continues to prepare a particular type of youth for college. Predominantly middle class and of European American descent (see Table 2.2), these students, like Ryan, are known for their domination of school-sanctioned extracurricular activities, enrollment in a particular set of advanced classes, and maintenance of high grade point averages. As the ESL aide notes above, when combined with the fact that European American youth spend their lunch hour in sections of the school where they are removed from classmates of color, this works to create the impression of "two schools."

In chapters 3 and 5, I considered Explorer's patterns of social separation and reproduction from the points of view of youth who do not fit this conventional model of social advancement. In this chapter, I look at the situation from a new angle, considering factors that work upon youth who fit Explorer's stereotype of the college-bound student. In considering these factors, my purpose is to provide insight into the ways in which school-based practices and procedures contribute to the formation of conformist ideologies. Through disciplinary technologies that provide youth with glimpses of the benefits associated with conformity, a discourse that works to communicate the dangers of intellectual independence, and practices that silence critical voices, Ryan and his peers are immersed in a system which teaches that access to power and privilege are best attained, as Ryan puts it, through "fitting in."

*Access to Academic Privilege: The Benefits of Conformity*

It's—you're not challenged a lot of times, at least
I'm not, in my classes where it's not accelerated.
Very rarely is there a challenge. There's a lot of busy
work. Like I spent an hour in science doing graph-
ing. I know how to do a graph. .... There's very
few things that I learn there. (ES37STB:714–731)
                                              —Ryan Moore

Upon entering Explorer as a ninth grader, Ryan, as well as his peers, became part of an experiment designed to foster social integration while simultaneously appeasing demands from the parents of college-bound youth. With the exception of ESL students, all incoming ninth graders were enrolled in two integrated courses (general science and social studies), while students with the highest achievement test scores were placed in accelerated English and more advanced mathematics courses. For Ryan's class cohort, this experiment began to dismantle during sophomore year, when the most academically successful general science students moved on to biology (others took life science). By junior year, academic tracking was fully restored, with the thirty most academically successful sophomores (of approximately 340) continuing on to AP History. Likewise, the forty to fifty most successful science students from Ryan's cohort were enrolled in chemistry.

Ironically, though detracking was meant to work toward breaking down the social and academic borders that separate Explorer youth, in fact, Explorer's social experiment has delivered two messages. Through comparisons between his advanced and integrated courses, Ryan has observed first that academic winners are rewarded with differential access to a curriculum that is not only labeled as being more prestigious, but is in fact both more challenging and more interesting than that encountered by the majority of youth at Explorer. Second, Ryan has had the opportunity to learn that the most academically successful youth have access to more information about future possibilities than do their general track peers. These factors have combined to strengthen Ryan's resolve to attend classes in which he is socially segregated, thereby pressuring him to accept less than ideal academic situations in general track classrooms in order to ensure his eventual admission to advanced courses.

Though students in Ryan's social studies and science courses were integrated, there was little attempt to make the curricular and pedagogical changes necessary to ensure the engagement of youth with a diverse array of abilities. Teachers at Explorer have received only minimal training in heterogenous grouping, and minimal instruction in designing the types of tasks most effective for encouraging learning in these types of settings. Thus, the first and most primary difference between the advanced and general courses Ryan attended was in the area of curriculum. It was not simply that Ryan's advanced courses required more work. Rather, students were afforded opportunities for different types of thinking within these courses. Two of Ryan's teachers, both from his more advanced classes, describe some of these differences below:

> *Advanced English teacher:* I do a lot of critical thinking [with the advanced class]. We try to focus in on logic. .... Not that I don't teach it to the other classes, or touch on it, but I think that I want these—I think these students are going to use it more ... and I could be wrong. I think I see more potential to use it in this class. And so I will spend a little bit more time on it, because I feel that they're better able to use it, better able to go further with it. (ES014ST2:177–219)

*Biology teacher:* This is part of genetics here [in biology], there is genetics in here [in life science]. But what we might take two weeks with here [in biology] we cover lightly in three days here [life science] and then have puzzles and da-de-da, lower-level activities. So [in biology] this is more thought-provoking, more concept-oriented, more application. You know, where you, like where you're given a problem and you have to say, 'Well, given this concept of dominance and recessiveness and multiple alleles, and I'm getting something that I'm not supposed to have, then something else must be happening, this must be it.' .... Logical interpretation, reasoning, where they're not just memorizing facts. (ES057ST1:567–591)

Observations of Ryan's classrooms confirm his teachers' descriptions. In general science and social studies classes, students spent the period completing worksheet exercises that focused primarily on recall and definition, reading from and answering questions posed in their text, and listening to the teacher. (See chapter 5 for a description of the norms, behaviors, and expectations encountered by students in general track classrooms.) In contrast, while students completed conventional exercises in English and biology classes, they were also provided with opportunities to engage in self-directed, investigative activities requiring both creative and analytical thought. In biology, for example, students carried out an investigation designed to mimic the ways in which biologists sample populations in an open environment. In addition, they worked on a long-term group project in which they were asked to analyze a pond located behind their high school, collecting water and plant samples to determine what life forms were present, then generating questions for further study. Similarly, in English class, in addition to completing more conventional assignments in which they analyzed and assessed pieces of literature, students were asked to design and present "talking book reports" on texts of their own choosing. Youths worked in pairs, choosing and analyzing a song, poem, or book of their choice, then making a presentation to their classmates. These observations are in accordance with large-scale studies of academic tracking, which indicate that teachers in advanced courses expect different kinds of behavior from their students, including critical thinking, individual work, active participation, self-direction, and creativity (Oakes, 1985).

A second and more subtle difference between Ryan's advanced and general track courses lay in the access to information each provided. During the first semester of Ryan's ninth-grade year, teachers in integrated social studies did spend some time reviewing the various requirements for college attendance. However, after this introduction, talk concerning such matters in general classrooms ceased. In contrast, in advanced English classes, specific information relevant to youths' post-high school plans continued to be woven into classroom talk. For example, Ryan's teacher was careful to announce the dates and to provide a general description of the meaning of upcoming achievement tests to the students in her class:

> *Teacher:* I want you to know about a PSAT seminar that I will be running with Mr. Thomas. The PSAT is a practice test for the SAT, but it is also important because it qualifies you for a National Merit Scholarship. We'll run the seminar on two Saturdays. We'll do one and one-half hours' practice on the verbal, one and one-half hours' practice on the math each Saturday, and we'll give you practice work in between. If you have any questions, I'll be here after class and during lunch. (ES47STO7:p.1)

During the twenty days I attended general track and ESL courses, over the same time period I heard no references to similar information. Consistent with my observations, during interviews with eleven Explorer students enrolled entirely in general track and ESL classes at the end of the year, seven said they had encountered little information relevant to future prospects in their first two years of high school.

As indicated in the quote that opens this section, Ryan is well aware of the differences between his advanced and general courses. He describes his experiences in general courses as mind-numbing: ".... I can get a lax attitude in that class .... when one class is like boring, you punch out the home-work—brainless—like a machine. And then you almost end up doing that in all your classes just because you're in that mind set" (ES37STB:777–794). As a result of his desire for additional challenge, and his awareness that advanced courses are looked upon favorably in the college admissions process, Ryan describes himself as working to ensure that he will be admitted to advanced courses during his sophomore and junior years. Advancement is dependent on both academic performance and the recommendation of teachers from general track courses, a factor of which Ryan is well aware: "Basically your teachers recommend your next year, your continuation on, your AP or reg-ular" (ES37STD:767–769). Thus, while Ryan expressed his frustration with general courses, he was also careful to complete his academic work and did not engage in behaviors that might cause teacher resentment.[1]

*Discourse on the Dangers of Intellectual Independence*

> I like writing, except that writing is fun until you
> have to do it for a grade. Like I'll think of schemes or
> something for my ships, like a history, and I'll write
> it down. It's fun to write, but I always worry that I'm
> going to get a bad grade when I do it for school. So
> it seems like for school you have to write the way
> your teacher wants you to write. (ES37STAB:35–44)
> —Ryan Moore

While Ryan's classrooms differed substantially in terms of the types of thinking opportunities they provided, they were similar in the sense that the majority worked effectively to warn against independence in areas of intellectual endeavor. As Ryan notes in the quote above, for many of the tasks he encountered, form was as important as content. Further, youth were punished academically when they failed to live up to this part of the academic contract. Finally, because classroom discursive practices emphasized grades as a societal sorting technology, Ryan has come to believe that deviance from teacher-generated standards and too much time spent on intellectual pursuits of his own choosing may result in exclusion from future opportunities to gain power and privilege.

As emphasized in the preceding section, some of Ryan's courses provide students with opportunities to engage in creative tasks which they themselves direct. However, at the same time, for many of the assignments Ryan has encountered, there is a specific form to which students must adhere. This is particularly true for written assignments of a more serious nature. For example, during Ryan's sophomore year, students in advanced English worked frequently on expository writing, analyzing written text, and presenting their arguments in essays. In all cases, students had to complete these assignments in a five-paragraph essay form. Suggestions that they might do otherwise were clearly antithetical to classroom norms:

> *Teacher:* Okay, you will recognize this quote from chapter 11. "Courage is when you know you're licked before you begin but you begin anyway and see it through no matter what." [Your assignment is to] Explain how Jem's experience with Mrs. Dubois reflects and supports this idea. ....
>
> I would like you to write this [your essay] in the archetypal five-paragraph essay format. An introduction, trying to express in

the introduction your thesis statement, your idea, your main idea. And then the body of the essay is going to be the support that you give to show how and why that idea is true for you.
*Student:* Can we do a four-paragraph essay?
*Teacher:* (chuckles) I'd prefer that you didn't. (ES47STO1:pp.3–4)

Similarly, in social studies, when students were asked to complete a research paper, their grades depended not only on the product they produced, but also on following each of the steps specified by the teacher as necessary to complete the task. Much to Ryan's distress, students who failed to provide such evidence were penalized academically:

.... like when we had our big paper due, Mr. Kula said, 'I can't answer questions, sorry, turn it in, I can't answer questions.' So I turned it in. [I asked] 'Did you want that paper?' He goes, 'Yeah, don't worry about it, I'll just knock you down a couple of points.' So it's like if you'd answer my question I could have put the paper in. (ES37STB:815–825)

Ryan says on the rare occasions when he has attempted to do things in a manner different than that specified by a teacher, adults' reactions have been disappointing. For example, in social studies, students were expected to keep track of points awarded for their academic work, and they were given explicit instructions on how to do so. Ostensibly, this was so students might cross-check the teacher's accounting. Ryan, discovering what he believed was a more efficient way to tally his totals, did so. When at the end of a grading period he arrived at a point total different than that of his teacher, he discovered his teacher was unwilling to consider his evidence because he had failed to keep his records as specified:

.... my point sheet said that I had an *A*. And I'd been keeping track. Well I took it to him and he said, 'Well you got a *B*.' He discounted my evidence because my point sheet was in a different order than his. I didn't tally it—it has four columns, it's points, possible points earned, total possible, total earned. Well I didn't always total the total possible and total earned until like halfway down, cause it didn't seem worth it. I totaled it at the end, so that the end result was the same. But I didn't do it right [the way that he wanted], so therefore I must have had a *B*, just because I didn't total that one column the whole time. (ES37STB: 1009–1030)

The message was that there is a right and wrong way to do things, that such matters are determined by those in authority, and that experimentation with the system may result in punishment.

Complementing this message is the fact that there is rarely time for students at Explorer to engage in extended intellectual exploration of topics of their own choosing. Ryan describes an increasing workload that has precluded his ability to pursue either his hobby of model boat building or his interest in history: "I'll just come home and do my homework and go to bed" (ES37STD:101–102), "My hobby of model boatbuilding I've hardly worked on at all. It's just sitting in our garage. There are projects that are half done that I just don't have time" (ES37STD:1431–1435). Further, classroom discourse warns of serious consequences should students fail to carry out the instructional tasks defined as necessary by teachers:

> .... as soon as we came here, 20 million teachers would go, 'Your grades are important.' Basically, without saying, they told us you had to ace everything or you'd get turned down for college. ... They said, 'Your grades are really important and there's no time to screw around now. They're [colleges] turning down straight *A* students and you just have to ace everything.' .... It bothers me because it makes messing up even harder to take. Because now you think more and more, 'Gee, now it's not just my grades, it's my future.' ....
>
> I don't think anybody would admit it if you asked them, because I don't think they realize what they're doing. I think they want to instill a value to get grades and to realize that it affects your future, but it's almost overkill because you get so scared. (ES37STD:50–87; 208–217)

Though a 3.5 GPA does not necessarily preclude admission to a prestigious university, it is clear Ryan does not doubt or question his teachers' warnings. Rather, he views them as serious speech acts; knowledge to be learned and acted upon. ("... now you think more and more, 'Gee, now it's not just my grades, it's my future.'") Ryan believes academic perfection is expected. As a result, he has increasingly come to focus on discerning and memorizing the content he knows his teachers will require of him: "I'll bury myself in the notes because I want to ace the test. And in every class you listen so much that you try to get everything down and then at night you stay up and you study it all again just because you want to make sure. As a result, I don't relax too much" (ES37STD:93–101).

Knowing that experimentation and risk-taking may result in short-term penalties (a poor mark) that could harm his eventual grade, believing he will be evaluated for college almost entirely on his academic record, Ryan pays attention to discerning what it is that his teachers want of him, sacrifices continued growth in areas of personal interest, and adjusts his academic work products to meet teachers' expectations.

## THE SILENCING OF CRITICAL VOICES

> .... they always say like if you have a problem, talk
> to them. That's the biggest—that's—you come and
> talk to them and they're like—and they're still right.
> You might have a problem, but of course they're
> right, they're right from the start and they end up
> right in the end. Even if you're right, they're
> right—they say we'll talk and we can work it out.
> Well sure we can work it out if you're right. That's
> like there's only one way to work it out. It ends up
> that they're right and whatever your problem was—
> it gets discredited. (ES37STB:992–1007)
>
> —Ryan Moore

During Ryan's sophomore year, a rather newsworthy disciplinary event occurred. One of Explorer's most academically successful and involved students, an African American female with a 3.9 GPA, was suspended. As a member of the school's student council and in her position as editor of the school newspaper, this young woman was known for her active role in the school. However, on the day a Republican politician was scheduled to visit Explorer, she wore a sweatshirt that called for his recall and made references to lesbian rights, advocated the elimination of capital punishment, and criticized proposals to decrease funding for state universities. Her activism proved too much for the administration. Asked to change her sweatshirt, she refused, and as a result was placed on suspension.

Through public displays of power such as the one above, as well as more mundane actions, adults at Explorer communicate that neither significant acts of protest nor more mundane student critiques are in keeping with the model of student conformity they seek to promote. Though Explorer has moved increasingly toward a model of site-based decision making, there are no formal structural means for youth to register protests or raise concerns about the system. Further, when major decisions that impact students are made, student input is not solicited. For example, as teachers and administrators pondered the elimination of a homeroom period during Ryan's sophomore year, students were not asked for their opinions. Similarly, when seeking a way to create a safer school environment, administrators did not involve student stakeholders in the decision-making process but instead announced and instituted a new disciplinary system. Ryan is well aware of this facet of his school environment. As he sees it, "If you get in good and have a reputation for changing things that you don't like, that you're a doer, then pretty much people will listen to you. But I haven't seen a way that the ordinary person, quiet and to himself, if he doesn't like something there really isn't a way to say, 'This is not good, this does not suit me, this is discriminatory' or something. There's no outlet for that at all" (ES37STD:872–883).

As a youth involved with student government, one whose parents are known and recognized by school administrators, Ryan is one of the few students who has been able to "get in good" and thereby access the administration. Yet, even he has come to believe that youths' comments and critiques matter little to those with power in the environment: "There's a lot of, 'Thank you very much, we'll write this down,' and I don't know where the notes go after the meeting" (ES37STD:891–893). For Ryan, such conclusions stem not only from observations about the ways in which acts of student protest are handled, but from personal experience. As a ninth grader, Ryan became increasingly concerned about aspects of the integrated social studies course he attended. Knowing the course had been dubbed experimental, Ryan and a friend approached the principal, asking to voice their concerns to members of the social studies department. The teachers responded first with requests to delay the meeting for two weeks, then with a request to survey the students in the class for their opinions. Weeks later, when the survey was not carried out, Ryan and his friend again requested to be heard. At this point, a brief meeting with the principal and members of the department was scheduled. However, according to Ryan, the presentation prepared by himself and a friend was effectively short-circuited:

> .... they [the teachers] brought in a whole bunch of other students to give their view. And these students were like plants. And they gave all these views like, 'Yeah, that was a good program.' .... [The social studies teachers said] 'Well these—all the

students—they've always had good stuff to say so we figure we can listen to them too.' Well we had this whole, like, case prepared. We had the course outline, that was highlighted good and bad. And we had a sheet for each of them [the teachers]. And the girls that were there, 'Oh, I like this program.' And then they didn't even—we didn't even have time really to go into it [the outline prepared by Ryan and his friend]—[or] let out what we wanted to say. It was like both of us got outside, we stopped, we said, 'I wasn't able to say anything I wanted to say.' (ES37STAB:499–518)

The lesson learned from Ryan's point of view is that students have little ability to affect change, leaving Ryan with little motivation to fight further for the opportunity to voice his opinions.

In all, over two years of high school, Ryan has observed and experienced the benefits that come with conformity and the sanctions that may be applied when youth stray from adult expectations. Ryan sees that true opportunities to extend himself academically, to grow and get better, can only be had by proving his superior adaptability within his school's ranking system. He learns that intellectual independence, manifested either in academic experimentation or in the pursuit of individual intellectual interests, may be irrelevant and perhaps harmful to his success in the system. Finally, Ryan receives no indication that youths might contribute to reforming the system that does exist. Together, these factors combine to reinforce Ryan's belief that "fitting in" is the most assured means to future success.

## REFLECTION

Ryan, involved in his school and an excellent student, is in many ways the embodiment of the all-American youth. Praised by school authorities as a model student, his behavior defined as the norm others should seek to emulate, Ryan could be viewed as the antithesis of Sonia. Yet, there are aspects of Ryan's response to his situation that are identical. Like Sonia, Ryan accepts and reproduces definitions present in his environment, sometimes enacts social categories without question, and distances himself from others who are perceived as being different. And like Sonia, who accepts a set of meanings about what it means to Mexican, Ryan conforms to a set of behaviors authorities define as necessary for success in mainstream America.

I have demonstrated that many aspects of Ryan's ideology and behavior are conformist, and argued that Ryan's experiences in high school have contributed to producing these aspects of his All-American persona. First, for example, over two years at Explorer, Ryan has become less likely to engage in intellectual exploration on his own terms, as he worries that time taken from specified academic endeavors will harm his long-term chances for future success. He expends energy on assessing the wants and desires of his teachers and adjusts his work products accordingly. Ryan links these behaviors to his fear that external indicators of excellence (grades) will determine his future, a message that has been emphasized by his high school teachers. His compliance is likely also encouraged by the fact that particular teachers will influence his ability to access the academic opportunities available in advanced courses. Ironically, though teachers praised Ryan for his initiative, in fact, their emphasis on extrinsic rewards appeared to produce an academically compliant student who has become increasingly oriented toward suppressing his own curiosity and interests.

Second, Ryan has come to believe he must beat others if he is to make it within the system. Ryan's observations of the academic and social divisions within his high school, and the intellectual benefits that accrue to youths who outperform their peers, have arguably contributed to this belief. Knowing that there are limited slots available for admission to advanced courses, and that youths who gain admission will be provided with more interesting activities and information relevant to post-high school plans, Ryan is determined to be one of those who is provided access to such opportunities.

Finally, Ryan has become increasingly skeptical about the ability of those without power to affect reform, at least within his local high school. On the one hand, Ryan describes himself as a youth who believes in the possibilities of change, attributing this to parental socialization: "If it's affecting me I'll say, 'I've got to change this just because I figure, why sit around when you can change it.' And if I'm mad enough I'll do it right away. .... It's always been kinda within me, it's also like my parents, from the beginning, you know, 'If you want something, go out and change it'" (ES37STAB: 554–564). It was this conviction that supported Ryan's willingness to approach school administrators with his concerns about integrated social studies. However, for the short term, Ryan has resigned himself to functioning according to the dictates of the system and abiding by the decisions of administrators. His resignation is undoubtedly produced by personal experiences with silencing and observations of how adults deal with other critical voices in the environment.

In the end, the environment works to produce stereotyped manifestations of excellence in Ryan. Ironically, though expertise in the area of boat modeling distinguishes him from his peers, Ryan suppresses these interests in favor of projecting an image he hopes will be acceptable to his teachers and to the universities to which he applies. As a result, the figure Ryan shows most publically is partial, only its more conventional aspects portrayed. Ryan is praised, but the price for this includes suppression of his personal interests and an increasingly narrow world view.

# PART IV

# Empowering Speech Acts:
# Encouraging Transcultural Identities

# CHAPTER 7

# Johnnie Betts on Recasting the Self

.... when I think about being Black, I'm happy, you
know, I think about cool. .... I'm proud because we
have a lot of, *lot* of famous Black people, Black
stars. Black people dominate sports, Black people
dominate the music industry. I like it because we
have a lot of Black, intelligent, fearless leaders like
Malcolm X, Martin Luther King, all those guys,
and you know. And I just like it because our background, you know, some you can't be proud of
them and some you can. I like it because you
know—a lot of people think well there's only
White queens and this and that, but there's a lot of
Black, beautiful African queens, you know. I like
that. .... Queen Nefertiti and all those. I'm proud.
I'm proud of my background and heritage and I
could never sell out. That's what I'm proud of.
(RA27STC:1229–1260)

—Johnnie Betts,
sophomore student,
Huntington High School

It is a damp, grey morning. Tired and a bit discouraged after meetings with
two soft-spoken students, I lean against a counter in the administrative area,
fiddling with my tape recorder as I wait for Johnnie Betts, then a ninth
grader at Huntington High School.

"Are you the person I'm supposed to talk to?" Looking up from my
fiddling, I turn to meet a six-feet, barrel-chested young man. I cannot see
his eyes, veiled behind dark sunglasses, but with chin raised and weight

thrust back on his heels, Johnnie looks nervous. I smile at the sunglasses and introduce myself. Johnnie nods hello, then asks, "How many times am I supposed to talk to you?" Laughing outwardly, groaning inwardly, I respond: "Four. But you don't have to talk to me at all."

I needn't have worried. Cautious of trouble, Johnnie employed a modified version of the stance he was later to describe as typical of that used by youth in the inner-city neighborhood where he spent his middle school years. Yet Johnnie's sunglasses, signifying caution, also veiled a gregarious nature and ready humor. Living up to his teachers' descriptions of a highly social youth, he was eager to talk.

Johnnie came to California from an inner-city community in St. Louis, where death, dropping out, and unemployment were far more common than school success. Interactions with teachers only confirmed Johnnie's belief that being Black in St. Louis meant certain failure: "Cause they know in St. Louis growing up as a young teen you don't do nothing no way because that's really how it is. Can't get a job. No good jobs there" (RA27STB: 1459–1463). In such an environment, attending high school and working to succeed academically were inconsistent with a pro-Black identity:

> Well it ain't really cool, you know. Being Black and going to school in St. Louis really doesn't exist. .... like in the city, the city. Nobody goes to school. .... I mean cause if you do, usually everybody will cop you off and all this other stuff. They don't really focus on school, and if they do it's just to get out of high school or whatever. (RA27STC:695–697, 717–736)

Consistent with this orientation, Johnnie earned *D*s and *F*s through middle school and repeated his sixth-grade year.

Things are very different in California, explained Johnnie. In a school where teachers communicate high expectations and African American students see school involvement as legitimate, being Black can take on other meanings. Speaking Black English and having African American friends can go alongside doing well in school, taking pride in making the honor roll, and participating on the football team. For Johnnie, such differences have led to a fundamental recasting of self, from oppositional gang banger to "cool" schoolboy. During his ninth-grade year, Johnnie earned 3.17 and 3.33 GPAs in remedial courses and made Huntington's honor roll. In tenth grade, after moving to general track classes, he maintained a 2.17 GPA and earned district honors for his performance on Huntington's junior varsity football team. At the same time, Johnnie continued to make clear the allegiance he asserts to his background, in the quote that opens this chapter. At lunchtime and while in the halls, Johnnie spent time with fellow African American males, using African American English vernacular almost exclusively. He chose clothing styles preferred by his African American friends. In the classroom, he moved just far enough into mainstream American standard English and behavior to suit his various teachers. In less-structured classrooms, Johnnie blended mainstream and African American English vernacular grammatical patterns, sprinkling street slang into his conversations with friends as well.

For Johnnie, the ability to maintain and project a pro–African American identity, while adopting pro-school behaviors, has been critical to his willingness to engage academically. This chapter explores the significant speech acts and environmental conditions which have enabled Johnnie to recast himself.

## WHERE IS JOHNNIE COMING FROM?

Johnnie's family and history are not contained in a single geographical area, but rather in a kinship network centered in two neighborhoods differentiated by social class and culture. Johnnie's mother, a beautician, lives in an inner-city St. Louis neighborhood with Johnnie's two brothers, twelve and thirteen years his junior. Johnnie's uncle, who works for the FBI, lives in the suburban, middle-class area that surrounds Huntington High School with his wife and three children. Both Johnnie's mother and uncle grew up in St. Louis, with Johnnie's uncle departing for college in California soon after his high school graduation.

Though in touch with his biological father, Johnnie's uncle has been the primary father figure in Johnnie's life: "…. he knows me a lot man, he's always been there. Even before he was married, before he had kids, he always knew me and he's always kept me and everything, and I have been his closest nephew" (RA27STB:985–990). Johnnie has moved between California and St. Louis five times, frequently spending periods with his uncle's family. While Johnnie's movement between two households and his close relationship with his uncle might appear extraordinary, both are representative of general survival and kinship strategies employed by the African American community. African American families—particularly when money is tight—often rely heavily on friends and family in raising children and sustaining a household (Omolade, 1986; Stack, 1975).

Parental concern for education underlay at least three of Johnnie's moves to California. In early elementary school, at the end of his fourth-grade year, and during middle school, Johnnie's mother sent him to California to remove him from schools where he was doing poorly. Both Johnnie and his mother believe his uncle is better able to set and enforce rules that enable Johnnie's academic success. Johnnie explains:

> .... she sent me out here because my uncle—he works for the state, he's an FBI agent, and so she thought if I came out here and stayed with a police officer or something like that—my uncle—I won't get in trouble. .... she wanted me to come out here because she always said if I go to California—every time I come out, I go to school, I do real good. When I go there [St. Louis] I do really bad. (RA27STA:101–106, 969–984)

While at his uncle's home, Johnnie adheres to a strict set of guidelines. For example, Johnnie is well aware that he must select his friends carefully: ".... he'll say, 'I don't like that crowd you're hanging with,' and I know I have to get rid of them. Cause if he sees me with them again I probably won't be going out for a bit" (RA27STC:1005–1009). Honesty is also key:

> He knows too when I, when I'm not being straight with him. Man he'll say, if I go, 'No, no, no' he'll say, 'Johnnie, you got to be straight with me. I got to help you. I can't help you if I don't know what's wrong with you.' That's when I feel guilty not telling. He knows. Every time he's like, he's there and he'll always figure out what the situation. (RA27STB:1021–1030)

During our interviews, Johnnie spoke of being put on restriction for trying to sneak out of the house to go out with a friend, avoiding parties that might get broken up by the police, and being forced to endure lectures and housework when he became involved in a conflict with a teacher that resulted in a two-day suspension at the end of his ninth-grade year. Johnnie's aunt and uncle also call the school when he has problems with a grade, attend parent-teacher conferences, and were both present at Johnnie's suspension meeting. Both teachers and administrators at Huntington commented on Johnnie's "strong support network."

While his aunt and uncle have helped Johnnie develop the academic aspects of his new California identity, both his mother and grandmother have worked to instill pride in his African American heritage. In St. Louis, Johnnie is immersed in a community oriented toward the cultural aspects of a southern African American existence. He is expected to attend a "straight, hard, down, bible-stomping gospel" church. (Johnnie continued to do so after arriving in California.) His grandmother, from Arkansas, often cooks foods she enjoyed during her childhood: sauerkraut, greens, pig's feet, and chitlins. His mother and grandmother speak a southern version of African American English vernacular and expect Johnnie to do so as well:

> My mom, she'll tell me, if I go home and I be talking all crazy and like a White kid or something like that, she'll tell me, 'You've been hanging around too many White kids, huh?' That's what my grandmother tells me, 'You're even starting to talk like them.' I don't know, cause well we kind of like in St. Louis, everybody talks like everybody, and you really hear no proper talk [mainstream American standard English]. It's like down South. (RA27STEN:178–189)

According to Johnnie, anything that might be construed as a negative comment toward African Americans is sharply rebuked. Because many of Johnnie's girlfriends have been of Latino or European American descent, for example, his grandmother is particularly sensitive to anything Johnnie says about African American women:

> If like I say something wrong, or 'She's ugly, she's ugly' my mom will say, ahm [I mean] my grandmother, 'Why you always talking about Black people? Any time any Black commercials come on you talk about them.' And she's all, 'Don't ever be ashamed. Don't ever be ashamed to be Black, cause you have some great, great ancestors.' (RA27STEN:104–112)

Much of Johnnie's positive emphasis on his African American identity and knowledge about major African American leaders appears to come from this part of his family.

In sum, Johnnie arrives at Huntington with a strong commitment to his heritage and is well aware of his family's desire for his academic success. Yet, his family's support has not always been enough to ensure this. I turn now to Johnnie's memories of his elementary and middle school experiences.

## "THAT WAS THE OLD ME": THE ORIGIN AND EXPRESSION OF A "GANGBANGING" SELF

> I was always getting in trouble in school. I mean, this is the best years I had ever! The best school years. I was, school, my mom used to say, 'I'll be

glad when you're out of school. Going up here
every other week. Every school you go to you get
kicked out of.' (RA27STEN:992–999)
                                        —Johnnie Betts

For Johnnie, school—particularly in St. Louis—has never been easy.
By the end of fourth grade, he had attended four elementary institutions.
Things did not go smoothly during these early years:

> *Johnnie:* I didn't like preschool. Go one day and you take naps
> and you eat graham crackers. ... And they used to spank us. And
> they used to spank us if we were noisy.
> *Interviewer:* How about elementary school? What was that like
> for you?
> *Johnnie:* I didn't like it either. They used to spank me too! I was
> always getting in trouble in school. .... Oh, my teachers always
> against me. Talking, not doing my homework, getting bad
> grades, not studying, not doing homework. And when someone
> yells at me, I get a mental block. I just black out my thoughts.
> (RA27STEN:976–993, 1008–1025)

According to Johnnie, things improved after his mother sent him to California, at the end of fourth grade. (Because of Johnnie's frequent moves, no elementary school record data are available.) However, in the middle of sixth grade, Johnnie returned to St. Louis because he learned his great-grandmother was dying.

Johnnie's memories of his middle school years in St. Louis center on violence, trouble, and death. (In four interviews, Johnnie associates the word *trouble* seven times and the word *death* two times with living in St. Louis.) Many of these memories are associated with Johnnie's membership in the neighborhood Crips gang, which he joined as a twelve-year-old:

> *Johnnie:* .... we went to parties a lot. Stuff happened like ... we
> even got sent to juvenile cause it was like, that was back in the
> days when everything was just crazy and we didn't care. And
> before we realized who we were, where we were going, we
> were just, you know, out there, floating around.
> *Interviewer:* Really?
> *Johnnie:* Yeah, just gang banging and all that kind of stuff. We
> was downing colors and all this, but now, it's changed.

*Interviewer:* Can you describe to me—you know when you talk about gang banging and colors and going down to juvenile—can you give me an incident or something to help me understand what your life was like then?

*Johnnie:* Yeah, cause I never went to juvenile, that's the only place I stayed out of, but a lot of my friends, they always got caught and stuff. But like, when we talk about gang banging, it's like you just sit around the block and all your boys and your friends be drinking and stuff and you might see some group of kids, group of other dudes that they don't like. Could be old, young, could be anybody except like girls. But they'd just be walking by and looking at you and even if they don't look at you, one of your partners says, 'Let's get 'em man,' and they already wasted and stuff so they just rush 'em and then they take out their little rags or whatever and throw them around. (RA27STB:138–180)

Johnnie joined the gang out of a desire for protection: ".... something happen, I just call my homeboy. They were like always at your back" (RA27STB: 469–471). A desire for companionship was also relevant, for without membership, Johnnie explained, "I'll just be like a loner. .... I would have to move to like a county and like an area instead of neighborhood" (RA27STB: 490–498). Johnnie's rationale is similar to that given by East Los Angeles gang members; toughness provides gang members with some relief from the fear omnipresent in street life, while gang camaraderie provides emotional support and a sense of responsibility as members work to earn that support (Vigil 1988; 1993).

School was not a priority during these middle school years. Johnnie and his friends rejected academics, celebrating suspensions and ostracizing peers who tried academically:

.... when I was in sixth grade down there, the teachers was all— they were strict man, they'll hit you, grab you. My teachers they hit me with a ruler and I said, I took the ruler and I broke it, and I left the class. And they were like going, 'Suspend him,' but I didn't care cause I didn't want to go no way. So it was really—when you got suspended in school in St. Louis it was like, 'Yeahhh, I got suspended!' (laughter) It was like, 'Yeah, alright!' you know. (RA27STB:1382–1400)

Kids that went to school there are like suckers man. .... They were stupid for going cause most of the kids who were into

school and stuff they got jumped. They got beat up or something like that. You felt sorry for them after awhile, but after
awhile you got used to it. (RA27STB:1473–1480)

Johnnie's grades are in accordance with this description. He earned mostly
Ds and Fs through middle school, repeating his sixth-grade year. Summing
up his perspective on this experience, Johnnie emphasizes that schools in St.
Louis are not places where one goes for academic learning: "In St. Louis
you can go to school but you can't get a good education, cause it's like
schools are, schools are death zones. You go to school, it's like, the only time
you go to school is really to hang out and stay out of class and talk to
everybody" (RA27STB:1323–1330). Johnnie's ninth-grade CTBS scores
reflect his academic history. He scored in the 16th percentile in reading, the
27th percentile in language, and the 15th percentile in math.

In explaining his and his friends' disengagement, Johnnie speaks
adamantly about the reality of the local economy and the role his teachers
played in communicating its hopelessness:

> *Johnnie:* Strict teachers in St. Louis, that's their *main* object is to
> tell the student that you're lower than trash, you're nothin'.
> Teachers here, they help you. They help you a lot. There they
> just like, 'Whatever … whatever you want to do.' Cause they
> know in St. Louis growing up as a young teen you don't do
> nothing no way because that's really how it is. Can't get a job.
> No good jobs there.
> *Interviewer:* How do you think that makes the students there feel
> toward school?
> *Johnnie:* Like 'Ahh, the hell with it.' They don't care. (RA27STB:
> 1448–1469)

Again, Johnnie's descriptions are consistent with previous studies of gang
involvement. Distinguishing among regular, peripheral, temporary, and situational gang members, Vigil (1988) points out the "degree of gang
involvement can usually be gauged by how severe and deep-rooted the
effects of racial and cultural discrimination and poverty have been on an
individual, or how family and school authorities have failed to influence and
guide" (p. 422).

By the end of his seventh-grade year, Johnnie's mother was suffi-
ciently worried to arrange for his return to Mostaza. In speaking of this
decision, Johnnie expresses both relief and a newfound optimism. For exam-

ple, the first thing Johnnie told me was that he came to California to get out of trouble and into school; throughout our conversations he emphasized his desire to beat the odds:

> *Johnnie:* My thing is just to get out of high school alive.
> *Interviewer:* When you say alive, what do you mean by that Johnnie?
> *Johnnie:* I mean like, it's hard to go to school, to make it. Black kids, usually they drop out. A lot of them don't make it, a lot of them do. And I want to be the one of them that makes it. And a lot of them die because there's a lot of killing between Blacks and Blacks. When I say alive, I mean alive. Just that. (RA27STEN:308–312, 326–340)

Johnnie's memories of trouble, death, and academic failure in St. Louis are integral to understanding the serious manner in which he approaches academic tasks at Huntington. He did not want to return to St. Louis and felt that doing well in school and staying out of trouble were ways to prevent this.

## SUCCEEDING WITHOUT SELLING OUT: JOHNNIE'S "COOL" SCHOOL SELF

> .... things that I do, you can't tell that I'm kind of like a good—I get good grades. You straight out look at me you'd be like, 'Oh God! Man, this kid is ...' Cause if you see somebody that's trying to act cool or whatever, and you see somebody 'What's up?', and you see somebody like that and you see them catwalking and you're like, 'Look at that!' You can almost—you can tell by the character. (RA27STA:629–633)
>
> —Johnnie Betts

Johnnie's "cool" school self—the self who combines academic achievement with street-stylized behaviors which Johnnie views as appropriate to a pro-Black male identity, the self who speaks happily about making the honor roll but who criticizes African American youths who make too much effort to conform—is Johnnie's public identity, his ideal presentation of self. Johnnie takes pride in the fact that he succeeds without "selling out." His assertion of this self is ever-visible in his day-to-day social interactions.

It can be seen, for example, in the street-smart fashion style Johnnie has adopted. His saggy pants, dark sunglasses, gold chains, and a gold-capped incisor go alongside an athletic duffle bag stuffed with textbooks.

It can be seen in the cool nods Johnnie sends his male friends in the hallway and the jokes he makes about my presence: "Hey Johnnie, who's that?" "My mom, man."

It can be seen in the verbal jibes Johnnie casts at his African American friends, even as he participates in class. Johnnie often engaged in signifying, a type of ritual insult found particularly among males in the African American community:[1] "Oh, you got *crowned* Jack!" "Hey, you're just about as dumb as you look, you know that?" "You don't know *none* of the answers, you just raise your hand every time."

It can be seen in the way Johnnie switches linguistic codes, as he moves to African American English vernacular grammatical patterns when engaged in social, as opposed to academic, conversation with teachers in the classroom: "Why come they're in the hall?"; "I don't know Ms. Ashton, if somebody did a murder you gonna' take everybody to jail?"; and "So, all we doin' is writin' out the word for word for simulate?"

Johnnie's "cool" school self is most visible in his English class, where he often competes with others for the attention of his teacher. Not wanting to blow the street-smart aspects of his identity, Johnnie is both serious and flippant in the way he approaches classroom tasks:

> *Teacher:* Did anybody else want to *really* do something, but you're just too busy and can't find the time?
> *Johnnie:* I wrote uhm, 'No, I don't think this is true because I always do, find time for what I want to do. Maybe on Verna I wouldn't because I wouldn't want to do anything but sit back and be happy.'
> *Donna:* Oh how pretty!!
> *Naomi:* Ohh.
> *Martha:* Alright Johnnie.
> *Teacher:* What are you able to find time to do specifically Johnnie, what are you able to do?
> *Johnnie:* I don't know.
> *Teacher:* What do you do in your spare time? If you can tell us.

*Johnnie:* Work, I don't know.

*A.J.:* Work?! Oh yeah, come on!

*Teacher:* What kind of work honey?

*Johnnie:* I don't know, just work.

*Naomi:* Where do you work?

*Johnnie:* Helpin' the old people. Want to see 'bout the ill people at the hospital.

*A.J.:* He lyin'. He just tryin' to make the girls feel happy for him.

*Teacher:* Donna, do you believe Johnnie?

*Donna:* No, but I think that would be something nice he could do.

*Johnnie:* End my life helpin' old ladies cross the street. (RA029OB5: p.9)

Johnnie is not about to publicize his job at McDonald's. Backing away from academic language, he moves into African American English vernacular and employs blatant sarcasm to avoid looking overly compliant.

For Johnnie, not "selling out" is of vital importance. He is highly critical of fellow African American youths who reject their background:

*Johnnie:* I'm proud. I'm proud of my background and heritage and I could never sell out. That's what I'm proud of.

*Interviewer:* What would be selling out Johnnie?

*Johnnie:* It's like you see some people around here, like they'll try—they're Black, they're Black as day. And they'll try to go around saying like—we had this one girl here who was—her father was Black and she would call you a nigger in a minute. She was half Black—her father was Black but her mom was White—so I guess she didn't like Black people. And that's what you call a sellout: somebody that is ashamed of their background. .... Selling out would be like leaving your own to go to somebody else's. (RA27STC:1258–1275, 1284–1286)

While Johnnie has friends in European American and Latino peer groups and dates a Filipina student, he spends most of his time with African American males who support his pro-Black orientation. He and his friends mark their identity through the kind of music they listen to, their use of African American English vernacular, the clothes they wear, and the words they use (which Johnnie describes as "street slang"):

*Johnnie:* .... it's different, cause usually when you see a White guy, he's got his pants all rolled up, and his legs are pegged, and he'll be all tight, and his pants'll be way up, and he'll have some funky disco shoes on or something like that. Some toe socks or something like that. (laughs) And then, you know, they don't expect you to dress like that. But how you dress is how you dress. We have some Black kids that dress like that, but label them as 'discos.' ... A loner.

*Interviewer:* Okay. So there is a definite way you're supposed to dress?

*Johnnie:* Dress how you want to dress is what they going to say. I mean you can dress that way, but they're going to talk about you, every Black kid in school is going to talk about you. (RA27STEN:434–460)

According to Johnnie, status is achieved through prowess on the sports field and through the development of relationships with the opposite sex. In contrast, his friends define the hostile, territorial aspects of Johnnie's St. Louis persona as antithetical to a pro-African American identity:

.... when I come back, they be like, 'Oh yeah, glad to have you back,' and they take me out and stuff and we just kick it or something like that. And they be like, 'Man Johnnie, you changed man, you changed. I remember when we used to go to school out here and you wasn't crazy like this and everything. Talking about all this crazy stuff [gangs].' And it was like, my one, I got a friend here named Tommy, and he's really cool and everything, and he was telling me too. .... He's all 'Man, we don't want none of that gangs bothering us, cause all it is is brothers killing brothers and it's low man. Why you going to shoot another dude that's your own color?' (RA27STB:567–597)

According to Johnnie, Huntington in characterized by low levels of conflict between ethnic and racial groups and a friendly social environment. In this context, manifestations of territorialism are incongruous with the social situation.

When I first came back, when I was a teen? I was—cause I had been in St. Louis for a long time and I was gang banging it, so I thought I was pretty bad. I came here and I was like, 'Why are all these people nice to me??!! Why?' I mean, I looked at them mean and everything, I was mugging them and everything, I'm like, 'Why do you want to be my friend?' Okay? .... it was like, 'Why do you want to be my friend? I don't like you.' You know, 'I'm from a different set [a block[s] in a neighborhood associated with a particular gang]. I'm cool.' .... So my one friend Damian was a senior last year, and he goes, 'Well, you know, I want to be your friend, it's cool.' So that's how I—if it wasn't for him, I'd probably be a loner, I wouldn't know nobody. (RA27STC:652–664, 683–686, 669–674, quote reordered for clarity)

While African American students at Huntington can sell out by rejecting their background or dressing inappropriately, Johnnie is emphatic that academic success is not antithetical to peer group norms. While he appeared familiar with this idea, he rejected it forcefully when I suggested it as a possibility:

*Interviewer:* So when you do well in school, you don't feel like you're rejecting your heritage or anything like that?
*Johnnie:* No. I don't like it when people say that! Cause what people are trying to say is that I'm supposed to mess up, I'm not supposed to go to school and climb. I don't like it when people say that. Cause a lot of Black kids, they get like five or six scholarships. Like my uncle, he had twelve scholarships: at UCLA, [and] he had a scholarship to Miami State. And this was academic and sports. So I get offended when people say that. (RA27STEN:868–899)

During our interviews, Johnnie spoke happily of making the honor roll ("I felt great!") and of having proved what no one in his family thought possible, that is, that he could get good grades while continuing to have a good time. More indicative, he and his friends frequently discussed their academic status:

*Johnnie:* Well the big thing this year was how we're going to be eligible to play sports. And they'll ask me, 'Are you going to be eligible?' and I'll say, 'Yeah.' And they'll ask me and I'll say, 'I got a C.' 'You got a C? I got a B! Well like maybe you can do this, maybe you can read this paper and I'll help you and we'll start doing this to earn extra credit and she'll give you a B.' And he goes, 'Alright.' And I was telling my other friend, 'I got a C.' And he goes, 'What!? I got a D.' 'Oh man!'
*Interviewer:* What about last year when you were getting like straight *A*s?

*Johnnie:* They—first they were amazed, they were like—well everybody wanted me to help them out, I was kind of like setting a role model for them and everything. But, this year they're setting a role model for me. Because my classes are harder. (RA27STC:888–919)

In contrast to St. Louis, where suspensions were a cause for celebration, helping one another stay in school at Huntington High is the norm: "If I get into trouble they'll help me get out, they'll do anything to keep me from getting kicked out of school" (RA27STC:837–839).

In sum, Johnnie's words and actions indicate that, in contrast to St. Louis, academic achievement is consistent with the expression of a pro-African American identity at his high school. He expresses no ambivalence about his academic achievement, no discomfort about his social status. Clearly, differences between Johnnie's peer groups in Mostaza and St. Louis are essential to his ability to add academic achievement to his identity. However, a series of actions on the part of school personnel have also been critical to Johnnie's redefinition of himself. I turn now to consider significant speech acts at Huntington High.

## THE REDEFINITION OF JOHNNIE: SIGNIFICANT SPEECH ACTS AT HUNTINGTON HIGH SCHOOL

*Interviewer:* Can you talk a little bit about what it's like to be a student here as opposed to St. Louis?
*Johnnie:* Well, first of all you get to live. Second of all, the school is better and the teachers are better. You don't have to worry about walking down the street, getting shot, or walking down the street getting gang banged, getting jumped, getting your clothes taken away. Here, you're walking and you're cool with everybody. You either settle it yourself, usually it doesn't get in a fight, or you go to a teacher and they get suspended. St. Louis, you're walking, you have a fight, you get jumped by the whole school. .... And here it's not like—it's better. You know? (RA27STC:627–653)

—Johnnie Betts

When I first met Johnnie, he had only good things to say about Huntington. Compared to the experiences he'd had in his St. Louis middle school, everything appeared better. Over time, as Johnnie became more aware of some of Huntington's negative aspects, he did become more critical. However, in many ways, Johnnie's ability to develop the academic aspects of his "cool" school self reflects a series of positive encounters and decisions made by school officials and teachers.

Johnnie entered the school district as an academic failure. Overage and with little to show for his years of extra schooling, Johnnie appeared as a prime candidate for eighth-grade remedial courses. Despite his record, however, Johnnie was given a "social promotion," skipping from the eighth- to ninth-grade remedial classes. (From Johnnie's description, it appears this switch was made because of his age and size.) Upon arriving at Huntington, Johnnie describes himself as being bombarded by messages from teachers in his remedial classes. Always, the expectation was that he should move upward and onward to general courses:

> *Interviewer:* In thinking about your teachers, the ones you have now, what do they expect out of you?
> *Johnnie:* Expect me to graduate, and to go to college, and to be something.
> *Interviewer:* How do you know that?
> *Johnnie:* Cause they tell us! Tell us, they say something like, 'I want you to do good this year so you can pass my class so you can go into a higher class and so you won't be back here.' (RA27STB:1493–1507)

One year later, Johnnie's remedial teachers recommended his move to the general track. Over the course of two years, through a series of sorting decisions, Johnnie was redefined, from an overage eighth-grade middle school student to a tenth grader on the general path toward high school graduation.

Paralleling Johnnie's movement were varied institutional speech acts which served to publicize and legitimate his academic accomplishments. Once a semester, Huntington publishes a newsletter that lists students who have made the school honor roll. This letter is mailed to parents and posted in the building. Youth from honors, general, and remedial courses are not differentiated or distinguished; thus, Johnnie's name appeared alongside peers from general and advanced courses. A more formal awards assembly, open to parents, also served to mark Johnnie's newfound academic identity. Conversations with teachers and observations indicated such publication efforts worked to inform others of his achievements:

> *English teacher:* He was in an awards assembly where he was awarded a certificate for getting a certain grade point average. He was all dressed up. He looked wonderful, just wonderful. (RA029ST1:254–259)

> *Discipline principal:* I know Johnnie doesn't want to go back to St. Louis. He had a real funny look on his face when we were talking about that. So there's fear. And there's also success for Johnnie. Johnnie's a smart guy. Johnnie made the honor roll. Johnnie's nobody's fool, Johnnie's unique. (RA092ST1:p.4)

> *Homeroom class:* Students are receiving their quarterly report cards; Johnnie sits at a table with three European American girls that I do not recognize from his other classes. The sub asks the students if they want their grades. Half say yes, others scream no! Johnnie definitely wants to see his report card, and studies it closely when it arrives. Johnnie announces, "I got four *F*s, a *D* and a *C*." "No, you didn't Johnnie, you're a nerd!" says a girl at the table. Johnnie laughs and smiles. "Why you say I'm a nerd?" (RA27STO1:p.17)

Teachers and administrators in the environment differed in their assessments of Johnnie's intelligence. However, the majority interviewed during Johnnie's freshman year recognized and commented on his academic success.

While sorting decisions and institutional speech acts served to redefine Johnnie's academic status in the school community, such redefinition would not have occurred if Johnnie had not responded with homework, attendance, and other manifestations of academic effort. Motivated by fear, Johnnie also linked his renewed efforts to a discourse of possibility which he perceived as permeating the school environment. On three separate occasions, Johnnie compared claims asserted by teachers in St. Louis and California, arguing that teacher exhortations and expectations functioned in his mind as significant speech acts which served to define alternative futures:

> .... teachers [in St. Louis], they were like, they didn't care, they didn't care what you do and how you do it or where you end up cause they be like—some our teachers they actually tell us you

going to be nobody. And they'd—if somebody keeps telling you you're gonna' be nobody, you're going to take that in and you're going to say, 'Well damn, I'm going to be nobody. Look at my grades, they're right.' But, they don't tell you that you have a chance to make it, like they don't tell you that you have a chance to get yourself together and get on the good foot, and get on the right track. They tell you, 'You going to be nothing, you going to the streets, you're going to be working at 7-11.' You're going to be doing this and you're gonna to be doing that.

Teachers here, they do it too [warn kids that they're messing up], but they'll tell you, they'll be like, 'You can make something of yourself.' 'You don't have to do this,' 'You don't have to do that.' .... they don't really stress on you can't be anything. Strict teachers in St. Louis, that's their main object, to tell you that you're lower than trash, you're nothin'. Teachers here, they help you. They help you a lot. There, they just like, 'Whatever ... whatever you want to do.' (RA27STB:1395–1420, 1446–1454)

For Johnnie, such messages are significant not only because they suggest options, but also because they remind him to stay on the right track: "Every time I get in trouble I think about something that somebody already said ... cause I know I'm in trouble and I say, 'Well, she just said, 'Well don't do this' and I did it anyway.' So, therefore, I can be like, 'Well he was trying to really keep me out of trouble, he wasn't just talking mess to me,' like that" (RA27STC:459–468). Though teacher discourse and Johnnie's responses were undoubtedly buttressed by his observations of the local community, the point is such discourse appeared to shape Johnnie's perceptions of future possibilities and his subsequent motivation.

A final factor perhaps relevant to understanding Johnnie's willingness to invest in school is the relative stability of Huntington's local African American student population. While, as previously discussed, a wide achievement gap exists between Huntington's African American and European American youths (see chapter 4), African Americans tend to maintain their small representation at Huntington and to graduate in numbers consistent with their representation in the population. For example, between freshman and junior years, the percentage of African American youths in Johnnie's class cohort remained almost stable, falling from 5 to 4.8 percent. Similarly, looking at the two class cohorts which preceded Johnnie's, African American youths comprised, on average, 4.8 percent of their sophomore classes, and 4.6 percent of their graduating seniors classes. (Overall, as indicated in Table 2.2, the attrition of African American students from the class cohorts which preceded Johnnie's averaged 29 percent between sophomore year and graduation, compared to 23 percent for European American students.)

## POWER AND IDENTITY: PEDAGOGICAL INFLUENCES ON JOHNNIE'S "COOL" SCHOOL SELF

> It wouldn't surprise me to see him go into a regular
> class and see him get a *B*. It depends on who he gets
> for a teacher, too. Diane Ingalls, who is here, is very
> strict. And if he happened to get in her class it would
> be all over for him. He couldn't handle that. If he
> got in someone else's class who would let him do a
> little bit more of what his thing is then he might do
> fine. He has to be in the right situation. He might
> end up telling Ingalls to go stick it somewhere. I
> wouldn't put that past him. (RA063ST1:pp.5–6)
> —Social studies teacher

For the most part, Johnnie is described as being polite, highly social, and academically concerned by teachers and other adults at Huntington. In "student-centered" classrooms, where teachers work to develop relationships with students, provide one-on-one assistance, and encourage student participation, Johnnie appears especially pleasant:

*English teacher:* He's a very mature boy, I mean young man. I don't think of him in terms of being a boy. Very mannerly, somebody has instilled in him a lot of thank-you, and yes, ma'am, and that kind of behavior. (RA029ST1:217–223)

*Life science teacher:* Johnnie, very pleasant personality, both in the classroom and on the football field. .... He could come up with something pretty funny. Everybody really enjoyed him, and I think that was either football or the classroom. .... Everybody didn't appreciate his effort at times, his effort at times was from my perception not what it could have been, and that goes for both places too, in the classroom and on the football field. But he was a fun type guy. (RA057ST1:28–51)

Yet, Johnnie could look quite different in classrooms where teachers distanced themselves from students, particularly in situations where teachers demanded and exerted strict control. Highly sensitive to the ways in which adults exercise and assert power, Johnnie's "cool" school self was virtually submerged in the latter settings. In its place, a youth who looked bored, uncomfortable, and sometimes angry emerged. The way in which adults in the environment conceptualized the student-teacher relationship and exerted power were thus variables relevant to the emergence and continued existence of Johnnie's cool school self.

To illustrate this pattern, I describe Johnnie's response to two classes. The first, remedial English, represents the type of setting in which Johnnie's cool school self was often visible. Also a setting which Johnnie referred to when describing teachers who voice clear expectations for student progress, English provides a more specific portrait of speech acts and behaviors that Johnnie viewed as relevant. In the second class, pre-algebra, a different Johnnie emerged. There were no "thank-yous" or "yes, ma'ams" from the youth in this course. Pre-algebra thus illustrates some of the pedagogical factors that constrain Johnnie's ability to construct a cool school self.

### Remedial English

> Miss Ashton, she'll go all off on the board and she'll
> tell you, you know, 'If you think you can't even
> spell this word, think you're going to go in the
> English class next year?' And then she'll say well,
> she'll talk to you. She won't put you down. She'll
> talk to you and she'll go, 'Yeah, you know I love
> you. You know I want you to make something out
> of yourself, so stop messing around in class.'
> (RA27STB:1526–1537)
>
> —Johnnie Betts

Remedial English best represents a place where Johnnie's ideal school persona appeared. During the five times I observed his English class, Johnnie readily tossed out verbal definitions to vocabulary words, including "imbecile," "fidgeting," "preliminaries," and "simulate." He identified authors' uses of similes in his reading. He volunteered to read the complete sentence answers he had written as part of his short reading assignments. He was praised by his teacher for his general academic demeanor. At the same time, Johnnie moved between African American and mainstream standard English vernaculars, frequently engaging in a series of one-line insults with his African American classmate A.J., even as he worked toward academic success.

Johnnie's teacher, Wendy Ashton, organizes her curriculum around short reading activities, which students complete themselves, and novels, some of which she reads out loud. (*Where the Red Fern Grows, Of Mice and Men*, and *Someone is Hiding on Alcatraz Island* are among the novels Ashton uses.) Drawing on content from reading activities, students in Ashton's class develop vocabulary lists, write short essays, and hold frequent in-class discussions in which they are pushed to develop their descriptive abilities, make inferences, and identify various writing techniques, such as a flashback. In addition, Ashton emphasizes oral participation, auditory activities, and reading for understanding, because of her belief that the way in which many classrooms are organized impedes many students' academic success. Ashton criticizes teachers who assume their students arrive with well-developed reading skills and who do little or nothing to help them become good readers: "For instance, when I started *Of Mice and Men*, this one boy, who came from another teacher to my class, said, 'Gee Ms. Ashton, you go through things.' He said, 'When we were given this book in another class,' he said, 'all we were told to do is read the book and answer the questions she gave us on ditto sheets.' That was reading" (RA029ST2:274–283).

Ashton's classroom is organized to promote interaction, both between students and between students and the teacher. Youths sit three or four to a table; the tables are arranged in a semicircle, allowing students to see one another as well as the teacher. Ashton believes it is critical to establish relationships with and between students to earn their trust and to establish a productive working atmosphere. Describing herself as student-centered, Ashton has organized time in such a way that she is able to see and visit with students. She circulates before class begins and during work periods, visiting briefly with the students who attend. She seats quieter students who tend to fade into the woodwork in the front of the room, "So I have a lot of eye contact and I can touch them every once in awhile, just briefly touch them, to make contact with them" (RA029ST2:506–509). In addition, discussions occur frequently. Rather than waiting to be called upon, students are encouraged to respond to and build on each other's comments.

The majority of Ashton's students arrive in her course because of low reading scores. In some instances, Ashton also inherits youths who "could not make it" in general courses; frequently, these students are viewed as having behavioral problems. In general, however, while some of Ashton's students are verbal and rambunctious, she does not experience significant management difficulties. It was rare for Ashton to become angry; rarer still for her to remove a student from the classroom to spend the period in the hall. In order to achieve this balance, Ashton negotiates for attention, using affectionate teasing and humor to push students who stray from academic discourse back on track. She feels a good sense of humor and an ability to laugh with students are important to maintaining the flow in her classroom: "I think it carries me along with them. I find them funny. And they need to laugh more" (RA029ST2:492–495).

As Johnnie notes in the quote that opens this section, Ashton also pushes her students. Over five classroom periods, she pressured students who answered 'I don't know' to attempt an answer four times and to expand on their answers twenty-three times. The example below, in which Ashton encourages Johnnie to make an inference from his reading, is typical of this pattern:

*Johnnie:* I had trouble with number one.
*Ashton:* Johnnie, I want you to look at your paragraph, because the answer to that is in your paragraph. It was a hard one, but it was in your paragraph as far as how Black players differed from White players. .... Who owned the presses for each team?
*Johnnie:* Oh, okay.
*Ashton:* So what is the answer to that question honey?
*Johnnie:* Uhm, that, got to think about it. ... White people owned the press?
*Ashton:* And therefore what is the conclusion you can draw, if White people owned the presses? They weren't about to do what?
*Johnnie:* Uugh, uhm, let it out. (laughs)
*Ashton:* Let what out?
*Johnnie:* About the Black baseball players.
*Ashton:* How're you gonna say that in a complete sentence?
*Johnnie:* Uhm ...
*Ashton:* Why isn't there much current history about the Black baseball players?
*Johnnie:* Because ...
*Ashton:* Because?
*Johnnie:* Because the press was all White.

*Ashton:* Was *owned* by.
*Johnnie:* Oh, because the press was owned by Whites and ....
Reporters didn't report Black baseball leagues. (RA029ST03:p.16)

Willing to assist her students as they grapple to assemble their knowledge into more coherent understanding, Ashton does not tend to spoon-feed but rather to guide her students as they reason their way through academic problems. As Johnnie saw it, "I could understand her. I like the way she talks, she talked better to me. And she broke it down" (RA27STC:145–147). Explaining her behavior, Ashton asserts: "They're in here to learn, and I'm not going to let them—to me, I might as well let them put their head down on the table, if I let them get by with 'I don't know'" (RA029ST2:744–750). Though her students sometimes complained ("Man Ms. Ashton, you bug!"), Johnnie appeared to view Ashton's behavior as an indication of her desire for students to advance academically.

For Johnnie, who has well-developed oral skills and the desire to maintain his high-profile identity, English class appeared to be an engaging learning environment. Over the course of the five classroom sessions I observed, Johnnie volunteered sixteen answers and raised three content-related questions. He not only paid attention, but sometimes fought to participate:

[Ashton has asked the students to describe a central character from a short story they've read for homework. A.J. and Johnnie are clamoring to answer.]
*Ashton:* Okay, A.J. do you want to get in?
*A.J.:* Yea, that if he was all that warm ... junk ... he'd have a lot of friends—
*Ashton:* —What junk?
*A.J.:* Warm stuff, and all that stuff, he'd have a lot of friends, but he doesn't have no friends or nothing so I don't think he must have been.
*Johnnie:* Can I read what I had?
*A.J.:* He must be like real mean and ... Well, I mean he could be nice and everything, but I don't think he's really friendly and things.
*Donna:* He's lonely. He doesn't have friends.
[Naomi and Johnnie are clamoring to answer, their hands waving in the air.]
*Ashton:* Alright, I'd like to hear first from Naomi, then Johnnie, and then from Matt.

*Naomi:* Okay, I think he is a man that doesn't appreciate what he has. He's lonely and then he's also timid.

[Naomi, A.J., and Donna begin to argue this point and Johnnie, losing his patience, calls again for a turn.]

*Johnnie:* Let me read, let me read, let me read!

[Ashton nods her assent.]

*Johnnie:* Okay, I put 'I think he's a very lonely guy. He had no friends, and he had not enough money. He probably feels like he's left out of the world. Charlie Evans seems like a very discouraged guy.'

*Naomi:* Is he making this up? Let me see that, you didn't write all that! (RA029ST05:pp.11–12)

With much classroom social interaction revolving around academic participation, Johnnie speaks up. Able to understand Ashton's explanations and wanting to be part of the class, he participates eagerly and actively.

### Pre-Algebra

Johnnie's pre-algebra class presented a very different context than did his English class, and revealed a very different Johnnie. During the days I observed this class, Johnnie volunteered no answers. He often looked disengaged, doodling on notebook paper, poking at classmates, and tossing things surreptitiously at friends. He also appeared lost and confused, sometimes voicing his frustration aloud: "Three??!! How'd you get three?" "I did every one of them wrong. I got them all wrong."

Johnnie's teacher, Denise Singer, was young and European American. Though she declined to be interviewed, Singer did allow me to observe. During the days I attended, students completed warm-up drills consisting of simple algebraic problems (e.g., $x + 12y + 3x + y$), reviewed homework, listened to brief explanations of mathematical problem-solving strategies (e.g., "Solving Equations Using Two Properties"), and performed work at their seats. According to Johnnie, these activities were typical of general classroom practice.

Students in pre-algebra sat in rows of desks, facing forward. Singer generally stood at the front of the classroom, facing her students at all times and working from an overhead. Students were expected to remain silent during work periods and classroom explanations. Singer monitored behavior closely, and any off-task behavior was seen as highly disruptive. During the days I observed, for example, two students were sent to the discipline principal's office because they popped their gum, two others were sent for no reason that I could discern, and another student almost made the same trip after dropping a piece of chalk loudly on the chalkboard ledge. The teacher expressed frustration with her students, who struggled with relatively simple subject matter: "You're still having problems for the reason that you're not listening" (RA27ST03:p.4). Her comment to me on the first day I attended class also indicated her frustration: "Be ready. This is a horrible class."

Relaxed and engaged in English class, the Johnnie in pre-algebra appeared to strain against behavioral constraints. For one thing, rather than focusing on the task at hand, Johnnie engaged in conduct that was clearly out of line with behavioral norms:

> Singer goes to the overhead. Johnnie begins to toss a piece of chalk at the boy in front of him. He, in turn, tosses it back. They play this game stealthily, and Singer doesn't catch them.
>
> Singer moves onto reviewing the notes she gave the students yesterday. Meanwhile, Johnnie's friend, trying to return the chalk the two of them have been tossing to its place on the chalkboard ledge, drops the chalk loudly. Singer turns around eagerly and begins to write a referral. As she bends over her desk, Johnnie puts his hands in his ears and wags them at his friend. (RA27ST04:p.3)

Secondly, Johnnie did not appear polite or respectful in this class. Rather, he expressed veiled sarcasm, disdain, and even hostility in his interactions with Singer:

> The class is generally quiet as Singer turns the lights off and the overhead on. The students are supposed to work on a drill. Johnnie, however, is chatting quietly.
> *Singer:* (rising intonation) Johnnnnie?!
> *Johnnie:* (mimicking her tone exactly) Yeesss? (RA27ST03: p.4)
>
> Singer is collecting homework.
> *Johnnie:* Uh-oh, some of us didn't get it done. (RA27ST03: p.5)

Johnnie earned a *B*− in math and managed to remain in this class without once fully losing his temper, but the frustration that such an environment created in him was apparent. In a class Johnnie attended as a freshman, where norms of behavior were similar, Johnnie was not so fortunate. Arriving late to that class, Johnnie was asked to sit in the back of the room. When he protested, Johnnie was further reprimanded and ordered to leave the room. According to Johnnie, he refused this request because it was cold and he had no coat. After the teacher came to the back of the room and placed a hand on his shoulder, Johnnie bristled, allegedly calling his teacher a "faggot" and demanding his teacher remove his hand. The school's discipline principal describes the incident below:

> *Discipline principal:* Johnnie Betts, I got a referral on Johnnie Betts from a teacher that's been teaching for twenty-three years. He wrote a note that said, 'In twenty-three years,' is what he started with, 'I have never felt physically threatened as a teacher. And today I felt physically threatened. I felt that I was in jeopardy of something ill happening to me in the classroom.' .... So, and this guy [the teacher] is about 6'5", and he's not a guy that's easily intimidated. .... the credibility of this teacher is extremely high, with me anyway, and he wouldn't even write this. He's the kind of guy who never writes referrals, he handles everything himself. So it was a big deal. (RA092ST1:p.2)

Backed into a corner, Johnnie does not retreat but will assert himself even at the risk of jeopardizing his position in the school community.

The ways in which teachers wield power in their classrooms and the relationships they develop with their students affect the extent to which Johnnie can reveal the verbal, playful aspects of his "cool" school self. When these relatively well-developed aspects of Johnnie's identity become irrelevant, Johnnie becomes discouraged, bored, and less willing to take academic risks. If combined with a highly controlling environment, Johnnie may also become oppositional, struggling against attempts to control and constrain.

Given this situation, it is probably important that Johnnie encountered a contingent of teachers during his ninth-grade year, with a relatively flexible set of norms for classroom behavior. This provided Johnnie with the space necessary to develop and construct his unique classroom persona, convincing him that he could participate productively in the academic aspects of his school community. As Johnnie moved into more traditionally structured classrooms as a sophomore, he encountered a different set of conditions: students tended to work and to produce answers individually, oral participation was de-emphasized in favor of written performance, and laughter and teasing were rarely heard. In these settings, Johnnie struggled to pay attention and frequently appeared unengaged in the task at hand; nevertheless, he continued to attend regularly, to complete his homework, and to pass his courses. I often wondered what would have happened had Johnnie moved directly into such classes as a ninth grader, when his sense of academic self had not yet emerged.

## REFLECTION AND CAVEAT

Johnnie's experience offers a clear and vivid picture of how movement into a new school environment can cause a fundamental reorientation in the way in which identity is conceptualized in relationship to schooling. Johnnie's response to an environment in which he feels safe and supported and where he perceives some hope for the future serves to remind us that alienated youth might choose other options if not in a situation where doing so seems both hopeless and fruitless.

In considering Johnnie's academic transformation, it is critical to take into account the local economic situation and its probable impact on peer group norms. For example, Johnnie's academic achievement and transition to the general track were not politically charged. His African American friends did not accuse him of selling out, but rather appeared to support, even value, his academic achievements. Were the local economy not growing, were there no jobs available for high school graduates, Johnnie's peers might respond quite differently to his academic endeavors.

Still, Johnnie insisted that simple actions and words at the school level also had some influence on his transformation. Coming to his high school from an inner-city middle school in which African American youth were expected to fail, Johnnie describes the culture shock he experienced upon moving to his new environment. Much to his surprise, Johnnie found high school graduation and academic engagement expected of African American and European American youth alike. He viewed it as relevant that Huntington teachers communicate that "you have a chance to get yourself together and get on the good foot, and get on the right track." In Johnnie's case, such words were buttressed by institutional moves. By making efforts to structure Johnnie quickly into the mainstream, adults arguably communicated their belief that Johnnie could get himself together. Further, rather than belittling his academic success by disqualifying him from the honor roll because of placement in remedial courses, adults rewarded Johnnie with public recognition.

Even so, there is a disturbing underside to Johnnie's story of transformation. For one, the drop in his grade point average, as well as conversations
with some of his sophomore teachers, revealed that Johnnie struggled in his
transition to mainstream classrooms. His difficulties were exacerbated by
the premium general track teachers placed on a narrow set of cognitive
skills and behaviors. However, Johnnie's struggles also reflect his poor elementary school education and its subsequent impact on his basic academic
skills. Johnnie found it difficult to take notes, for example, not knowing
what to write down. Reading was also laborious. There was nothing in
Huntington's environment to address this issue, save remedial classrooms,
which emphasized remediation rather than acceleration. (Further, because
the difficulty and amount of work required in such courses is less challenging than that which is required in general courses, remediation may actually
contribute to transition problems as students fall further behind their peers.)
Thus, though Johnnie was encouraged to succeed, there was little present in
the environment to empower him to do so. Johnnie's frustration with this
situation was reflected in his interview discourse, which became increasingly
critical as his sophomore year progressed: "We got counselors here and
they don't even counsel you. What are they here for? We have teachers
here on the student councils and all these people here are supposed to help
you and they just sit up there in their office. .... They don't go out and see
which students are having problems. Here, like the teachers expect and
they try to help everybody. So that's what's good. As far as counseling and
helping out, they don't really do that" (RA27STEN:595–605; 624–628).

Equally important, because the speech acts Johnnie encountered were
not oriented toward altering academic differentiation at his high school or
toward the empowerment of youths of color, their long-term impact on the
school in general and Johnnie's ideology in particular were limited. As
noted in chapter 4, significant academic divisions between European American, African American, Latino, and Asian-descent youths are a prominent
feature of Huntington's environment. Johnnie's recognition of the divisions
in his environment was reflected in his discourse. On the one hand, Johnnie
critiqued teachers at Huntington, whom he felt had generally lower academic expectations for African American youth. On the other hand, Johnnie argued that Asian-descent students were smarter than Mexicans and
Blacks, citing as evidence his observation that "you don't cheat off a Mexican's or Black's paper" (RA52ST05:p.2).

Johnnie's beginning understanding of the links between student disengagement and local conditions offers the starting point necessary for

grounding conversations about societal divisions. Recall, for example, that Johnnie linked St. Louis teachers' low expectations to the local context: "…. they know in St. Louis growing up as a young teen you don't do nothing no way because that's really how it is. …. No good jobs there" (RA27STB:1459–1463). However, there were no curricular opportunities for Johnnie and his classmates to build on such personal understanding and to move toward analyzing societal factors that impede the progress of people from certain groups. Indeed, discussions concerning inequality, social stratification, and the mechanisms of power were not present in Johnnie's classrooms. Thus, though Johnnie was left changed, his is the story of individual comeback and new faith in the possibilities present in the existing system, rather than one of heightened political consciousness and collective transformative effort.

# CHAPTER 8

# Patricia Schmidt on
# Alternative Discourse

*Interviewer:* What do you think of yourself? I mean, do you identify more as a White, or a Latina, or as Chinese, or what?

*Patricia:* I ... that's one thing that sort of gets me mad that, you know on applications and stuff, they have different sections? And, I really, in my mind I'm not really White, Mexican, just one solid thing. But since, you know, my appearance looks Hispanic, I do have to put Hispanic. The one time I did put down White on my application, they go, 'Oops, you made an error,' and they erased it and put Mexican. ....

So, I don't really enjoy doing that part of the applications. But I can't really consider myself one thing. And if I say to my Mexican friends or someone, you know, people who are more Mexican than me, say that I'm White, they'll call me 'gringa,' like a White person. And if I say to a White person that I'm Mexican they'll call me a beaner. Either way, you know, you're just like stuck. So I just say, I'm a lot. When they ask me, 'What are you?' I say 'A lot.' (laughs) .... Cause I don't really believe that I'm one race. (VA17STEN:14–31, 56–72, 87–88)

—Patricia Schmidt,
sophomore student,
Maple High School

189

A striking blonde appears at the door of Yvonne Haight's counseling office. I look up, then away. It is May 1990, and Yvonne, in charge of 300 students at Maple High School, has many visitors. Some come to sign the college scroll she has in her room, others come because teachers have sent them from their rooms on referrals. This student must be here to see Yvonne.

The blonde, clad in close-fitting faded jeans, boots, and a stylish blouse, looks at me, looks at Yvonne. Yvonne swivels in her chair. "Oh, hi Patricia." I startle to alertness and look again. Under the blonde hair, there are round brown eyes that smiled at me three months ago. Then, Patricia's face was framed by brown wisps, falling from a messy brunette ponytail. "Patricia!! I didn't recognize you." "It must be the hair," laughs Patricia in response.

It was more than the new hair color. Patricia's clothing, gold jewelry, and coral lipstick had also thrown me. In February, during our first interview, she wore baggy sweats, a puffy team jacket, and little makeup or jewelry. From tousled ponytail to high-top sneakers, she'd looked much like the stereotype of the all-American tomboy. But, as Patricia emphasizes in the quote that opens this chapter, she does not like social categories. The daughter of a Mexican immigrant mother of Chinese-, French-, Portuguese-, and Spanish-descent, and an American-born father of Eastern European ancestry, Patricia resists social categories even as others, including myself as an interviewer, seek to push her into them.

Patricia's struggle goes beyond changing her hair color and adopting different dress styles. Every morning, she is one of the more than 300 students who arrive at Maple from "Northside," an area composed primarily of low-income barrios. At home, Patricia speaks both Spanish and English and spends the majority of her time with her Mexican immigrant boyfriend. At school, Patricia maintained a 3.83 GPA during her sophomore year, with a challenging academic course load, including advanced English, geometry, computer science, and second-year Spanish. In her academic achievement, Patricia is among a small group of Latino-descent youth at Maple who stand out academically. During the fall of Patricia's sophomore year, 13.5 percent of Maple's Latinos had GPAs between 3.0 and 4.0.

However, Patricia is more than someone who beats statistics. Among teachers, for example, she is known for her independence and outspokenness. Patricia was recognized for her strong desire not just to achieve but to learn: ".... even after I have my career, I'm still going to look into other fields, I'm still going to be educating myself in different things. I don't think education ever stops. You can never know enough" (VA17STD:290–297). Most notable of all, Patricia does not simply cross social borders, but works to blur them with creative flair. In both her self-presentation and her voice, Patricia resists hiding either the "schoolgirl" high-achieving aspects of her character from her Latino working-class peers, or the working-class Latina aspects of her heritage from her European American middle-class peers. "Crisscrossed by multiple identities," Patricia shows a capacity to blend cultural elements, which Rosaldo (1989) refers to as "transculturation."

## WHERE IS PATRICIA COMING FROM?

Every weekday of her sophomore year, Patricia rose at 4:30 A.M. She was dressed and ready by 4:45 to greet her boyfriend Roberto, who brought Patricia breakfast and visited with her until 5:30, when he left for his early morning job. At 6:00 A.M., Patricia left Northside, where she grew up, for the fifty-minute bus ride to Maple High School. As Patricia makes this journey, she moves across socioeconomic and cultural borders. In 1990, housing prices in Republic (Northside's major city) averaged $115,000. In comparison, housing prices in the neighborhood surrounding Maple ranged from $330,000 to several million dollars.

Northside has always been Patricia's home. Her mother, who grew up in Veracruz, Mexico, emigrated to the United States when she was twenty-six years old. Divorced three times and the mother of six children, she earned her GED at an American city college. While working as a waitress in a local cafe to support her family, she met Patricia's father. Patricia's father joined the navy immediately after graduating from a high school in Montana and returned to a local city college for vocational training after his marriage. Currently, he works as a machine distributor, while Patricia's mother stays at home. She has never worked during the marriage. Patricia and her younger brother are the last of her mother's eight children.

The play of Mexican and American cultures is a central feature of Patricia's home life. Multilingual conversations are not uncommon, as Patricia's brothers and father understand Spanish but are uncomfortable speaking the language, while Patricia's mother understands English but prefers to speak Spanish. (Patricia speaks Spanish with her mother, English with her father and brothers.) Patricia's mother has retained strong ties to her large extended family, and Patricia has fond memories of spending almost every weekend in Mexico with aunts and cousins during her elementary and middle school years:

.... the country, I don't [know], it seems peaceful, more peaceful. Even though, you know, it seems more dirty. I don't know, it's just a peaceful environment to be in. Cause when you drive there you can see all the grass and the ocean and everything. I don't know, I like it down there. .... family down there was closer. You know, they had more fun together. Activities and stuff .... everybody chipped in. With the housework and everything. (VA17STEN:244–253; 221–226)

Patricia's interest in the Mexican aspects of her heritage and her desire to maintain and improve her Spanish language skills developed during this period. Patricia, explaining why Spanish is her favorite course, referred to her early childhood experiences:

I've got a real interest in Spanish because I want to learn about it and its culture. .... It's because when I was growing up my mom and various others—well she spoke about her hometown, Veracruz, since I was little and I've been wanting to go there. So that got me interested a lot in Mexico and then a lot of my Mexican relatives, they still live in Mexico, and we used to go over there a lot and we stopped.

Then no more Mexico and then so it was like I've had this interest for a long time. It's just, I never wanted to speak— well [when I went to Mexico] I wanted to speak Spanish but I was embarrassed I would say something wrong. So since I was little I knew how to speak it and everything but I just didn't want to. (VA17STC:18–20; 246–281)

Patricia views her Spanish course as a means to develop the Latina aspects of her transcultural identity, a means to improve her Spanish language skills and thereby gain the confidence necessary to display the linguistic aspects of her heritage when she crosses the Mexican border.

Aspects of Patricia's home life also reflect her mother's Mexican upbringing and values. In particular, Patricia's mother expects her children to place the family before self-interest (two of Patricia's older siblings give her mother half of their paychecks to help support the family) and asks Patricia, rather than her brothers, to stay at home to help her with the housework and baby-sit her niece. On the other hand, independence and self-reliance are supported by Patricia's American-born father. According to Patricia, these differences are reflected in her parents' varied cultural expectations for proper female adolescent behavior:

My mom, she sort of got mad at my dad because he lets me do what I want. And she—my mom—told him, 'A Mexican dad would never do this.' And my dad did not like it for anything! He said, 'This isn't a Mexican family, remember? You didn't marry a Mexican, you married me.' He goes, 'I want to raise people the way I want to. And I want to—I trust my daughter.' So, that's like the main thing that ever happened with my parents. .... Maybe it might be true but he didn't like it for nothing! (VA17STEN:412–426)

Trying to satisfy her mother's demands, while at the same time developing her independence, has been difficult for Patricia her first two years of high school.

I don't want to stay home! You know, I'm at that age where I want to go out. But, I clean around the house and I help her with the house and everything. And I feel like, you know, I help her with the house and everything, and I should have that privilege to go out since I already helped. .... She likes to stay at home just sitting there. Just sitting there! Not doing nothing.

But, I don't know, maybe it's one of those Spanish traditions, where the girl stays in. And I just, that's what I think most of it is, that she grew up in a family that girls stay home, guys go do whatever you want to do. But I don't know, it just gets me frustrated, because you know, it's the United States. You have certain—you know, it's not like that. You know, equal, equality! And I'm just frustrated, God! (VA17STD2:816–849)

While it is clear Patricia values many aspects of her Mexican heritage, she criticizes and resists traditions which circumscribe her movement and status, claiming what she views as the contemporary U.S. vision of the female role.

Patricia describes her parents as consistent advocates of her educational efforts. During her elementary years, Patricia recalls her father and mother quizzing her on spelling and vocabulary and praising her academic achievements. Patricia's father still readily contacts the school if she runs into difficulties or if he feels she has been treated unfairly: "My dad, he calls—he called Miss Haight (Patricia's counselor) about the back injury [I had], about the grades, he wasn't satisfied either, he thought I deserved more and then they discussed it" (VA17STC:1396–1402). Because neither of Patricia's parents has an advanced education, they have become increasingly unable to assist her with her advanced schoolwork: "…. they don't really help me in my studies. Cause I'm really—in my studies, I'm independent. I've become very independent, unless I really, really need the help" (VA17STC:1373–1377). However, within her family, Patricia can look to her stepbrother Martin, who graduated from Maple and attends a local state university, for support. Through her ninth-grade year, Martin helped Patricia with math, while she, in exchange, helped type his essays for college. In addition, it continues to remain clear to Patricia that her parents expect much from her:

> …. they expect a little bit more out of me than the rest, my brothers and sisters, they always really did. And sometimes I just get frustrated. Like when they saw the Cs and they started yelling at me and I got mad, because I was trying and, well, I knew I could do better, but I was putting my effort into it. And I was really mad, because I remember when my brothers and sisters got Cs on their report cards they didn't really mind. 'That's good, at least you didn't get an F.' And they told me, 'What's wrong with these Cs, why aren't they As?' (VA17STA:698–735)

As Patricia notes above, she and Martin stand out in the family for their academic achievements. Of Patricia's stepsisters, the oldest lives in Mexico and operates a store, the second dropped out of college during her first year to marry into the military, and the third has borne three children and lives on public assistance. Patricia has never met her oldest stepbrother, but believes he went to college. A second stepbrother works in Adobe Viejo and is estranged from the family.

A review of Patricia's early school record provides insight into her parents' high expectations. Through elementary school, teachers cited Patricia's excellent attitude and academic ability: "She readily accepts responsibility for completing daily assignments and is eager to help others," commented her first-grade teacher. "What an excellent young lady to have in class!! I expect great things to continue to happen to Patricia" added her third-grade instructor. Patricia's CTBS scores also reflect steady educational progress. Upon entering elementary school in kindergarten, she tested in the 45th percentile in language and the 72nd percentile in mathematics. By the end of her sixth-grade year, these scores had increased to the 88th percentile in math, the 72nd percentile in language, and the 64th percentile in reading. In third grade, Patricia was identified to participate in GATE (Gifted and Talented Education). In middle school, she maintained a 3.53 GPA and received sixteen "excellent," three "good," and four "satisfactory" marks in citizenship over a two-year period. Her CTBS scores in seventh grade again reflect improvement: Patricia scored in the 99th percentile in mathematics, the 95th percentile in language, and the 77th percentile in reading.

In sum, Patricia arrives at Maple with a positive orientation toward aspects of both her Mexican and European American heritages and successful elementary and middle school histories. Navigating varied cultural demands on a daily basis within her own family, Patricia is also accustomed to coping with demands from differing social worlds.

## A "REBEL" WITH A CAUSE: BLURRING SOCIAL BORDERS

> The rebel. (laughs) They call me the rebel because
> I'm always alone .... most of the time I'm alone
> unless somebody walks up to me and starts talking
> to me. The rebel. (VA17STEN:895–899)

> My self-esteem is up there ... If I don't like some-
> thing—how I look or something—I'll just work
> around what I have until I like it. And that's it.
> (VA17STC:1091–1097)
>
> —Patricia Schmidt

Patricia's transcultural identity cannot be easily categorized. As her friends aptly assert, Patricia is a rebel—resisting strict allegiance either to Latino working-class or European American middle-class peers. Patricia cannot be called a "sellout," for she does not reject or try to hide the Latina aspects of her heritage, nor does she spend all of her time at school with European Americans. At the same time, while Patricia chats and jokes with peers from her neighborhood, she does not fit in with a group and does not identify any peer at school as a close friend. As a rebel, Patricia is independent, yet not antisocial; uncompromising, when it comes to her education. As a rebel, Patricia will sit quietly in class, yet suddenly rise to challenge the ideas and assumptions of her peers. As a rebel, Patricia refuses to hide either her multiethnic heritage or her allegiance to Maple High. A member of her high school swim team and the top fund-raiser in her class during ninth grade, Patricia also readily speaks Spanish in hallways and classrooms and dresses in a style typical of young women from her community. Patricia's "rebel" self reveals itself both in her self-presentation and in the voice she adopts for social interactions.

The self was visually displayed in the stark black hearts that decorated her bright yellow notebook. Here, Patricia played with words from two cultures to proclaim her romantic attachment: Patricia con Roberto, Patricia and Robert, Patrice y Roberto.

It was aurally displayed, as Patricia moved without inhibition between English and Spanish, while speaking with Latino peers in an advanced English classroom dominated by European American peers.

It was displayed in the interests Patricia expressed during class. During a work period in Spanish, for example, she moved across the room to sit with Latino peers who wanted her to participate in their assessment of the various cars ("cruisers") displayed in *Lowrider* magazine. Later, she moved back to her seat to continue her seat work, resisting her friends' requests that she stay: "I want to finish my work."

Patricia's rebel identity was also present in our interviews, both in terms of content and in form:

> *Interviewer:* Do you ever feel like you kind of have to change the way you act around certain friends ... Do you have to put on one face for some people, and another face for other people?
> *Patricia:* No, I really don't think I have more than one face. I, you know, they're all—I really think of it as if they don't like me for who I am, *I ain't gonna change for 'em.* It's just me. And maybe in time I might evolve into something else, but, until that time I ain't just gonna snap my fingers and say, 'Hey, start acting like this cause that's how, the way they want to see you.' That's just what I plan to do; what I want to do. (VA17STEN:763–784, emphases mine)

Patricia not only emphasizes her independence, but uses speech patterns characteristic of her community, to add force to her words. Just as she won't "snap her fingers" and behave as her peers expect, she does not move into mainstream standard English vernacular simply because a European American woman from a university is interviewing her.

Patricia's teachers' comments indicate that her independent thinking shines through in the classroom as well. "I had a student teacher the first semester, so I could sit back and observe. And within two days, I could tell Patricia was a top student. She'll kind of sit back and watch and then just ... (*Bam!?*) Yeah!" says Patricia's advanced English teacher. "She writes beautifully. Her communication skills are way above her level. .... She is a fine advocate of other people, as well as herself," adds another. "I've talked to Patricia some about who she hangs out with, and she describes herself as a loner. But, she's not antisocial. She talks with people in the class and she gets along with all the students. I'd describe her as very independent," adds Patricia's Spanish teacher. From Patricia's comments, it appears that even her P.E. teacher views her as a leader: "…. every day it's like I'm just standing there waiting for the exercises, and he goes 'Patricia, get up there and lead them.' I go 'Again!?'" (VA17STD:901–911). In short, Patricia has not only mastered the competencies required for success in a wide variety of classrooms, but she stands out among her peers as a youth who possesses the confidence and assertiveness necessary to articulate a strong sense of self.

Patricia's rebel persona is particularly noteworthy in light of the fact that she experiences pressure to conform, most notably from male peers who are less academically successful than she:

> *Interviewer:* I wanted to know if you ever got a hard time for being a woman who is so successful. From any of your friends.
> *Patricia:* Ohhhh. A hard time? I heard, let's see, I guess they were playing around, but in a way, it was like, it's like ironic I guess you would say. Because they used to tell me, 'Oh, look at Miss Executive, getting all these high grades.' But, you know, they were actually trying [to say], you know, Miss Smarty Pants. I, I really don't care. I don't really care if, you know, they say it. I, hey, at least they know, at least I'm doing something about my life, you know. Like yesterday, I saw some friends with some report cards I couldn't *believe.* I could not, you know. *D*s, *F*s, straight down the line.
>
>   I guess people—this is what I noticed yesterday. People don't really expect me to be smart. You know, they don't see me as a smart person. …. They don't see me as someone, that, you know, that would get good grades. And they told me that, and I was *laughing.* I go, 'Not all blondes are bimbos, you know. My roots are brown.' …. And, I guess when they find out, it's like all of a sudden, they start calling me 'schoolgirl.' And then they forget about it, and then when report [card] time comes again, schoolgirl comes back. (VA17STEN:977–1059)

Patricia's peers suggest she is taking on behaviors and characteristics of another social class by calling her "Miss Executive." At the same time, it also appears Patricia does not fit their stereotype of the high-achieving sellout.

For example, Patricia maintains so many aspects of her home/neighborhood ways of interaction that these same peers frequently "forget" about her high academic achievement.

As Carla Chávez (see chapter 4) demonstrates, one strategy for crossing social borders is to play different roles in different settings—taking on the behaviors and language of European American peers in classrooms where they form the majority, dropping these behaviors when with other peers or at home. However, Patricia rejects this strategy: "I don't, personally I wouldn't want to be something that I'm not. I wouldn't, you know, try to play the role. Unless it's in a play" (VA17STEN:571–574). Her propensity to assert a "rebel" identity stems from both personal preference and a political agenda. First, Patricia appears to derive aesthetic enjoyment from playing with the feminine identity she projects:

> *Interviewer:* What about you Patricia? Do you have different looks?
> *Patricia:* Well yeah, I guess I do. …. If I feel like getting dressed up I'll dress up but, if I don't, if I don't care, I just [don't], you know. Like one time I was going to go to [the store]. I have my pajamas on? And I just put a pair of sweats [on] …. I just put on a pair of sweat pants! I still had my pajama shirt. …. that's like the look when I don't care. (laughs)
>     …. sometimes like, I have—there's like a look I want to get. You know how 'Pretty Woman?' …. I *love* that. And one time I had this outfit on, it was a black skirt, with like white, with like a ivory white little jacket? And I had my hat on. And I had my hair—you know how she wears her hat, that one hat, when she puts it on top with the ponytail? That's how my hair was. ….
>     And sometimes I like to wear tight things, you know. I guess my mom calls them taco dresses.
> *Interviewer:* Taco dresses?
> *Patricia:* Yeah, cause you know they just hug? You know, when they hug your body? And they're like spandex. And I still—sometimes I just want to wear that. And sometimes I like to be 'Pretty Woman.' And sometimes I just don't care. (VA17STEN:684–697, 709–729, 742–752)

Patricia moves, with ease and confidence, from the casual look she adopted during our first interview to the upper-class attire promulgated in the movie "Pretty Woman" to a sexy street look.

Second, Patricia is driven by her desire to challenge conventional notions concerning people from her community. From Patricia's perspective, the socioeconomic differences between Northside and Maple communities are translated into a set of negative expectations about what it means to be from her section of town. As such, a false Northside personality is promoted by Northside and Maple residents alike:

> *Patricia:* .... down there they don't really—nobody notices you.
> *Interviewer:* You mean Northside?
> *Patricia:* [nods and continues] Cause they don't want to be expecting too much. They just know you're there, it's not going to impress them. .... They don't give you credit for who you are. You're just there, cause like really if an older person sees you walking down the street, they go, 'Oh another low life.' (VA17STC:1183–1210)

> I guess I believe that, you know, the kids up here [from the neighborhood that surrounds Maple] have a stereotype of the kids that like get bussed in. You know, they're from Northside, they're gangs, they're violence. You know, they always do this. I don't really like it but I guess you can't really change someone's thoughts unless they want to change their thoughts and stuff. (VA17STD:1715–1724)

Patricia is highly critical of her peers' views on gangs, seeing them as one-dimensional and unjust: "... you don't see no vandalism around this school. If they [gang members] wanted to vandalize the school, they wouldn't wait until all the adults weren't in the way. .... They just want to be with their friends. But they don't do any harm to nobody" (VA17STD:1154–1160; 1171–1173). At the same time, Patricia's awareness of negative expectations fuels her desire to succeed in order to make a statement about residents from her community:

> I just want to get an education, cause I want to go—I want to break the line between, you know, like Northside and the whole—it's like two different kinds of communities. Like I just want to go over that line and show people that not all people where I live are low. They [say people where I live] have lowlife standards and it's not true. (VA17STC:461–474)

In sum, Patricia views educational achievement not simply as a means for personal advancement, but as a political act. Her individual achievement will help show others that their visions of Northside residents are false.

Patricia succeeds in asserting a multifaceted identity, which combines elements of her Mexican, working-class, and European American heritages with school-based behaviors she finds appropriate. In her use of language, self-presentation, and choice of conversations, Patricia has crafted a public persona her peers find difficult to pin down. As she presents her rebel self, Patricia also asserts her commitment to the idea that social categories, defined and enacted in interactions with others, are open for negotiation.

Because of the individualism embedded in much of Patricia's rebel discourse, it is easy to overlook the social matrix in which she operates. Yet, from the time Patricia entered high school, she has been exposed to significant speech acts that directly support aspects of her ideology by challenging theories that equate a Northside persona with academic failure. Further, because these speech acts have been linked to a set of strategies that confront the workings of sorting mechanisms at the institutional level, they have fostered the creation of social and psychological space conducive to the presentation and assertion of Patricia's transcultural self.

## SIGNIFICANT SPEECH ACTS WITH STRUCTURAL CONSEQUENCES: CREATING SPACE FOR PATRICIA

> We don't really have a solution to the problems, we
> don't really address problems in that way. We're
> interested in finding the components on which we
> can start to build solutions to the problems.
> (VA04501:51–57)
>
> —PEP teacher

To understand the existence and implications of the speech acts Patricia encounters during her school day, one must first appreciate Maple's sociohistorical context. Once viewed as one of the "big schools," "one of the best in the 1960s," Maple is now defined by its faculty as a school with "problems." Declining enrollment and drops in indicators of academic achievement, in conjunction with demographic change, form the basis for teachers' and administrators' perceptions.

Maple, located adjacent to one of the wealthiest areas in California, has changed markedly since its opening in the late 1950s. Then, Maple served primarily European American, primarily upper-middle-class students. However, as many of the area's wealthiest families moved south with increasing growth, a new high school was constructed. Completed in 1982, this school drew the majority of its students from surrounding neighborhoods. With this came a decline in one of the more politically salient indicators of school performance. Between the 1981–82 and 1982–83 school years, the percentage of Maple students taking the SAT dropped from 37.2 percent to 30.4 percent; average verbal and math scores dropped from 446 and 521 to 430 and 500, respectively. While the percentage of Maple students taking the SAT eventually returned to its former level (38.5 percent by 1987–88), performance indicators have decreased still further; scores averaged 405 on the verbal and 460 on the mathematics portion of this exam during 1987–88.

These changes have had a substantial impact on Maple's student body composition and a devastating impact on its enrollment. In 1980, Maple's total population was almost 2,000, with European Americans comprising 71.8 percent of the student body. In 1990–91, Maple's enrollment was just 950, less than half that of 1982. Youth of color, the majority of them (47 percent) Latino, made up 60 percent of the population. Almost 40 percent, like Patricia, were transported from Northside to attend the school. Of these, 23 percent were limited English-proficient (LEP) students and 29 percent qualified for free lunches. By 1986, Maple ranked fifteenth out of twenty district schools with regard to parents' educational background. Students, along with adults, are aware of Maple's changed reputation. As one student from Northside expressed, "We feel kind of down, because so many students from this area went to another school and they don't like this school, [they] make it seem kind of dumb. 'You guys are dumb to go to that school,' and 'They're not teaching there'" (VA14STC:616–622).

Maple's history, like that of Explorer's, provides a frame of reference for many of its adults, who compare and contrast the Maple that was with the Maple that exists today:

> *Teacher:* .... the teachers here are used to teaching White, middle-class students. It is really hard for a lot of them to adjust. An underlying attitude on the part of many teachers is that the minority kids are the problem. (VA00201:122–135)
> *Vice principal:* We have a school with declining enrollment, a school to the south that took the best, and we are not a magnet. Maple is considered a leftover school. (VA070001:136–141)

During interviews with thirty-five teachers, administrators, and staff (conducted by CRC staff in 1988–89), thirteen characterized their students as lazy and/or unmotivated, eleven characterized their students as lacking basic academic skills, and ten characterized their students as lacking parental support. In six cases, negative characteristics were linked explicitly to a Latino or minority background, with teachers asserting generalizations such as, "The Hispanic kids can't read dialect or decode," "What we have bussed in is not the same thing intellectually," and "The parents of these kids don't support us. It's all too far away" (VA01601:138–139; VA02701:58–59; VA04001:130–132).

In reaction to this discourse, a small but significant number of school personnel have banded together to resist the dominant definitions that permeate their school environment. Based on their belief that Northside students face borders that are structural as well as socioeconomic, these faculty and counselors have organized a variety of efforts designed to undermine institutional inequalities and disciplinary technologies that work to impede youths of color from succeeding academically. The most significant of these efforts is Maple's Personal Effort for Progress (PEP) program, which operates as a four-year, regularly scheduled class. Patricia has been enrolled in PEP since entering Maple in the ninth grade. In its design and operations, PEP can be characterized as an alternative discursive system, comprised of significant speech acts and practices which are designed to affect and challenge dominant ideas about Northside adolescents. As the program director explains, "I tell people around here who think Black and Hispanic students aren't going to achieve to walk into my room, and you see stereotypes dying all around you" (VA058ST1: 108–112).

PEP is an academic enrichment program. The program targets low-income students and youths of color who come from middle school as mid-level academic achievers, students like Sonia Gonzales (see chapter 5) who earned Bs and Cs in middle school. (Patricia's outstanding academic record is not typical of program enrollees; her parents asked that she be enrolled in PEP due to her older brother's success in the program.) As of the 1990–91 school year, ninety-eight students—eighty-eight of them youths of color—were enrolled at Maple, making up over 10 percent of the student body. PEP's goal is to empower traditionally underrepresented students to attend the University of California school system. Thus far, it has been successful. Between 1980 and 1988, for example, 99 percent of the 220 students graduating from PEP enrolled in post-secondary education; of these, 89 percent enrolled in four-year colleges or universities.

As a disciplinary system, PEP is organized to redefine program participants as college-bound and to assert the message that people of color can and do participate in significant intellectual activity. Norms and expectations, curriculum and social organization, combine to communicate these messages. First, program requirements and classroom atmosphere communicate the expectation that all PEP participants will engage in challenging academic work. All students are required to enroll in at least one advanced course; over the course of the year, the program director communicates regularly with students, discussing their academic triumphs and difficulties. With regard to essays completed as part of the PEP curriculum (see the following paragraph for further explanation), students earning less than a *C* redo their work, revising their papers with the aid of tutors until they are deemed worthy of an *A* or a *B*. Classroom decor conveys the idea that this is all part of preparation for eventual college attendance. As one program enrollee describes, "When you walk into that class you see all kinds of insignias or like initials of the colleges and like once you step into that class you know you're talking about college." College counseling is also a central aspect of the curriculum, contributing to this message. According to Patricia, these and other factors combine to make program norms and expectations explicit:

> *Interviewer:* What about PEP, what do they expect of you?
> *Patricia:* They expect you to go to college! Definitely! They expect you to get good grades cause they're there. You know, if there's something, an assignment you don't understand, they're there to help you, so they expect you to get good grades. (VA17STB:1517–1526)

Referring specifically to the behavior of the program director, Patricia laughed: "Mr. Berger, he pressures everybody into getting good grades. That's just—I guess that's his job" (VA17STD:893–896).

Amplifying its message, PEP employs a curriculum that both supports students' academic development and communicates the significant intellectual role played by people of color in America. Over a period of four years, students work their way through an increasingly difficult writing curriculum. Developed by the program director in collaboration with two of Maple's advanced English teachers, the curriculum centers on ten common writing techniques: autobiography, short story, description, explanation, compare/contrast, cause and effect, problem solving, evaluation, analysis, and persuasion. To demonstrate each technique, students are provided with "model passages"—many by writers of color. A brief biographical sketch follows each model passage. For example, as they prepared to write an essay that incorporated themes of cause and effect, Patricia and her class-mates considered the following model passage from "Letter from a Birmingham Jail," by Martin Luther King, Jr.:

> .... segregation distorts the soul and damages the personality. It gives the segregator a false sense of superiority and the segregated a false sense of inferiority. To use the words of Martin Buber, the great Jewish philosopher, segregation substitutes an "I-it" relationship for the "I-thou" relationship, and ends up relegating persons to the status of things. So segregation is not only politically, economically, and sociologically unsound, but it is morally wrong and sinful.

> *A Closer Look*: Martin Luther King, Jr. (1929–1968), winner of the 1964 Nobel Peace Prize, was an African American Baptist minister who led the civil rights movement in the United States. His nonviolent approach to his quest for racial harmony contrasts with his powerful literary voice. Other works by Martin Luther King, Jr. include: *Why Can't We Wait, The Trumpet of Conscience, Where Do We Go From Here: Chaos and Community.*

Each "model passage" is followed by an analysis of how the author uses a particular grammatical or stylistic technique to make his or her point:

> *Control*: Note King's use of the coordinating conjunction "and" and "but" in the underlined sentence above. The word "and" is used to connect the series of adverbs "politically," "economically," and "sociologically." The word "but" is used to connect the clauses, "So segregation is not only politically, economically and sociologically unsound," and "it is morally wrong and sinful." In your writing, use at least one coordinating conjunction to link words, phrases, clauses, or sentences.

Because sophisticated technical skills are linked explicitly to specific authors and diverse models of excellence are employed, the curriculum communicates the idea that excellence is manifested in a variety of ways by authors of all ethnic and racial backgrounds.

A third manner in which PEP communicates its message concerning possibilities and capabilities is by making use of older students and graduates, who demonstrate the effects of the program to younger students. Collaboration is a program norm, and because students are not grouped by grade level, seniors and juniors not only work alongside Patricia and her peers, but occasionally help them with work during designated tutorial periods. Amplifying this message, and providing more extensive academic support, recent graduates of the program, many of them youths of color who are attending state colleges in the area, are employed as tutors in the classroom. Two such program graduates work in the classroom each period, assisting individuals or groups of individuals with work. Classmates also are encouraged to work together; students sit four to a table and pair up when working on similar assignments.

PEP's academic impact on an individual level is revealed both in the numbers of students it prepares for college and its affect on grade point averages. (District-wide, PEP students earning GPAs of 2.0 or above increased from 74 percent, prior to enrollment, to 81 percent after enrollment.) However, because PEP's speech acts are partially communicated through practices that affect course enrollment, the character of academic differentiation also has been affected at Maple, impacting the patterns that often emanate from sorting technologies. As mentioned previously, each PEP student is required to take at least one advanced course (many take more). The impact of this can be discerned by considering comparable tracking statistics. For example, though Latinos and African Americans at Maple are underrepresented in advanced courses, the magnitude of their underrepresentation is far smaller than at Explorer or Huntington (see Table 2.1). In fall 1990, for example, Latino students made up 33.2 percent of Maple's fluent English-speaking population, and comprised 24 percent of its accelerated English classes. Thus, at Maple, fluent English-speaking Latinos were 72.3 percent as likely to take advanced English courses as one would expect, given their enrollment. This compares to figures of 33.3 percent at Explorer and 55.2 percent at Huntington. Statistics for African Americans are similar: these youth were 76.4 percent as likely to take advanced English courses as one would expect, given enrollment, compared to 31.9 percent at Explorer and 67.2 percent at Huntington. This pattern repeats itself when enrollments in advanced science and math courses are compared across the three schools.

As PEP devotes classroom time to college awareness and counseling activities, it also may play an important role in shaping school statistics on fulfillment of the University of California's (UC's) entrance requirements. During Patricia's sophomore year, for example, 14.1 percent of Latino students and 22.2 percent of African American students graduating from Maple met UC's requirements. When attrition rates are taken into account, 9 per-

cent of Latino sophomores and 16 percent of African American sophomores from the two class cohorts preceding Patricia's met these requirements
(see Table 2.2). While these figures are not particularly encouraging, they
compare favorably with those figures from schools with similar demographics. At Explorer, with attrition taken into account, 4 percent of Latino
and 10 percent of African American sophomores met these requirements.
Similarly, at Huntington, 4 percent of Latino and 5 percent of African
American sophomores did so.

For Patricia, enrollment in PEP has both political ramifications relevant to the assertion of a "rebel" persona and positive personal consequences. First, on a daily basis, Patricia is surrounded by other Northsiders
who are striving to achieve academic success, not only as she attends PEP
class (where Patricia was one of twenty-three youths of color enrolled) but
also as she moves into advanced classrooms. When Patricia went to English
class, for example, she was not isolated but rather one of thirteen youths of
color, out of a class of thirty-three students. Of those in advanced English
class, I recognized four who were from Patricia's particular PEP period. In
contrast to the classrooms attended by Carla Chávez (see chapter 4), Patricia's conversations in English ranged from the academic to the social, as
she and her friends moved between Spanish and English. Thus, manifestations of ethnicity were quite visible in the classroom:

> Students are working in groups, discussing a project they are
> doing on different authors.
> *Erica:* [to Patricia] Qué libro leyiste? (What book did you read?)
> *Patricia: The Color Purple.*
> *Erica:* What?
> *Patricia: The Color Purple.* Joyce me lo dijo. (Joyce told me about
> it.)
>
> *Diego:* Ey Patricia. Tenga un coche su novio? (Does your
> boyfriend have a car?)
> *Patricia:* Sí. (Yes.)
> *Diego:* What kind?
> *Patricia:* Es un Torres. (It's a Torres.) (VA17ST01:pp.5–6)

When I accompanied Patricia, she walked with PEP classmates during
passing periods, worked with PEP peers in class, and chatted with PEP
youths during lunchtime. In sum, while Patricia faces verbal criticism
from some Northside peers and disempowering stereotypes from mid-

dle-class students as she asserts her rebel identity, she also finds support for the academic aspects of this persona from peers in her environment.

Second, with neither of her parents having attended a four-year college, PEP has provided Patricia with a means to gain valued information, particularly about postsecondary educational opportunities:

.... they have these college videos, videos about different colleges, and you get to see the campuses, instead of going all the way out in la-la land. It's right there on tape. So you get to see the campuses and you get to hear about the programs and stuff .... and Mr. Berger discusses colleges also with us. (VA17STD:1417–1435)

Patricia's knowledge of the system has increased noticeably since she entered high school. For example, despite her excellent academic record, Patricia said in the middle of ninth grade she planned to go to a trade school and learn a skill that would enable her to pay her way through a four-year college. However, by the end of her sophomore year, Patricia realized scholarships were a possibility. With this, she set her sights on applying directly to four-year state and private universities upon graduation:

Every once in awhile they [my parents] ask me—my dad asks me about college. 'Which one do you want to go to?' and that. And you know, I told him either UC Adobe Viejo or Adobe Viejo State. And he was like, 'How do you expect to get there?' And I go, 'Good grades, scholarships, grants if I can. Financial aid.' (VA17STD:979–986)

Arguably, Patricia's access to such information has been important, not only because it has expanded her vision and increased her sense of efficacy, but also because it has increased her ability to direct and manage her future. In contrast to Carla Chávez (see chapter 4), who must listen to European American- and Asian-descent students for information about college, and has no means by which to assess the validity of the information she receives, Patricia can maintain her independence and demonstrate that she, like her peers, understands the workings of the system.

For Patricia, this latter aspect of PEP's impact has also been augmented and complemented by exposure to other support mechanisms in the environment. Maple has involved itself in a statewide consortium that focuses on informing incoming ninth and tenth graders about the classes they need to take to enter the UC system. In eleventh grade, students are also given assistance with college admissions tests, financial aid, and college applications. As a result of meetings with consortium personnel, Patricia arranged her classes in a manner more consistent with her goals. Upon entering Maple in ninth grade, for example, Patricia was enrolled in Algebra 1, first-year Spanish, advanced English, advanced world history, PEP, and P.E. As a sophomore, due to her interests in applied fields requiring knowledge of math or science, Patricia began computer science classes. Later that year, she also became interested in medicine. When Patricia met with consortium personnel as a sophomore, she expressed her interests. Noting Patricia had not taken science during her ninth- or tenth-grade years, personnel strongly recommended that she take biology during summer school so she could take physics as a senior. Patricia followed this advice, beginning advanced chemistry as a high school junior.

## REFLECTION AND CAVEAT

Patricia crafts a public "rebel" identity that blends behaviors and speech patterns characteristic of her working-class barrio and middle-class school communities. Aspects of her multiple worlds are visible in many of her interactions; even as Northside peers see Patricia's schoolgirl behaviors, youths from the Maple neighborhood see manifestations of Patricia's Northside identity. Based on her experiences with Mexican family and friends, European American father and teachers, Patricia cannot declare allegiance to one group: "I value all of the different things equally, it's not one more than the other. I can't see myself picking one thing out" (VA17STEN: 1244–1247).

I have argued that aspects of Patricia's rebel identity are enabled by significant speech acts that comprise the ideology of a program oriented toward the academic empowerment of low-income youths and students of color. PEP's speech acts, enacted through its explicit norms and expectations, curriculum, and a support network, have been employed to combat messages that emanate from disciplinary technologies and beliefs at Maple High School. As Patricia's PEP teacher insists his pupils enroll in advanced courses and provides them with access to cultural capital, he narrows the knowledge gap that may exist between students with identical grades and test scores. At the same time, because PEP's policies impact the character of academic differentiation at Maple and because PEP helps adolescents develop mutually supportive peer networks, it also supports Patricia's ability to assert the Northside aspects of her identity in mainstream cultural contexts. Thus,

PEP helps reduce the isolation that can render youths of color like Patricia silent and/or dependent, marginalized even as they participate in academic courses.

At the same time, even as efforts like PEP challenge dominant categorical meanings, it is important to note that a rationale for ignoring other parts of the environment is provided, distracting attention from salient issues. First, for example, while Maple employs some Latino and African American faculty, in general, students transported from Northside encounter adults who differ from them in terms of class and cultural background. By the end of her sophomore year, for example, Patricia had had just two teachers of color, out of a total of twelve. The potential importance of diverse adult role models for youths like Patricia can be seen in her interview discourse. For example, when discussing her favorite teacher, a male Latino, Patricia emphasized his ability to project an identity that manifested markers of both Mexican heritage and professional success: "He's got this real Mexican look, he likes nice things. He dresses real nice for a teacher, and expensive. (Laughs) .... He cares about his job, his students, and especially the way he looks" (VA17STC:111–129).

Second, with PEP being a separate program, and with PEP enrollees adapting readily to the academic and behavioral demands of their teachers in mainstream classrooms, it becomes easier for teachers to ignore their curricular and pedagogical practices. For example, data on Maple's suspension and grades indicate that teachers experience relatively more difficulty negotiating for the attention of African Americans and Latinos. (Students from both groups are more likely to be suspended than their European American and Asian-descent peers; Latino and African American youths are also disproportionately represented among those earning *D*s and *F*s, particularly during their ninth- and tenth-grade years.) Yet, as one teacher describes, some faculty at Maple resist frank discussions of strategies to address these gaps, feeling youths from these groups have already received ample attention:

> Let me tell you what happened in a meeting I was in last week. You know the district has made a commitment to empowering the African American male and the Latina female. And they were sitting there talking about this, and a guy sitting behind me said, 'God, haven't we given them enough?! What more do they want?'" (VA059ST1:122–131)

In sum, even as PEP challenges social categories, it may work to silence discussion and examination of more basic features of the school, including academic tracking, classroom pedagogy, and curriculum. One PEP director argued strongly that the program should not have to exist, in that the types of discourse and encouragement present in her classroom should be present in all classrooms. Yet, teachers do not come to the PEP classroom for ideas as much as they view the program as a solution to their school's problems.

Third and finally, with PEP functioning as a separate enrichment program, it may perpetuate the notion that Northsiders suffer from deficits, even as it generates discourse about possibilities and capabilities. Because one must be special to belong (low income or minority), PEP enrollees are defined as "different." In some cases, as the program director notes, this works to generate anger about the special attention received by individuals from this group: "I sometimes have to fend off people who believe the program might be an extravagant expense. Not so much here in the school but when I go out and people find out what I do and then find out it's focused on minorities" (VA058ST1:114–120). In others, it provides a reason for European Americans to question the validity of the Northside presence in their classrooms: "It's supposedly, quote, 'advanced English class,' but the students in there, are not supposed to be—should not be in advanced English class. You know, I mean they're just dumb. They're straight stupid students .... most of the class isn't even—it's a very Hispanic class. And the people are not qualified to be in that classroom. It's not because they're Hispanic, it's just that they shouldn't be in there" (VA20STC:484–494, 534–538).

Nonetheless, however, PEP does challenge the divisions and meanings that have come with desegregation, generating alternative discourse, which is opposed to commonsense notions that permeate the larger institutional environment. Because of PEP, Patricia navigates a context where meanings are challenged by a significant number of students. It is in this sense that Patricia's school experience differs from that of individuals like Sonia Gonzales (see chapter 5) and Carla Chávez (see chapter 4). Patricia finds space and opportunity for her resistance to become part of a greater collective statement about the capabilities of adolescents from her community. She is left with options, better able to publicize an identity that goes against the mainstream.

# PART V

# Epilogue

CHAPTER 9

# Epilogue

This book has considered the making and molding of ethnic and racial identities in varied curricular settings. Moving first from literature which suggests that school and classroom-level factors influence the behaviors and ideology of diverse students, I considered the perspectives of fifty-five high school adolescents, who named specific factors they considered relevant to manifestations of opposition and engagement. From here, I looked closely at six students in varied school settings, delving more deeply and specifically into the formation of identities. Consistent with previous research, individual's experiences suggest strong links between conceptualizations of identity and engagement in school. At the same time, the data suggest that dominant anthropological and sociological analyses of students' responses to school are overly narrow and limiting. First, it is apparent that "opposition" is not necessarily synonymous with academic failure, accommodation is not the sole route to academic success. Rather, opposition can be communicated in various and multiple ways. For example, Marbella, Patricia, and Johnnie participated in the academic life at their schools, but at the same time asserted unconventional identities which challenged and subverted the existing power structure. This is a type of opposition similar to that described by bell hooks, as she speaks of African American filmmakers:

> When most black people in the United States first had the opportunity to look at film and television, they did so fully aware that mass media was a system of knowledge and power reproducing and maintaining white supremacy. To stare at the television, or mainstream movies, to engage its images, was to

213

engage its negation of black representation. It was the oppositional black gaze that responded to these looking relations by
developing independent black cinema. (hooks, 1992:117)

As hooks argues, "Assimilation, imitation, or assuming the role of the rebellious exotic other are not the only available options and never have been"
(1989:54). Among these other available options are unconventional, oppositional identities which question and confront social stereotypes and presumptions.

Second, the cases reveal that student ideologies and behaviors emanate
not just from historically derived perceptions of economic and political
opportunity structures, but also from day-to-day experiences within institutional settings. As Marbella, Carla, Sonia, Ryan, Johnnie, and Patricia moved
through their first two years of high school, they encountered disciplinary
technologies, significant speech acts, and other factors that contributed to the
formation of social categories within the environment. Marbella's separatist
self, Johnnie's "cool" school identity, and Carla's daily behavioral shifts reflect
their readings of and responses to such categories, and thus their locations in
specific curricular contexts characterized by relationships laden with power
and meaning.

As a text, this can be read as one of several recent efforts (see also
Weis, 1990; Raissiguier, 1994) to encourage movement past purely "culturalist" perspectives on schooling. Throughout this text, my purpose has
been not only to detail the particular stories of particular youths, but to
demonstrate the importance of going beyond predicting and explaining
student ideology and behavior in terms of social class or minority status
characteristics. In the course of this exploration, three general factors
emerged as particularly relevant to the construction of identities. These
included disciplinary technologies, which divide and thereby marginalize,
bureaucratized relationships and practices, which silence and thereby dis-
empower, and speech acts, which serve to label groups positively or negatively. Thus, schools as institutions play powerful roles in shaping certain
parts of student identities. At the same time, this investigation has revealed
that individuals enter schools with preexisting ideologies that structure their
responses to and interactions with the environment. Schools cannot be said
simply to reproduce social categories. Rather, student ideologies and school
contexts exert a reciprocal influence on one another.

In this final chapter, I move beyond these general conclusions to discuss additional issues that arise from considering the data presented in this

book. I do not seek to summarize all major points, but rather to concentrate on the implications of youths' voices and experiences for four contemporary theoretical and policy debates. These debates include those concerning contemporary theories of race and ethnicity, the content and form of the multicultural curriculum, the curricular reorganization of schools, and approaches to student discipline. Finally, I review and summarize specific factors which students say contribute to the molding of identity in curricular settings, with the goal of drawing attention to processes that should be taken into account when considering school reform. My intent is to inform discussions, rather than to prescribe specific solutions. I believe the research reported here is quite relevant for those concerned with creating more inclusive and democratic schooling environments. At the same time, this investigation is oriented toward the illumination of processes contributing to various outcomes, rather than the discovery of solutions to educational problems.

## FLUID IDENTITIES IN TRADITIONAL SCHOOLS

During recent years, increasing numbers of scholars (Anzaldúa, 1987; hooks, 1989, 1992; Rosaldo, 1989) have challenged the notion of unified racial and ethnic identities grounded in single shared cultures. Rather than viewing social categories as sacred and inviolable, such scholars point to and praise individuals who challenge, cross and/or transcend social divisions. They suggest that rather than choosing between assimilation and cultural maintenance, individuals can blend cultural elements and, in the process, develop a more critical perspective on both their own and others' cultures. Paralleling this, some describe the potential of a "new ethnicity" that is post-tribal, allowing for "a capacity to enter into multiple perspectives, and to see the same matter from more than one point of view" (Novak, 1980: p. 45).

Growth can be described as an increase in an organism's ability to secure meaning from experience and to act in ways instrumental to the achievement of worthwhile ends (Dewey, 1938). Taking this definition, notions such as transculturalism and new ethnicity are particularly attractive because each implies bicultural fluency and border-crossing abilities, and therefore increased ability to secure meaning within an increasingly global society. With evidence that such blended cultural forms can arise within varied populations (Anzaldúa, 1987; Spindler & Spindler, 1984; 1993), these notions also have a basis in reality. Further, though manifestations of cultural creativity within populations often arise in conjunction with opposition to schooling,[1] this need not necessarily be the case. Recall, for example, the "rebel" persona that Patricia Schmidt crafts at Maple High School (chapter 8). Similarly, Foley (1991) describes a group of academically successful middle-class Mexican American high schoolers who, like Patricia, integrate Chicano cultural forms of expression with pro-academic and traditional Mexican behaviors.

Yet, the voices of individuals like Marbella Sanchez and Carla Chávez (chapters 3 and 4) raise serious questions about the potential for transcultural identities among typical teens navigating typical school settings. As youths who seek to challenge constraining societal categories, neither Carla nor Marbella encounters support for the assertion of a nonstereotypical persona. Further, while both are committed to resisting others' categories, each in some way also conforms, limiting the expression and assertion of their ethnic selves. Their experiences are not unique. As indicated in chapter 2, many participants in the Students' Multiple Worlds Study felt compelled to hide their ethnic and racial selves while in segregated classrooms, a factor which rendered the manifestation of transcultural identities rare. Similarly, African American and Latino authors and professionals reflecting on their experiences in school refer to pressures impeding the assertion of race and ethnicity (Gray, 1985; Neira, 1988; Rodriguez, 1982). Speaking on the behavioral effects of her isolation in advanced classes during high school, for example, Jacquelyn Gray, a project officer for the United States Information Agency, writes:

> Except around my family and friends I played the role—the un-black. To whites, I tried to appear perfect. I earned good grades and spoke impeccable English, was well-mannered and well-groomed. ... I had heard white parents on TV, grumbling about blacks ruining their schools; I didn't want anyone to think that I, too, might bring down Sacred Heart Academy. So I behaved, hoping that no one would associate me with "them" [other African Americans]. (1985:E1,E5)

Pressures to conform appear to emanate first from the presence and acceptance of categorical meanings about what it takes to succeed within the environment, second from the ability of a relatively powerful majority to assert and enforce these social definitions, and third from a variety of practices that depict behaviors and expectations associated with white ethnicity as culture free norms from which others deviate.[2] In short, even as students find locations where they might assert identities that challenge others' expectations, social meanings work against the emergence of behaviors that might challenge or expand others' views of what it takes to succeed.[3]

One inroad to supporting the expression of transcultural identities lies in creating a social and political base for individuals interested in mounting challenges to dominant theories that equate making it with "fitting in" to northern American middle-class standards for self-expression. We have seen how Maple's PEP program (chapter 8) provides one model for this approach. By creating a mutually supportive peer network, PEP helps reduce the isolation academically oriented students of color can experience and also offers a forum in which youths can discuss and develop strategies to cope with the social and academic problems they encounter. Further, because PEP provides information about the ways and means to postsecondary education, as well as academic assistance, it guards against youths becoming dependent on middle-class peers for help and information. PEP bears resemblance to a second successful model, the University of California at Berkeley's Professional Development Program (PDP). Like PEP, PDP highlights the strengths of its students by building a community of academically oriented African Americans. Students are socialized to believe that success is contingent on willingness to help others. Predicated on the notion that African Americans attending college often enter with an extreme and ultimately self-defeating commitment to individualism and self-reliance, PDP works to foster collaborative working relationships through the use of a group-centered approach to learning and problem solving. African American students who came to Berkeley prior to PDP, according to the program's founder, did not lack academic motivation or the support of their communities. Nevertheless, many failed prerequisite math and science courses, even if they came from academically reputable high schools. Several years after PDP was established, African Americans who were enrolled in the program outperformed a similar group of Asian American students in Berkeley's first-year calculus classes (Treisman, 1983, 1985; cited in Fordham, 1991).

A second approach to this issue is a curriculum that asks students to examine the making and enforcement of social borders (see Banks, 1993; Giroux, 1992; McLaren, 1994). In naming social borders which structure behavior and inhibit creativity, students arguably take the first steps toward developing the insight necessary to act against them. This approach is described in greater detail in the section that follows.

## CURRICULUM DEBATES:
## PARTICULARISTIC VS. HOLISTIC APPROACHES

Scholars, policy makers, and classroom teachers who are concerned with diversity have expended tremendous efforts during recent years debating multicultural curricula. Debates on the meaning of the term reveal that scholars disagree on issues of content. While some argue that a curriculum should strive only to foster an appreciation of diversity, others argue that it must also help students understand and gain the skills necessary to challenge social stratification (Sleeter & Grant, 1987). Yet, recent furors over the adoption of texts indicate that many agree on one point. They look at *what* gets put in front of students in the form of textbooks as key to accomplishing their social goals (California, 1991; Sleeter & Grant, 1987).

In signifying particular constructions of reality and particular ways of organizing and selecting knowledge, written curricula send strong messages about who and what is considered important (Apple, 1992). Moreover, the "null curriculum," what schools do not teach, has an important influence on the options youths consider and the perspectives from which they can view a situation or problem (Eisner, 1985). Yet, the individuals in this text argue that they and their peers draw meanings about diversity from far more than the texts and assignments they encounter in class. Of the schools studied, none had adopted a coherent multicultural mission. Further, of the thirty-two classrooms I attended regularly, just four included curricular content relevant to either social diversity or stratification. However, the vast majority of students did not note these gaps, and the few who did failed to protest these omissions. Rather, when speaking of curriculum relevant to race and ethnicity, students referred to a constellation of relational and institutional factors that communicate implicit meanings 1) about the possibilities of working and communicating with others who are socially different than themselves and 2) their place and the places of their peers in the structure of society. In short, youths can be described as drawing meanings both from an explicit (written) curriculum, and from the relational and differentiating aspects of a curriculum implicit to the environment (Davidson, 1994).

Students' voices reveal the importance of taking a holistic rather than a particularistic approach to the democratization of school environments. Factors such as the patterns that emanate from academic tracking and the manner in which adults use power as they seek the attention of diverse pupils may work to strengthen or weaken conceptions about social differences, as well as subvert messages embedded within the explicit curriculum. This point was reinforced for me as I attended a heterogeneously grouped social studies class during the study year. Here, a politically liberal teacher voiced frequent concerns about America's increasing social stratification and referred often to economic and political oppression. He exhorted his students to think critically about their text and the world around them, e.g., "Why are we not the favorite people in the world? Why, when I go to Calcutta or Delhi, and they don't know yet I'm an American. .... What do they see, what's their perspective? [As a European American] I'm a conqueror" (ES034OB2: p.6). At the same time, the teacher delivered his curriculum via sermon-like lectures, managed his classroom through intimidation, made no effort to develop positive educational relationships with his students, and did not challenge the stratification that continued to permeate his detracked classroom through the use of cooperative grouping or other alternative pedagogical approaches. This had consequences for the messages his students took from his curriculum. The teacher was uniformly criticized by the five youths we interviewed who attended his course, with students of color reading his descriptions of the social system as manifestations of racism rather than as attempts to encourage them to look more critically at the world around them:

> *Rosa, Mexican American:* .... to me he was putting down Mexicans saying stuff—like he would actually say, 'Mexicans are the ones that are mostly in low-class jobs and low-class houses and welfare and stuff.' It was like, I don't know, he just like put Mexicans down a lot. (ES40STC:55–61)

The teacher's hidden curriculum subverted the views he expressed. Rather than encouraging a critical perspective, he tweaked the most sensitive aspects of his students' identities.

The example above is not meant to suggest that educators should not attempt hard discussions in their classrooms. Rather, it highlights the importance of structuring activities so that explicit and implicit curricular messages remain consistent. For example, Banks (1993) and Giroux (1992) have argued that a multicultural curriculum should equip individuals to critically examine how knowledge is constructed as part of a more general effort to deepen understanding of racism, as well as political and economic oppression. Following this line of reasoning, it is inconsistent to tell students what to believe, as does the teacher in the example above. Alternatively, youths might be given the responsibility for working with and critically examining materials that incorporate information about the workings of culture and social stratification, with teachers working to facilitate student exploration. So, for example, students might investigate varied descriptions of similar events in order to consider "how cultural texts are regulated by various discursive codes . . . also how such texts express and represent different ideological interests" (Giroux, 1992:135).

Scholars concerned with a more radical approach to multicultural education also advocate encouraging students to express feelings about race and ethnicity from their vantage points, that is, to discuss how they have seen and experienced oppression and social injustice (Giroux, 1992; McLaren, 1994). McLaren (1994) suggests, for example, giving students the opportunity to develop oral histories through interviews with members of their communities, and inviting students to analyze youth protest as expressed through music and other forms of popular culture.

The outcomes that emerged when I and my colleagues inadvertently took a modified version of this type of approach with a group of twelve diverse high schoolers shed some light on its potential (Phelan & Davidson, 1994). Seeking to test the validity of findings emerging in the Students' Multiple Worlds Study, we invited students to work with us as researchers, that is, to read, discuss, and critique three-page versions of case studies we had constructed about individuals in the study. The cases presented information about differences among students' family, peer, and school worlds, as well as information about pressures emanating from cultural differences and social stratification. The materials elicited substantial conversation, as student researchers began to describe the racism they had seen or experienced at their high schools, adopted a more critical perspective on student grouping patterns, discussed the labels they attached to students in different academic tracks, and pondered the social forces that perpetuated social divisions. After several study sessions, we presented the youths with an analytical typology we had designed to summarize patterns emerging from our data (Phelan, Davidson & Yu, 1993). The students critiqued the typology, pointing out its limitations and biases. They then revised and improved it, using their experiences to transform the typology into a more fluid model and alerting us to other patterns of student adaptation. Some continued to critique the general approach, pointing out that the model could still be used negatively when considering human behaviors:

> *East Indian male:* I believe the best advantage to "our" model is that it helps us understand where people do come from and problems that are associated with their personal lives. If this

model will enable us to be more tolerant and understanding of other people then more power to it. But, if this model leads to the grouping of individuals and separation of people then there must be a better way to study the problems and personalities of people. I think the best thing about this model is that it creates a space for everyone, but everyone should *not* be confined to their space. I think it is safe to say that people can and will change. (Phelan & Davidson, 1994: 56–57)

In sum, by offering individuals the opportunity to make sense of cultural and social issues with the aid of diverse peers, it appeared to us that students began to move toward more complex understandings concerning social borders and more critical perspectives about the production of knowledge.

Looking to the data presented in this text, two alternative models provide examples of how teachers have worked to create democratic and empowering classroom environments where implicit and explicit curricular messages combine holistically to subvert dominant stereotypes about diverse students. The PEP program provides the first model. The messages from PEP stem not only from its written curriculum, but also from speech acts which redefine enrollees as college-bound and the employment of diverse role models (tutors) who combine academic achievement with manifestations of ethnic identity. Further, PEP affects meanings throughout the school environment by altering the patterns of enrollment in advanced classrooms and by filling potentially marginalizing gaps in the knowledge base of its participants.

The second model can be seen at the classroom level, most notably in the example of Sergio Vargas (chapter 3). As the social studies teacher for Explorer's ESL students, Vargas has created an environment where youths perceive respect and encouragement for both manifestations of ethnicity and educational engagement. Here, three factors are critical. First, Vargas' immigrant students encounter a worthwhile explicit curriculum which requires them to engage in substantive long-term projects and which incorporates an examination of cultural diversity, Mexican culture and history, and aspects of the American opportunity structure. Second, Vargas employs significant speech acts to effectively communicate high expectations for his students. In addition to providing challenging academic work, Vargas takes youths on trips to universities, encourages his students to consider more academically oriented courses, and provides students with information about postgraduate opportunities. Third, Vargas has encouraged and supported his students as they engage in minor acts of resistance against their marginalization. For example, by helping his students institutionalize ballet folklórico as a curricular offering, Vargas assisted students in forcing the school to take a first step toward recognizing and validating the legitimacy of their cultural presence.

## CURRICULAR ORGANIZATION

I have argued throughout this book that the structure of the typical American high school works to exacerbate social divisions by segregating European American and Asian-descent youths in exclusive academic environments. Students of color from underrepresented groups who move into such classrooms are separated both physically and psychologically from peers who understand their culture and background, a practice anthropologist Signithia Fordham (1991) refers to as "peer-proofing." As discussed, isolation is not only emotionally painful, but also makes it more difficult for underrepresented individuals to challenge the stereotypes of their majority peers. Academic segregation has educational consequences for European American and Asian-descent students as well, for it prohibits them from getting to know their African American and Latino peers and thus fosters stereotypes, that is, the idea that they are more intellectually able.

Critiques of academic tracking are certainly not new. Scholars point out first that students in advanced academic tracks have greater access to the kinds of knowledge that may enable long-term access to social and economic power, and second that the nature of student-teacher relationships in lower track classrooms is likely to promote alienation from the schooling experience (Oakes, 1985). Further, while tracking is predicated on the notion that students will learn more when grouped together for instruction, in fact it is apparent that 1) the learning of those in low and average groups is generally inhibited and 2) students in advanced groups do not consistently do better as a result of their isolation (Oakes, 1985).[4] Such findings have led to calls for the elimination of tracking, and some districts have responded accordingly, grouping students heterogeneously for some or all of their academic instruction.

While I favor detracking, at the same time the data presented in this text, as well as numerous studies of classroom teaching, lead me to question whether elimination of academic tracking, in and of itself, will do much to affect youths' sense of marginalization within the academic environment. I base this argument on two concerns. First, detracking is again a particular-istic approach. Due to its emphasis on curricular structure, it cannot and does not address many sources of ethnically relevant meaning emanating from more general features of the institutional environment. For example, Sonia Gonzales (chapter 5) navigates a school setting that works essentially to confirm her conviction that individuals of Mexican descent are prone to deviance and academic failure. Her conclusions are supported not just by a stratified academic environment, but by a disciplinary system that targets Latinos and adults who appear to take the disengagement of Latino-descent students for granted. Even if complete detracking were to occur, these meanings would remain in the environment.

Second, there is substantial evidence to suggest that teachers adhere to a pedagogical model that will work effectively to reproduce stratification within heterogenous settings. Teacher-dominated, whole group instruc-tion is the norm in classrooms (Goodlad, 1984; Hoetker & Ahlbrand, 1969; Sirotnik, 1983), and in whole group settings, individual opportunities for interactions with the teacher tend to fall disproportionately to students per-ceived as more academically able (Herreshoff & Speidel, 1987). Moreover, in traditionally structured learning environments (classrooms characterized by similar tasks, limited materials, and limited methods), status differences are highlighted as youth compare performances on uniform products (Hertz-Lazarowitz, Kirkus & Miller, 1992). This implies that if youth of all academic backgrounds are simply placed together, those with stronger aca-demic training will focus on the academic weaknesses of peers who come from less prestigious academic environments. Finally, as discussed in chapter 2, teachers' perceptions of academic ability tend to vary along ethnic and racial lines, with teachers looking for and reinforcing achievement behaviors in European American students (Baron et al., 1985; Cooper & Baron, 1977; Cooper & Tom, 1984: Good, 1981). Taken as a whole, this literature sug-gests that youth who enter detracked classroom settings are likely to observe patterns that confirm rather than challenge their convictions and stereotypes. This was the case for Ryan Moore (chapter 6), as he attended detracked classrooms during his ninth-grade year.

The increasingly extensive literature on heterogenous grouping iden-tifies factors that may help to prevent simple replication of status relations in detracked classrooms. It is clear that the way in which learning tasks are structured is critical to achieving this goal, as low-status students are typically less active and less influential in heterogenous work groups (Cohen, 1986). A first step to addressing this issue involves placing youths in cooperative groups characterized by 1) a cooperative incentive structure and 2) tasks that demand multiple cognitive and social abilities (Cohen & Lotan, 1995; Slavin, 1984). The critical feature here is that youths are not simply placed together, but are interdependent for a reward they will share as a group. Further, it is critical that group rewards are based on the sum of individual learning performances and that individual efforts are identifiable, so that pro-performance norms will be applied to all group members (Slavin, 1984).[5] Finally, complex multiple ability tasks help provide opportunities for meaningful contributions from the broadest array of youth (Cohen & Lotan, 1995).

Secondly, in order to help subvert group domination by one or two students, teachers can make active efforts to assign competence to low-status individuals (Cohen & Lotan, 1995). In this case, a teacher watches for instances when low-status students perform well in some area relevant to success on a classroom task, then praises that student publicly and specifically. It is critical that this praise occur only when the student performs well on a particular ability, so that both high- and low-status students will find the treatment believable (Cohen & Lotan, 1995). In investigating this approach in thirteen elementary school classrooms, Cohen & Lotan found that equal status treatments, coupled with more frequent use of multiple ability tasks, were associated with more equal status interactions.

Finally, cooperative structures should be designed to reduce the salience of categorical meanings and to maximize opportunities for students to establish a classroom identity based on personal attributes. The literature suggests the following principles for design (Miller & Harrington, 1992). First, group members should be trained in group process skills (e.g., turn taking, listening, offering criticism and praise). This encourages self-disclosure, which can help decrease the salience of categorical membership and may direct attention toward social as well as cognitive abilities relevant to production, particularly if these skills are given weight in the classroom assessment system. Second, intergroup competition should be avoided, as failure may lead to the seeking of a scapegoat. Third, teachers should avoid composing teams that highlight categorical status (i.e. ethnicity, gender). In particular, unequal numerical representation on teams is associated with reduced intergroup acceptance, a finding that suggests teachers should avoid placing a single individual of color on each heterogenous team. Rather, teachers may equalize the frequency of category representation, rotate team membership, and/or recategorize students along a different dimension, for example, by interests in certain aspects of the subject matter or unique attributes.

## APPROACHES TO SOCIAL CONTROL:
## SEGREGATION VS. ASSIMILATION

Approaches to social control have long been a primary concern for U.S. educators, as evidenced by the vast literature on classroom management. In the past decade, worries have escalated. Real and cinematic accounts of gang activities, the rising teenage homicide rate, and statistics concerning students who carry weapons to school[6] are but part of the cultural discourse that has left many who work with today's adolescents nervous and disheartened. As of 1991, 15 percent of city teachers reported that they felt unsafe in their school buildings after-hours and 15 percent said they had been threatened with injury (National Education Goals Panel: Exhibits 60, 61). Schools have responded with a variety of measures, ranging from the installation of metal detectors to training students in conflict resolution.

As described in this text, a frequent and popular response to improving social control involves surveillance and segregation; administrators try to control the school environment by watching and constraining student movement, suspending or expelling troublesome students, and isolating "at-risk" students in special programs. Though this approach may succeed in containing and constraining some deviant activities, the data presented in this book suggest that in the long term it has drawbacks. First, it inhibits the integration of adolescents into the school and prohibits them from contributing in meaningful ways, thus contributing to a sense of social estrangement. Second, because youths do not encounter alternative models for addressing conflict, it reinforces rather than challenges the notion that social control can only be achieved through exhibitions of force. Finally, this approach may produce the very behavior it is meant to prevent. Schools which have closed climates, typified by teachers and administrators who foster the use and abuse of power as a means of control, have students and teachers with higher levels of alienation (Calabrese, 1987). Similarly, disorderly schools are characterized partially by teachers with punitive attitudes and rules that students do not perceive as fair and clear (Gottfredson, Gottfredson & Hybl, 1993).

Alienation theory and empirical studies concerned with reducing manifestations of student alienation provide one basis for considering alternative approaches to social control. First, because alienation is a multidimensional and situational phenomena associated with feelings of powerlessness, social estrangement, and meaninglessness (Mau, 1992), some have suggested altering school environments in order to address these issues.

Specifically, they advocate reforms which will 1) involve all students (including those most deviant) in the school institution 2) promote inter-age and inter-peer integration and 3) enfranchise youth by giving them a voice in the decision-making process (Calabrese, 1987; Crase, 1981; D'Amico, 1980; Steele, 1978; Tjosvold, 1978). Testing these ideas, Calabrese and Schumer (1986) developed a program for ninth grade students which was designed to encourage participation in community service activities and to provide access to significant adults. As part of this program, twenty-five students were told to independently develop a community service project which could be used as a model for other communities. Meeting in small groups, the students planned, developed, and implemented their project. Four volunteer faculty and the principal facilitated the process, acting as advisors. In comparison to a control group, these students showed significantly reduced levels of both alienation and discipline problems.[7] Peer mediation programs, which train students to facilitate and resolve student-student and, in some cases, student-teacher conflicts, are a second example of an approach that promotes inter-age and inter-peer integration and enfranchises youth. Preliminary studies show positive results both for reducing behavior problems and resolving student-student conflict (Johnson et al., 1995; Stomfay-Stitz, 1994).

A second promising approach to social control involves changing classroom instructional practices in order to enable success for a broader array of students. Many approaches to classroom discipline are custodial, emphasizing control through curricular forms of disciplinary technology. For example, studies suggest teachers can achieve order by giving students clearly defined tasks (e.g., worksheets, spelling tests) that constrain and structure their behavior (Gottfredson, Gottfredson & Hybl, 1993). Alternatively, however, some have tested an approach which emphasizes changing mainstream classroom instructional practices so lower-achieving students have greater opportunities for success, involvement, and learning. For example, Hawkins, Doueck & Lishner (1988) instituted a program which emphasized interactive teaching, cooperative learning, and proactive classroom management in fifteen seventh grade math classrooms.[8] They found a significant reduction in the rate of school suspensions and expulsions for low-achieving students enrolled in these math classes as compared to a control group. Further, after enrollment, students had more positive attitudes toward school in general and math in particular.

Finally, both this text and conventional studies concerned with improving student behavior suggest that it is critical to foster positive and supportive student-teacher relations in order to improve behavior. Gottfredson, Gottfredson & Hybl (1993), for example, worked with school improvement teams of teachers to implement a new disciplinary program in six middle schools. All of the schools took a rather conventional approach to revising their disciplinary technologies, clarifying their discipline policies, implementing computerized behavior management systems, and developing systems for rewarding appropriate behavior. Further, in all schools, students reported improvements in the clarity of rules and rewards. However, in the end, only schools that also 1) significantly reduced the amount of punishment students received and 2) from students' perspective, changed the school climate in the direction of respectful, supportive, and fair treatment, showed improvements in student behavior.

Though it is difficult to offer a recipe for improving student-teacher relations, one can look to exemplars such as Sergio Vargas (chapter 3) and Wendy Ashton (chapter 7) for guidelines. For example, Ashton developed positive relationships with a roomful of potentially oppositional students through three primary means. First, she organized her class to promote student-teacher and student-student interaction, both by arranging seating so students could see one another and circulating before class to visit briefly with each of her students. Second, she met classroom disruptions with a sense of humor and pointed, but affectionate, teasing, thereby moving discussions back on track. Finally, she insisted students attempt answers and told them she expected them to move ahead, thereby communicating high expectations. Though none of Ashton's moves are in and of themselves particularly striking, taken together, they created an atmosphere where learning rather than discipline was the primary focus.

## WHAT MATTERS: SEPARATING, SILENCING, AND LABELING

In this final section, I revisit and summarize the main points that emerge from consideration of the more fine-grained details presented within the case studies in this volume. Youths indicate it is these five points that educators and policy makers must keep in mind when seeking to design educational environments which are conducive to fostering the emergence of pro-academic identities in diverse students.

1. Marginalization, a sense of cultural estrangement, and alienation are enhanced by common practices that work to separate students along

ethnic, racial, and class lines and to valorize particular behaviors. Examples of such practices include delivering information to a diverse linguistic population in a single language, tracking youth by linguistic or academic status, and providing a curriculum that works effectively to communicate the idea that students in general or remedial track classes are not capable of significant intellectual activity.

2. Barriers to information further marginalize individuals from working-class and impoverished communities, where parents are less likely to have attended college. Barriers to information also foster a sense of powerlessness and meaningless, which can promote anger conducive to the expression of anti-academic identities.

3. Bureaucratic practices predicated on the notions of student management and adult control contribute to feelings of powerlessness and generate anger and frustration, conducive to disengagement from school.

4. Distant and depersonalized relationships with adults in authority, particularly when these relationships are authoritarian in tone, work effectively to silence students. This is particularly true when youths perceive differential treatment; that is, when students see adults apply power disproportionately to members of a specific ethnic or racial group. Adolescents suggest that distant and authoritarian relationships contribute to student alienation; therefore, it is important for adults to reach out to students, that is, to participate actively in the construction of relationships.

5. Speech acts that label and define emanate principally from teacher expectations, policies that highlight the behaviors of particular social groups, and differential treatment. More frequently, teachers and schools employ speech acts that work to confirm rather than counter oppositional identities by highlighting categorical membership and equating it with negative outcomes. However, teachers or programs may employ labeling strategically to counter and subvert stereotypical categorical meanings and manifestations of anti-academic identity. In the latter case, it is critical to layer and align actions, behaviors, and statements in order to define marginalized youths as capable and worthy of time and investment. It is also important that students find the emotional and cognitive support necessary to support their growth and development.

Meanings relevant to the construction of identity emanate from multiple contexts, reflecting not only peer group ideologies but also experiences within a school's varied administrative and curricular settings. Students imply that those interested in structuring schools for inclusion must think holistically, crafting environments where disciplinary technologies and speech acts combine to redefine conventional social categories.

## FINAL THOUGHTS

This book began on an optimistic note. Johnnie's description of his transformation indicates that youths conventionally dismissed may construct quite different personas, succeeding "without selling out," in altered educational circumstances. Much of the remainder of the text, however, has been sober. Though this study was carried out in "good" high schools in a relatively progressive region of the country, the stereotypes and constraints that structure student behavior are quite apparent. It appears schools do not often work to foster critical examinations of categorical meanings, or value expressions of difference. As the case study of Ryan Moore (chapter 6) reveals, it is conformity that brings praise. I have tried to make the implications of this situation apparent through students' voices.

We no longer live in neatly bounded, homogenous communities, nor do we operate in a purely national economy. For these reasons alone, the ability to challenge and negotiate social categories can be viewed as an ability worthy of encouragement. This text, by making categorizing practices and the conditions that support them explicit, is meant to contribute to the debate about how educators might do so. Young adults, like all of us, argue that they need the room and support necessary to express their emerging and sometimes critical selves. The challenge lies in translating this call, in responding to Marbella's wish that adults treat her and her peers like "civilized persons, not like some kind of objects."

# Notes

## INTRODUCTION: WAY TO AN INQUIRY

1. Drawing on data collected from sixteen secondary schools over a four-year period, The Center for Research on the Context of Secondary School Teaching aimed to specify ways in which the various contexts of secondary school teaching interact to shape and impact teachers' professional roles and dispositions and students' orientations toward schools and learning. Policy, district, union, school, department, subject matter, and students were among the primary foci. (For more on the CRC and its work, see Bascia, 1994; McLaughlin, 1993; McLaughlin & Talbert, 1990, 1993; Siskin, 1993; Talbert & McLaughlin, 1993.)

2. The students varied along a number of dimensions, including gender, ethnicity, social class, achievement level, immigration, and transportation status. An equal number of high- and low-achieving students were selected from each school. For details on the study design and sample, see Phelan, Davidson & Cao, 1991.

## 1. THE POLITICS OF IDENTITY

1. Data from the 1980 High School & Beyond ('HS&B') study indicate significant differences in dropout rates by race and ethnicity, with rates among the sophomore cohorts of Asian Americans (8.2 percent) and European Americans (14.8 percent) lower than those of their African American (22.2 percent), Latino (27 percent), and Native American (35.5 percent) peers (National Center for Education Statistics, 1989).

231

2. Jiobu's (1988) study of California ethnic and racial groups indicates similar patterns in income disparity. For example, while the educational distribution of African Americans in California is almost identical to that of European Americans, the proportion of African Americans in higher occupational and income categories is not. Similarly, while the level of Filipino education is, on average, higher than that of European Americans, fewer Filipinos occupy managerial positions and their income also falls below that of European Americans.

3. Several excellent studies comparing children's interactions at home and in the classroom have been carried out. Among these are studies of African American (Heath, 1982), Mexican American (Delgado-Gaitan, 1987), Native Hawaiian (Au, 1980; Au & Jordan, 1981), and Native American (Philips, 1972, 1982) youths.

4. Fordham and Ogbu's emphasis on the potential importance of peer pressure is backed by quantitative studies of peer influence. A synthesis of the research indicates a consistent correlation (.24) between peer influence and educational outcomes, with a trend toward higher correlations with older (tenth through twelfth) grade students and students in urban environments (Ide et al., 1981).

5. In addition to ethnographic information from the United States, there is also cross-national evidence that supports Ogbu's theory. Studies of Buraku Japanese (a social group that is outcast on the basis of occupation) show that they do poorly in Japanese schools compared to dominant Ippan students, but do equally as well as Ippan immigrants when in the United States (DeVos, 1973; Ito, 1967). Koreans, stigmatized in Japan, show a similar contrast in academic performance after immigrating to the United States from Japan (DeVos, 1983; Rohlen, 1981). Similarly, in Sweden, where Finns are viewed as inferior to Swedish children, they fail in school more often than do Swedish children; in Australia, they do equally well as other Scandinavian immigrants (Cummins, 1986).

6. According to one study, in 1982, the dropout rate among Central American students was 11.4 percent, compared to 21.2 percent for their Mexican American and Puerto Rican peers (Hispanic Policy Development Project, 1984).

7. Of European American youth participating in HS&B, those in the lowest income quartile dropped out more often than comparable African American and Latino peers (Fine, 1991), indicating that class status may be a more important predictor of opposition than immigrant status. On a regional level, a study of Californian adults age twenty-five and older indi-

cates that African Americans are more likely to complete high school than several of their immigrant counterparts, including Chinese Americans, Filipinos, Vietnamese, and Mexican Americans (Jiobu, 1988). (While Chinese and Filipinos are more likely than African Americans to gain collegiate or post-collegiate education, they are also more likely than their African American peers to leave school before the eighth grade.) Were immigrant status solely to account for orientation toward schooling, one would not necessarily predict this pattern of performance.

8. These findings are consistent with general research on private school effects. While about half of the difference in higher college attendance rates of non-Catholic, private school students can be accounted for by socioeconomic status (Coleman, 1987), the balance of college attendance differences is accounted for by a school's curricular and extracurricular activities, academic standards, value climate, formal and informal communication networks, staff orientation, and the resources it devotes to advising college-bound students (Alexander & Eckland, 1977; Falsey & Heyns, 1984).

## 2. YOUTHS' FRAMES ON ENGAGEMENT

1. Sociologists have demonstrated that powerlessness and meaninglessness are significant indicators of workplace alienation (Blauner, 1964; Mottaz, 1981), while social isolation has been related to chronic school absenteeism and dropping out (Finn, 1989).

2. For further details on the Student Multiple Worlds Study sample, see P. Phelan, H. Cao & A. Davidson, *Students' Multiple Worlds: Study Design, Sample Description, and Summary of Record Data* (Stanford, CA: Center for Research on the Context of Secondary School Teaching, 1991).

3. With the exception of the youths enrolled in the ESL track (all Mexican immigrants), youths of all backgrounds are represented in each academic track and achievement category depicted in Table N.1 below. Achievement refers to grades received during the first year of the study. Students earning mostly *A*s and *B*s were designated *high*, students earning mostly *C*s were designated *medium*, and students earning mostly *D*s and *F*s were designated *low*.

4. To indicate whether the student was born in the United States or abroad, I follow each ethnic designation with the descriptor "American" or "immigrant."

Table N.1. Academic Placement and Achievement:
Students' Multiple Worlds Study Sample

| Track | Achievement Level | | | |
|---|---|---|---|---|
| | *Low* | *Medium* | *High* | *Total* |
| Advanced | 2 | 1 | 19 | 22 |
| General | 9 | 3 | 2 | 14 |
| Remedial | 2 | 0 | 4 | 6 |
| ESL | 0 | 1 | 3 | 4 |
| Mixed | 3 | 3 | 3 | 9 |
| TOTAL | 16 | 8 | 31 | 55 |

5. In all, 18 percent of the sample said that tracking contributed to the establishment of borders between peer groups, while an additional 22 percent of students said that an opportunity to interact with diverse youth in shared work settings (e.g., common classes, sports teams) enabled them to develop cross-ethnic friendships. (As one student explained, "The ability for two people to do exactly the same thing and work together erases visual presumptions" [OR05STD:2170–2172].) Students' comments are in accord with studies of cooperative learning, which indicate that students liking others from different racial backgrounds can increase with involvement in carefully structured cooperative activities (Hertz-Lazarowitz, Kirkus & Miller, 1992).

6. Further, the standards teachers define for practice may be positively influenced by the character of their professional community (McLaughlin, 1993).

7. Explorer, Huntington, and Maple, each located in a large, urban high school district, share similar histories and demographics. All are situated in predominantly European American, middle-class neighborhoods and all saw their populations transformed by desegregation in the 1980s. As of 1990–91, as indicated in Table N.2 below, the schools were characterized to various extents by populations that were culturally, economically, and linguistically diverse.

Table N.2. School Demographics

| School | Race/Ethnicity | | | | *Percent LEP Total/Latino* | *Percent Reduced Lunch* | *Percent Transported* |
|---|---|---|---|---|---|---|---|
| | *African American* | *Asian Descent* | *European American* | *Latino* | | | |
| Explorer | 3.2% | 12.2% | 42.2% | 40.6% | 31%/25% | 31% | 36% |
| Huntington | 5.4% | 22.7% | 50.3% | 20.7% | 15%/4% | 23% | 19% |
| Maple | 6.8% | 8% | 42.4% | 45.4% | 23%/21% | 29% | 40% |

### 3. MARBELLA SANCHEZ ON MARGINALIZATION AND SILENCING

1. All interviews were conducted in Spanish by a male European American interviewer. I was usually present as well.

2. "Cabrón," literally translated, means "billy goat" or (derogatory) "cuckold." The translation above is taken from a glossary which defines various Latino urbanisms (Rodríguez, 1993).

### 6. RYAN MOORE ON FITTING IN

1. Ryan's participation across varied classrooms has served not only to foster his conformity to academic circumstances that are less than ideal, but also to deepen the stereotypes he holds about others. Because Ryan's advanced courses are dominated by European American youth, similar in background and beliefs to his, he has become further convinced that he and his like peers are the ones primarily interested in growing and getting better. Ryan blames the curriculum he encounters in integrated classrooms on his classmates, rather than considering whether alternative forms of pedagogy might provide more challenging experiences: "If it's an accelerated class the teacher can teach. If it's a general class the teacher can teach. But when it's a mixed [heterogenous class] it's basically all general" (ES37STB: 737–743).

### 7. JOHNNIE BETTS ON RECASTING THE SELF

1. When signifying, one delivers a personal insult, ideally in the form of a quick one-line comeback to someone with whom one is intimate and friendly.

### 9. EPILOGUE

1. Groups who develop secondary cultural differences may claim and exaggerate certain behaviors, symbols, events, and meanings as appropriate for the group because they are not characteristic of members of another population (Ogbu, 1987). Among these may be anti-academic behaviors that demonstrate resistance to schooling.

2. For further discussion concerning general failures to call into question the norm of whiteness as an ethnic and racial category, see Giroux (1992).

3. In addition to precluding educational opportunities in the classroom, submerging ethnic and class identities may also create substantial psychological stress (Spindler & Spindler, 1993, 1994). When forced to adopt the "situated self" expected and required by more powerful others, youth are in constant danger of damaging their inner core, or "enduring self" (Spindler & Spindler, 1993; 1994).

4. Literature concerning the positive long-term effects of desegregation on the educational and occupational attainments of African Americans also provides support for this argument (Wells & Crain, 1994).

5. In contrast, if the group grade depends only on a final group product, pro-performance norms may be directed toward those deemed most valuable to its production, thus leading to simple replication of preexisting status relations.

6. In 1993, 11 percent of eighth graders, 10 percent of tenth graders, and 8 percent of twelfth graders reported that they had brought a weapon to school at least once during the previous month (National Education Goals Panel: Exhibit 56).

7. When the principal ceased involvement with the project, discipline problems returned to their former levels, suggesting that connections between youths and a significant adult are an important aspect of improving the disciplinary climate.

8. Interactive teaching requires students to master specific learning objectives before proceeding to more advanced work. Teachers determine grades by considering mastery and improvement over past performances, rather than through comparison with other students. This approach also emphasizes frequent checks for understanding on the part of the teacher. Proactive classroom management is based on two primary ideas: rewarding attempts to comply with rules and giving clear and explicit instructions for behavior (Hawkins, Doueck & Lishner, 1988).

# References

Alba, R. D. (1990). *Ethnic Identity: The Transformation of White America*. New Haven: Yale University Press.

Alexander, K. L., and Eckland, B. K. (1977). High School Context and College Selectivity: Institutional Constraints in Educational Stratification. *Social Forces* 56.

America's Immigrant Challenge. (Fall 1993, Special Issue) *Time Magazine*, pp. 3–9.

Anzaldúa, G. (1987). *Borderlands/La Frontera: The New Mestiza*. San Francisco: Spinsters/Aunt Lute Book Company.

Apple, M. W. (1992). The Text and Cultural Politics. *Educational Researcher*, 21, 7, 4–11.

Au, K. H. (1980). Participant Structures in a Reading Lesson with Hawaiian Children: Analysis of a Culturally Appropriate Instructional Event. *Anthropology and Education Quarterly* 11, 2, 91–115.

Au, K. H., and Jordan, C. (1981). Teaching Reading to Hawaiian Children: Finding a Culturally Appropriate Solution. In Trueba, H.T., Guthrie, G.P., and Au, K.H. (Eds.) *Culture in the Bilingual Classroom: Studies in Classroom Ethnography*. pp. 139–152. Rowley, MA: Newbury House.

Au, K. H., and Mason, J. M. (1981). Social Organizational Factors in Learning to Read: The Balance of Right Hypothesis. *Reading Research Quarterly* 17, 1, 115–152.

Bacharach, S. B., Bauer, S. C., and Conley, S. C. (1986). Organizational Analysis of Stress: The Case of Secondary and Elementary Schools. *Journal of Work and Occupations* 13, 7–32.

Banks, J. A. (1993). The Canon Debate, Knowledge Construction, and Multicultural Education. *Educational Researcher* 22, 5, 4–14.

Baron, R. M., Tom, D., and Cooper, H. (1985). Social Class, Race, and Teacher Expectations. In Dusek, J.B. (Ed.) *Teacher Expectancies*. pp. 251–269. Hillsdale, NJ: Lawrence Erlbaum Associates.

Bascia, N. (1994). *The Role of Unions in Teachers' Professional Lives*. New York: Teachers College Press.

Bell, D. (1975). Ethnicity and Social Change. In Glazer, N., and Moynihan, D.P. (Eds.) *Ethnicity: Theory and Experience*. Cambridge: Harvard University Press.

Bereiter, C., and Engelmann, S. (1966). *Teaching Disadvantaged Children in the Preschool*. Englewood Cliffs, NJ: Prentice-Hall.

Blauner, R. (1964). *Alienation and Freedom: The Factory Worker and His Industry*. Chicago: University of Chicago Press.

Bourdieu, P., and Passeron, J. C. (1977). *Reproduction in Education, Society, and Culture*. CA: Sage Publications.

Brophy, J. (1983). Research on the Self-Fulfilling Prophecy and Teacher Expectations. *Journal of Educational Psychology*, 75, 631–661.

Calabrese, R. L. (1987). Adolescence: A Growth Period Conducive to Alienation. *Adolescence* 22, 88, 929–938.

Calabrese, R. L., and Schumer, H. (1986). The Effects of Service Activities on Adolescent Alienation. *Adolescence* 21, 83, 675–687.

California Rewrites History. (1991, October 27). *This World: San Francisco Examiner*, pp. 7–10.

Cazden, C., and John, V. P. (1971). Learning in American Indian Children. In Wax, M.L., Diamond, S., and Gearing, F.O. (Eds.) *Anthropological Perspectives on Education*. pp. 252–271. New York: Basic Books.

Clifford, J. (1988). *The Predicament of Culture: Twentieth Century Ethnography, Literature, and Art*. Cambridge: Harvard University Press.

Cohen, E.G. (1986). *Designing Groupwork: Strategies for the Heterogenous Classroom*. New York: Teachers College Press.

Cohen, E.G., and Lotan, R.A. (1995). Predicting Equal-Status Interaction in the Heterogenous Classroom. *American Educational Research Journal* 32, 1, 99–120.

Coleman, J. (1987). Social Capital and the Development of Youth. *Momentum* 18, 4, 6–8.

Cooper, H. M., and Baron, R. (1977). Academic Expectations and Attributed Responsibility as Predictors of Professional Teacher's

Reinforcement Behavior. *Journal of Educational Psychology* 69, 409–418.

Cooper, H. M., and Tom, D. (1984). Teacher Expectations Research: A Review with Implications for Classroom Instruction. *The Elementary School Journal* 85, 1, 77–89.

Corcoran, T. B. (1990). Schoolwork: Perspectives on Workplace Reform in Public Schools. In McLaughlin, M., Talbert, J., and Bascia, N. (Eds.) *The Contexts of Teaching in Secondary Schools: Teachers' Realities.* pp. 142–166. New York: Teachers College Press.

Crase, D. (1981). Declining Health Behavior of Adolescence: A Measure of Alienation. *High School Journal* 64, 213–216.

Cummins, J. (1986). Empowering Minority Students: A Framework for Intervention. *Harvard Educational Review* 56, 1, 19–22.

D'Amico, J. (1980). Reviving Student Participation. *Educational Leadership,* 44–46.

Davidson, A. L. (1994). Border Curricula and the Construction of Identity: Implications for Multicultural Theorists. *International Journal of Qualitative Studies in Education* 7, 4, 335–349.

Davidson, A. L., and Phelan, P. K. (1993). Cultural Diversity and Its Implications for Education. In Phelan, P., and Davidson, A. (Eds.) *Renegotiating Cultural Diversity in American Schools.* pp. 1–26. New York: Teachers College Press.

Dawson, J. A. (1985). School Improvement Programs in Thirteen Urban Schools: A Report of a Four-Year Documentation Study. Philadelphia, PA: Research for Better Schools.

Delgado-Gaitan, C. (1987). Traditions and Transitions in the Learning Process of Mexican Children: An Ethnographic View. In Spindler, G., and Spindler, L. (Eds.) *Interpretive Ethnography of Education: At Home and Abroad.* pp. 333–362. Hillsdale, NJ: Lawrence Erlbaum Associates.

Deutsch, M. (1967). *The Disadvantaged Child: Selected Papers of Martin Deutsch and Associates.* New York: Basic Books.

DeVos, G. A. (1983). Achievement Motivation and Intra-Family Attitudes in Immigrant Koreans. *Journal of Psychoanalytic Anthropology* 6, 1, 25–71.

——— . (1973). Japan's Outcastes: The Problem of the Burakumin. In Whitaker, B. (Ed.) *The Fourth World: Victims of Group Oppression.* pp. 307–327. New York: Schocken Books.

Dewey, J. (1938). *Experience and Education.* New York: Macmillan Publishing Company.

Duffy, G. G. (1981). "Teacher Effectiveness Research: Implications for the Reading Profession." In Kamil, M. (Ed.) *Directions in Reading: Research and Instruction: 30th Yearbook of the National Reading Conference.* pp. 113–136. Washington, DC: National Reading Conference.

Eisner, E. W. (1985). *The Educational Imagination: On The Design and Evaluation of Educational Programs.* New York: Macmillan Publishing Company.

———. (1991). *The Enlightened Eye: Qualitative Inquiry and the Enhancement of Educational Practice.* New York: Macmillan Publishing Company.

Falsey, B., and Heyns, B. (1984). The College Channel: Private and Public Schools Reconsidered. *Sociology of Education* 57, 2, 111–122.

Fine, M. (1991). *Framing Dropouts: Notes on the Politics of an Urban Public High School.* Albany: State University of New York Press.

Finn, J. (1989). Withdrawing from School. *Review of Educational Research* 59, 2, 117–142.

Fiske, S. T., and Taylor, S. E. (1978). Salience, Attention, and Attribution: Top of the Head Phenomena. In Berkowitz, L. (Ed.) *Advances in Experimental Social Psychology: Volume II* (pp. 249–288). New York: Academic Press.

Foley, D. E. (1991). Reconsidering Anthropological Explanations of School Failure. *Anthropology and Education Quarterly,* 22, 1, 60–86.

Fordham, S. (1991). Peer Proofing Academic Competition Among Black Adolescents: 'Acting White' Black American Style. In Sleeter, C.E. (Ed.) *Empowerment Through Multicultural Education.* pp. 69–94. Albany: State University of New York Press.

Fordham, S., and Ogbu, J.U. (1986). Black Students' School Success: Coping with the 'Burden of Acting White.' *Urban Review* 18, 3, 176–206.

Foucault, M. (1979). *Discipline and Punish.* New York: Pantheon.

———. (1983). "The Subject and Power." In Dreyfus, H.L, and Rabinow, P. (authors), *Michel Foucault: Beyond Structuralism and Hermeneutics.* pp. 208–226. Chicago: The University of Chicago Press.

Gallimore, R., Boggs, J., and Jordan, C. (1974). *Culture, Behavior, and Education: A Study of Hawaiian Americans.* Beverly Hills, CA: Sage Publications.

Gibson, M. A. (1987). Punjabi Immigrants in an American High School. In Spindler, G., and Spindler, L. (Eds.) *Interpretive Ethnography of Education: At Home and Abroad.* pp. 274–281. Hillsdale, NJ: Lawrence Erlbaum Associates.

Giroux, H. (1992). *Border Crossings: Cultural Workers and the Politics of Education*. New York: Routledge.

Glazer, N., and Moynihan, D. P. (1975). Introduction. In Glazer, N., and Moynihan, D.P. (Eds.) *Ethnicity: Theory and Experience*. Cambridge: Harvard University Press.

Goldenberg, C. (1992). The Limits of Expectations. A Case for Case Knowledge About Teacher Expectancy Effects. *American Educational Research Journal* 29, 3, 517–544.

Good, T. L. (1981). Teacher Expectations and Student Perceptions: A Decade of Research. *Educational Leadership*, 38, 5, 415–421.

Goodlad, J. (1984). *A Place Called School*. New York: McGraw-Hill.

Gottfredson, D. C., Fink, C. M., and Graham, N. (1994). Grade Retention and Problem Behavior. *American Educational Research Journal* 31, 4, 761–784.

Gottfredson, D. C., Gottfredson, G. D., and Hybl, L. G. (1993). Managing Adolescent Behavior: A Multiyear, Multischool Study. *American Educational Research Journal* 30, 1, 179–215.

Gray, J. (March 17, 1985). A Black American Princess: New Game, New Rules. *The Washington Post*. pp. E1, E5.

Hall, S. (1987). Minimal Selves. In *ICA Documents 6: Postmodernism and the Question of Identity*. London: ICA.

Hawkins, J. D., Doueck, H. J., and Lishner, D. M. (1988). Changing Teaching Practices in Mainstream Classrooms to Improve Bonding and Behavior of Low Achievers. *American Educational Research Journal* 25, 1, 31–50.

Heath, S. B. (1982). Questioning at School and at Home: A Comparative Study. In Spindler, G. (Ed.) *Doing the Ethnography of Schooling: Educational Anthropology in Action*. pp. 102–131. New York: Holt, Rinehart & Winston.

Herreshoff, M. J., and Speidel, G. E. (1987). Child Talk in Large Group Storybook Discussions in Kindergarten. In Farran, D.C. (Ed.) *Kindergarten Project Team Research Design 1985–86*. Technical Report No. 143. Honolulu: Kamehameha Schools/Bishop Estate, Center for Development of Early Education.

Hertz-Lazarowitz, R., Kirkus, V. B., and Miller, N. (1992). Implications of Current Research on Cooperative Interaction for Classroom Application. In Hertz-Lazarowitz, R., and Miller, N. (Eds.) *Interaction in Cooperative Groups*. pp. 253–280. New York: Cambridge University Press.

Hiltz, S. R., and Turroff, M. (1993). *The Network Nation: Human Communication via Computers.* Cambridge, MA: MIT Press.

Hispanic Policy Development Project. (1984). *"Make Something Happen": Hispanics and Urban High School Reform.* New York: Hispanic Policy Development Project.

Hoetker, J., and Ahlbrand, W. P. (1969). The Persistence of the Recitation. *American Educational Research Journal* 6, 145–167.

Hoffman, D. M. (1988). Cross Cultural Adaptation and Learning: Iranians and Americans at School. In Trueba, H., and Delgado-Gaitan, C. (Eds.) *School and Society: Learning Content Through Culture.* pp. 163–180. New York: Praeger Publishers.

hooks, b. (1992). *Black Looks: Race and Representation.* Boston: South End Press.

———. (1989). *Talking Back: Thinking Feminist, Thinking Black.* Boston: South End Press.

Ide, J., Parkenson, J., Haertel, G., and Walberg, H. (1981). Peer Group Influence on Education Outcomes: A Quantitative Synthesis. *Journal of Educational Psychology* 73, 4, 472–284.

Ito, H. (1967). Japan's Outcastes in the United States. In DeVos, G.A., and Wama, H. (Eds.) *Japan's Invisible Caste in Culture and Personality.* pp. 200–221. Berkeley: University of California Press.

Jiobu, R. M. (1988). *Ethnicity and Assimilation.* Albany: State University of New York Press.

John, V. P. (1972). Styles of Learning—Styles of Teaching: Reflections on the Education of Navajo Children. In Cazden, C., John, V., and Hymes, D. (Eds.) *Functions of Language in the Classroom.* pp. 331–343. New York: Teachers College Press.

Johnson, D. W., Johnson, R., Dudley, B., Ward, M., and Magnuson, D. (1995). The Impact of Peer Mediation Training on the Management of School and Home Conflicts. *American Educational Research Journal* 32, 4, 829–844.

Kanter, R. M. (1977). Some Effects of Proportions on Group Life: Skewed Sex Ratios and Responses to Token Women. *American Journal of Sociology* 82, 5, 965–990.

Keefe, S. E., and Padilla, A. M. (1987). *Chicano Ethnicity.* Albuquerque: University of New Mexico Press.

Keith, T. Z., and Page, E. B. (1985). Do Catholic Schools Improve Minority Student Achievement? *American Educational Research Journal* 22, 3, 337–349.

Kondo, D. (1990). *Crafting Selves: Power, Gender and Discourses on Identity in a Japanese Workplace.* Chicago: The University of Chicago Press.

Labov, W. (1969). The Logic of Non-Standard English. *Georgetown Monographs on Language and Linguistics* 22, 1–31.

Louis, K. S. (1992). Restructuring and the Problem of Teachers' Work. In Lieberman, A. (Ed.) *The Changing Contexts of Teaching: Ninety-first Yearbook of the National Society for the Study of Education.* pp. 138–156. Chicago: The University of Chicago Press.

Lucas, T., Henze, R., and Donato, R. (1990). Promoting the Success of Latino Language-Minority Students: An Exploratory Study of Six High Schools. *Harvard Educational Review* 60, 3, 315–340.

Macias, J. (1990). Scholastic Antecedents of Immigrant Students: Schooling in a Mexican Immigrant Sending Community. *Anthropology and Education Quarterly* 21, 4, 291–318.

MacLeod, J. (1987). *Ain't No Makin' It: Leveled Aspirations in a Low-Income Neighborhood.* Boulder, CO: Westview Press.

Matute-Bianchi, M. E. (1986). Ethnic Identities and Patterns of School Success and Failure Among Mexican-Descent and Japanese-American Students in a California High School: An Ethnographic Analysis. *American Journal of Education* 95, 1, 233–255.

Mau, R. Y. (1992). The Validity and Devolution of a Concept: Student Alienation. *Adolescence,* 27, 107, 731–741.

McLaren, P. (1994). *Life in Schools: An Introduction to Critical Pedagogy in the Foundations of Education, Second Edition.* New York: Longman.

McLaughlin, M. W. (1993). What Matters Most in Teachers' Workplace Context? In Little, J. W., and McLaughlin, M. W. (Eds.) *Teachers' Work: Individuals, Colleagues, and Contexts.* pp. 79–103. New York: Teachers College Press.

McLaughlin, M. W, and Talbert, J. E. (1990). The Contexts in Question: The Secondary School Workplace. In McLaughlin, M. W., Talbert, J. E., and Bascia, N. (Eds.) *The Contexts of Secondary School Teaching: Teachers' Realities.* pp. 1–14. New York: Teachers College Press.

——— . (1993). *Contexts That Matter for Teaching and Learning: Strategic Opportunities for Meeting the Nation's Education Goals.* Stanford, CA: Center for Research on the Context of Secondary School Teaching.

Mehan, H., Hubbard, L., and Villanueva, I. (1994). Forming Academic Identities: Accomodation with Assimilation Among Involuntary Minorities. *Anthropology and Education Quarterly* 25, 2, 91–117.

Metz, M. H. (1986). *Different by Design: The Context and Character of Three Magnet Schools.* New York: Routledge and Kegan Paul.

Miller, N., and Harrington, H. J. (1992). Social Categorization and Intergroup Acceptance: Principles for the Design and Development of Cooperative Learning Teams. In Hertz-Lazarowitz, R., and Miller, N. (Eds.) *Interaction in Cooperative Groups.* pp. 203–227. New York: Cambridge University Press.

Moll, L. C., and Diaz, S. (1987). Change As the Goal of Educational Research. *Anthropology and Education Quarterly* 18, 4, 287–299.

Mottaz, C. J. (1981). Some Determinants of Work Alienation. *Sociological Quarterly* 22, 515–530.

National Center for Education Statistics. (1989). *Dropout Rates in the United States: 1988.* (NCES89–609) Washington, DC: U.S. Department of Education.

———. (1994). *Digest of Education Statistics.* (NCES94–115) Washington, DC: U.S. Department of Education.

National Education Goals Panel. (1994). *The National Education Goals Report.* Washington, DC: NEGP Communications.

Neira, C. (1988). Building 860. *Harvard Educational Review* 58, 2, 337–342.

Nielsen, F. (1985). Toward a Theory of Ethnic Solidarity in Modern Societies. *American Sociological Review* 50, 133–49.

Novak, M. (1980). Pluralism in Humanistic Perspective. In Peterson, W., Novak, M., and Gleason, P. (Eds.), *Concepts of Ethnicity.* pp. 27–56. Cambridge, MA: Belknap Press of Harvard University Press.

Oakes, J. (1985). *Keeping Track: How Schools Structure Inequality.* New Haven: Yale University Press.

Ogbu, J. U. (1978). *Minority Education and Caste: The American System in Cross-Cultural Perspective.* New York: Academic Press.

———. (1982). Cultural Discontinuities and Schooling. *Anthropology and Education Quarterly* 13, 4, 290–307.

———. (1987). Variability in Minority School Performance: A Problem in Search of an Explanation. *Anthropology and Education Quarterly* 18, 4, 313–334.

———. (1994). From Cultural Differences to Differences in Cultural Frame of Reference. In Greenfield, P.M., and Cocking, R. (Eds.) *Cross-Cultural Roots of Minority Child Development.* pp. 365–391. Hillsdale, NJ: Lawrence Erlbaum Associates.

Okamura, J.Y. (1981). Situational Ethnicity. *Ethnic and Racial Studies* 4, 4, 452–465.

Omolade, B. (1986). *It's a Family Affair: The Real Lives of Black Single Mothers*. Latham, NY: Kitchen Table: Women of Color Press.

Persell, C.H. (1977). *Education and Inequality: A Theoretical and Empirical Synthesis*. New York: Free Press.

Pettigrew, T. F. & Martin, J. (1987). Shaping the Organizational Context for Black American Inclusion. *Journal of Social Issues* 43, 1, 41–78.

Phelan, P. K., and Davidson, A. L. (1994). Looking Across Borders: Students' Investigations of Family, Peer, and School Worlds As Cultural Therapy. In Spindler, G., and Spindler, L. (Eds.) *Pathways to Cultural Awareness: Cultural Therapy with Teachers and Students*. pp. 35–59. Thousand Oaks, CA: Sage Publications.

Phelan, P. K., Davidson, A. L., and Cao, H. T. (1991). Students' Multiple Worlds: Study Design, Sample Description, and Summary of Student Record Data. WP–1005. Stanford: Center for Research on the Context of Secondary School Teaching.

Phelan, P. K., Davidson, A. L., and Yu, H. C. (1993). Students' Multiple Worlds: Navigating the Borders of Family, Peer, and School Cultures. In Phelan, P., and Davidson, A. L. (Eds.) *Renegotiating Cultural Diversity in American Schools*. pp. 52–88. New York: Teachers College Press.

Philips, S. (1972). Participant Structures and Communicative Competence: Warm Springs Children in Community and Classroom. In John, V. P., and Hymes, D. (Eds.) *Functions of Language in the Classroom*. pp. 370–394. New York: Teachers College Press.

———. (1982). *The Invisible Culture: Communication in Classroom and Community in the Warm Springs Reservation*. New York: Longman Press.

Raissiguier, C. (1994). *Becoming Women, Becoming Workers: Identity Formation in a French Vocational School*. Albany: State University of New York Press.

Ritts, V., Patterson, M., and Tubbs, M. (1992). Judgments on Attractive Students. *Review of Educational Research*, 62, 4, 413–426.

Rodríguez, L. J. (1993). *Always Running: La Vida Loca: Gang Days in L.A.* New York: Simon and Schuster.

Rodriguez, R. (1982). *Hunger of Memory: The Education of Richard Rodriguez*. New York: Bantam Books.

Rohlen, T. P. (1981). Education: Policies and Prospects. In Lee, C., and DeVos, G. (Eds.) *Koreans in Japan: Ethnic Conflict and Accommodation*. pp. 182–222. Berkeley: University of California Press.

Roosens, E. (1989). *Creating Ethnicity: The Process of Ethnogenesis*. Newbury Park, CA: Sage Publications.

Rosaldo, R. (1989). *Culture and Truth: The Remaking of Social Analysis.* Boston: Beacon Press.

Rumberger, R. W. (1987). High School Dropouts: A Review of Issues and Evidence. *Review of Educational Research* 57, 2, 101–121.

Schultz, J., and Erickson, F. (1982). *The Counselor As Gatekeeper: Social Interaction in Interviews.* New York: Academic Press.

Seeman, M. (1975). Alienation Studies. In A. Inkeles (Ed.) *Annual Review of Sociology: Vol. 1.* pp. 91–123. Palo Alto, CA: Annual Reviews, Inc.

Shamai, S. (1987). Critical Theory of Education and Ethnicity: The Case Study of the Toronto Jewish Community. *Journal of Education* 169, 2, 89–114.

Shulman, L. S. (1986). Those Who Understand: Knowledge Growth in Teaching. *Educational Researcher* 15, 2, 4–14.

Sirotnik, K. A. (1983). What You See Is What You Get: Consistency, Persistency, and Mediocrity in Classrooms. *Harvard Educational Review* 53, 1, 16–30.

Siskin, L. S. (1993). *Realms of Knowledge: Academic Departments in Secondary Schools.* New York: Falmer Press.

Slavin, R. L. (1984). Students Motivating Students to Excel: Cooperative Incentives, Cooperative Tasks, and Student Achievement. *Elementary School Journal* 85, 1, 53–63.

Sleeter, C. E., and Grant, C. A. (1987). An Analysis of Multicultural Education in the United States. *Harvard Educational Review*, 57, 4, 421–444.

Spindler, G. (1987). Beth Anne: A Case Study of Culturally Defined Adjustment and Teacher Perceptions. In Spindler, G. (Ed.) *Education and Cultural Process: Anthropological Approaches.* pp. 230–244. Prospect Heights, IL: Waveland Press.

Spindler, G., and Spindler, L. (1982). Roger Harker and Schonhausen: From the Familiar to the Strange and Back Again. In Spindler, G. (Ed.) *Doing the Ethnography of Schooling: Educational Anthropology in Action.* pp. 20–46. New York: Holt, Rinehart & Winston.

———— . (1984). *Dreamers with Power: The Menominee Indians.* Prospect Heights, IL: Waveland Press.

———— . (1993). The Processes of Culture and Person: Cultural Therapy and Culturally Diverse Schools. In Phelan, P., and Davidson, A.L. (Eds.) *Renegotiating Cultural Diversity in American Schools.* pp. 27–51. New York: Teachers College Press.

———. (1994). What Is Cultural Therapy? In Spindler, G., and Spindler, L. (Eds.) *Pathways to Cultural Awareness: Cultural Therapy with Teachers and Students.* pp. 1–33. Thousand Oaks, CA: Corwin Press.

Stack, C. (1975). *All Our Kin: Strategies for Survival in a Black Community.* New York: Harper and Row.

Steele, M. (1978). Enrolling Community Support. *Journal of Research and Development in Education* 11, 2, 84–94.

Stevenson, R. B., and Ellsworth, J. (1993). Dropouts and the Silencing of Critical Voices. In Weis, L., and Fine, M. (Eds.) *Beyond Silenced Voices: Class, Race, and Gender in United States Schools.* pp. 259–271. Albany: State University of New York Press.

Stomfay-Stitz, A. M. (1994). Conflict Resolution and Peer Mediation: Pathways to Safer Schools. *Childhood Education* 70, 5, 279–282.

Suarez-Orozco, M. M. (1989). *Central American Refugees and U.S. High Schools: A Psychosocial Study of Motivation and Achievement.* Stanford: Stanford University Press.

Suarez-Orozco, M. M., and Suarez-Orozco, C. M. (1993). The Cultural Psychology of Hispanic Immigrants: Implications for Educational Research. In Phelan, P., and Davidson, A.L. (Eds.) *Renegotiating Cultural Diversity in American Schools.* pp. 108–138. New York: Teachers College Press.

Talbert, J. E., and McLaughlin, M. W. (1993). Understanding Teaching in Context. In Cohen, D. K., McLaughlin, M. W., and Talbert, J. E. (Eds.) *Teaching for Understanding: Challenges for Policy and Practice.* pp. 167–206. San Francisco: Jossey Bass.

Taylor, S. E., Fiske, S. T., Etcoff, N. L., and Ruderman, A. J. (1978). Categorical and Contextual Bases of Person Memory and Stereotyping. *Journal of Personality and Social Psychology*, 36, 7, 778–793.

Tharp, R. G., and Gallimore, R. (1991). *Rousing Minds to Life: Teaching, Learning, and School in Social Context.* New York: Cambridge University Press.

Tjosvold, D. (1978). Limited Democratic Schools: A Social Psychological Analysis. *Educational Studies* 9, 25–36.

Tomlinson, S. (1991). Ethnicity and Educational Attainment in England— An Overview. *Anthropology and Education Quarterly* 22, 2, 121–139.

Treisman, P. U. (1983). Improving the Performance of Minority Students in College-Level Mathematics. *Innovation Abstracts*, 5, 17.

———. (1985). A Study of the Mathematics Performance of Black Students at the University of California, Berkeley. Unpublished manuscript.

Trusty, J., and Dooley-Dickey, K. (1993). Alienation from School: An Exploratory Analysis of Elementary and Middle School Students' Perceptions. *Journal of Research and Development in Education* 26, 4, 232–242.

Uribe, F., Levine, R., and Levine, S. (1994). Maternal Behavior in a Mexican Community: The Changing Environments of Children. In Greenfield, P,. and Cocking, R. (Eds.) *Cross-Cultural Roots of Minority Child Development*. pp. 41–54. Hillsdale, NJ: Lawrence Erlbaum Associates, Inc.

Vigil, J. D. (1988). Group Process and Street Identity: Chicano Gangs. *Ethos* 16, 4, 421–445.

———. (1993). Gangs, Social Control, and Ethnicity: Ways to Redirect. In Heath, S. B., and McLaughlin, M. W. (Eds.) *Possible Selves: Achievement, Ethnicity, and Gender for Inner-City Youth*. pp. 94–119. New York: Teachers College Press.

Vogt, L. A., Jordan, C., and Tharp, R. G. (1987). Explaining School Failure, Producing School Success. *Anthropology and Education Quarterly* 18, 4, 276–286.

Wehlage, G. G., and Rutter, R. A. (1986). Dropping Out: How Much Do Schools Contribute to the Problem? *Teachers College Record* 87, 374–392.

Weis, L. (1990). *Working Class Without Work: High School Students in a De-industrializing economy*. New York: Routledge.

Weis, L., and Fine, M. (1993). *Beyond Silenced Voices: Class, Race, and Gender in United States Schools*. Albany: State University of New York Press.

Wells, A. S., and Crain, R. L. (1994). Perpetuation Theory and the Long-Term Effects of School Desegregation. *Review of Educational Research* 64, 4, 531–555.

Willis, P. (1977). *Learning to Labour*. Westmead, England: Saxon House.

Zweigenhaft, R. L., and Domhoff, G. W. (1991). *Blacks in the White Establishment? A Study of Race and Class in America*. New Haven: Yale University Press.

# Index